The Daily Telegraph
ROOM SERVICE

The Daily Telegraph

ROOM SERVICE

Paddy Burt

BOXTREE

First published in Great Britain in 1994 by
Boxtree Limited, Broadwall House, 21 Broadwall, London SE1 9PL

Copyright © Boxtree Ltd
Text copyright © 1994 Paddy Burt

All rights reserved

1 3 5 7 9 10 8 6 4 2

ISBN 0 7522 1613 9

Text design by Blackjacks, London
Printed in Great Britain by The Bath Press, Avon

A CIP catalogue entry for this book is available from
the British Library

ACKNOWLEDGEMENTS

All the pieces included in this collection appeared first in the 'Weekend' section of the *Daily Telegraph*.

I would like to thank Bernice Davison (the-then Travel Editor) for commissioning me to write this hotel column and for her enthusiasm for getting it off the ground; and Gill Charlton, her successor, who's very nice to me too! Thank you also to Marsha Dunston, whose idea it was to call it 'Room Service'; to the *Telegraph* lawyers who've kept me on the straight and narrow; to the *Telegraph* readers who take such a personal interest in 'Room Service' and write such amusing/helpful/friendly letters. And of course to my eagle-eyed husband, Robin, whose company has made visiting all these hotels such fun – particularly the horrid ones.

But the *real* stars are all the hoteliers at whom I've poked a little fun and who have bounced back.

INTRODUCTION

If you need to know whether a hotel has courtesy coaches to the airport at 5am, trouser presses or conference facilities – you have picked up the wrong book.

This guide is different. It is aimed at people who want to visit hotels for pure pleasure. It is the only one in which every hotel has been stayed in by the same person – me. As *Telegraph* readers know, 'Room Service' is, quite simply, about staying in hotels and reporting on what happened. Oh yes: I always book in incognito and pay the bill.

My aim is to give the flavour of every establishment. While, inevitably, I have liked some better than others, all the hotels in this book are worthy of inclusion. In some cases, the justification for inclusion lies in the comments which follow the piece.

Some hotels have had to be omitted for reasons of space; a few did not want to be included; while others have changed ownership. I can only offer sincere apologies to any readers or hoteliers who are disappointed.

In my travels, I have discovered you cannot tell what a hotel is going to be like until you get there, when you may well find the claims it makes for itself are the result of the hotelier's rose-coloured imagination. 'This one's going to be good,' I think, having read a guide entry or its own brochure, only to discover indifferent food or indifferent staff... though a caring owner makes up for a *lot* of defects.

So what do I look for? Nice people or, as one hotelier put it, 'Being a host means treating your clients as guests, *never* customers'...and he did it with immense charm. You'd think this approach was obvious, wouldn't you, but it isn't always so.

Suppose it's dead of winter and we've checked in around 6pm and are taken to our room. Unreasonably, in some hoteliers' opinion, I actually expect someone to have bothered to turn on the heating beforehand. Yes, you'd be surprised how many cold bedrooms I've encountered. Is it forgetfulness – or *meanness*? Either way, it's the mark of someone who's not putting his heart into what he's doing.

Other things I look for: a clock; *two* bedside lights, it saves a lot of arguing; being able to decide what I want for breakfast *at breakfast* rather than being conned into ordering it the night before – who wants to decide between white and brown toast and Arbroath Smokies or scrambled egg before dinner?

My favourite proprietors are those who – let's be charitable – are idiosyncratic or, better still, completely potty. My ideal presides over a hotel dripping, though not literally I hope, with character, like the one in Derbyshire with its collection of hippy hats and feather boas. I prefer proprietors who *speak* – I've come across two who managed to utter not a single word all the time we were there, quite an achievement I thought. Clearly it did not occur to them that their behaviour may make guests uneasy, not to mention unwelcome – but if they don't like people, what are they doing in the hotel business anyway? 'The type of customer we attract would not appreciate an ebullient Mine Host,' sniffs the prissy representative of one of these silent men who was *still* in a sulk when invited to be in this book. On the other hand, save me from those who speak too much, usually about themselves, when I want to get my nose into their glossy magazines.

As for food, it goes without saying it should be good of its kind. I don't see why we should eat something that's obviously come out of a packet – we don't at home, why should we pay to do so? And without wishing to nitpick, I also expect to find that what's on my plate is the same as described on the menu – especially an expensive menu.

I remember the grand Home Counties hotel which was charging an outrageous £32.50 for its set four courses. Ordering 'brandysnaps filled with whipped cream and strawberries' for pud, I was miffed to be served brandysnaps filled with *ice*-cream, not the same thing at all. On mentioning this to the dim waitress, she looked nonplussed. 'Sorry, the chef must have got mixed up or something.'

The person in charge of this girl – being paid a pittance, no doubt – should understand that it's important that anyone employed to wait at table should be able to deal with a complaint or query. While I realize that some remote country hotels may have difficulty in finding suitable staff, there are others who are too stingy to bear the cost of training them or paying them properly.

Communal dining, or dining private-house style, as hoteliers often prefer to call it, is something that appals some people when all they thought they were getting was a quiet weekend. My own feeling is that this approach is fine when it works, embarrassing when it doesn't. At one hotel in Cumbria, we sat round a table with eight other people while the owners did the cooking *and* serving. Poor them. Poor *us*. Afterwards I got a puzzled letter asking why I'd given the impression of not liking the concept of dining together at their place yet had enjoyed the experience elsewhere? How difficult to tell someone they haven't the panache to carry off the occasion.

A little light entertainment is always welcome. I've fond memories of our Saturday night waiter at a Norfolk hotel, presumably once a chorus boy, who gave a splendid tum-ti-tum-ti-tum performance as he plonked down the plates. The owner *could* have been cross at some of my observations. But no. 'I've no doubt you get missives exploding with indignation, but we fell about laughing,' he said.

Then there was the stylish Hampshire hotel whose room had a style all its own. 'Drains,' declared the housekeeper. 'They've tried everything.' Shortly afterwards, at a City lunch, I met this room's owner holding his nose, pretending to search for the awful smell. I loved him for that. On the other hand, the man from one of London's most exclusive country house hotels wasn't as sporting. 'I'd like to pour a bucket of cold water over your head,' he growled.

One of the things that had upset them was my comment about the breakfast grapefruit tasting of garlic – no, it's not something I recommend.

Among my most fierce critics are hoteliers who think I have been too soft! My remarks on one country hotel prompted the following lively response from a neighbouring hotelier who must remain nameless. 'My wife and I checked the local competition a few weeks ago. Prices are exorbitant, the wine list nearer a 400% markup than the usual 200%, the bottom line of the credit card is left open (a practice I detest) and the service, which you describe as far too fussy or intrusive, caused my wife to declare that a second night's stay could well prompt the imminent demise of the hostess.' While I know hoteliers can't resist having digs at each other, I do wish some of them would realize just how restrained the 'Room Service' column sometimes is.

'It doesn't seem right that the writer of 'Room Service' is a woman,' grumbles a reader. 'You come across as someone with a henpecked husband. I deplore women who go to hotels and take all the initiative, leaving husbands looking silly.'

Never mind husbands – mine plays the role impeccably. But according to another letter, I made a *hotelier* look silly. My sin? I mentioned how bowled over I'd been when he kissed my hand. This man's best friend thought I was being condescending. 'While giving you the benefit of considerable doubt,' he wrote, 'I shall recommend to Tom that

he stifles his natural charm next time and bites your hand instead.' How kind. I'm sure Tom bites beautifully.

A stay in a hotel is supposed to be a treat. If it isn't, the visitor might just as well stay at home – and probably will next time. The following salutary letter was sent to me by a Brighton reader: 'Remember me?' it begins. 'I'm the man who arrived at your hotel feeling tired and who hung about in reception while you gave orders to your staff. I'm the man who wanted a drink, only the barman thought the needs of that group of businessmen were greater than mine. I'm the man who mentioned to the waitress that his fish was overcooked and she said she would tell the chef...only I never saw her again. You won't remember me because I'm the man who didn't complain. I'm also the man who'll never come back and who now watches, amused, as you spend thousands on advertising to get me back when I was there in the first place ...and all you had to do was make me feel I mattered.'

Everyone has different likes and dislikes which will make or mar a stay in a hotel. Some may not be apparent until too late. These suggestions should help you to make the right decision.

Information that seems unnecessarily repetitive is not given here. Some facilities and services are so common that, unless otherwise stated, they can be assumed.

The vast majority of hotels offer ensuite facilities, meaning that bedroom, WC, wash basin and either shower or bath are self-contained.

Room Service

Some form of heating, central or individual, is always provided. Remember, though, that I may have stayed during summer in a place that, in winter, might be unbearably cold. If in doubt, ask.

TV, radio, telephone and tea - and coffee-making equipment are almost universal in today's hotels. You will know from reading the pieces where I found that one or other was not available.

A cooked breakfast is traditionally included in the room rates in the vast majority of hotels. But if, as someimes happens, no breakfast or a continental one only is included, this is stated.

Credit cards are now the most popular means of payment. This book only tells you which hotels do *not* accept them.

Country hotels nearly always have off-street parking, but at some town hotels you may have to leave your car in the street.

Disabled people can often be accommodated in restaurants, but not always in bedrooms. I have indicated those hotels which have ground-floor rooms. Check for suitability before booking.

Vegetarian and other special diet foods are usually readily available – again, check before booking.

Where rooms are described as 'twin' or 'double', the price quoted is for two. Prices for single people in double rooms are quoted where the hotelier has been persuaded to part with the information.

Duvets versus blankets and sheets, bath versus shower, clock radios – if these things matter, ask before you book.

Some hotels have a pub-type bar, often open to locals. Others serve drinks in a lounge or drawing room. If a room in which to sit and browse is important, check it out first.

Many hotels offer substantial discounts (a) at weekends; (b) out of season and (c) for two or more night stays. *Always ask when booking.*

I have not given exact locations – from my experience, these can sometimes only tell half the story. Ask the hotel directly if you want to know how to get there.

Although there are no maps in this book, the indexing system has been designed to be helpful. Whether you know the name of the hotel you are looking for, the name of the town in which, or near, you would like to stay, or want to know what hotels there are in a given county, one of the indexes will help.

All factual information was provided by the hoteliers themselves and prices were correct at the time of going to press.

I hope that the reviews which follow will give a picture of what each hotel is really like, whether it is comfortable, what sort of food is on offer, what it is likely to cost and – most important – whether they make you feel like an honoured guest. Never forget...they *take your money.* I wouldn't be a hotelier, not in a million years, but I *do* love poking my nose into their hotels.

PADDY BURT

Any correspondence relating to this book should be addressed to me at PO Box 4264, London SW18 1XF.

AUSTINS HOTEL AND RESTAURANT

'There's a similarity between running a hotel and acting,' declares Robert Selbie, pausing for theatrical effect while we wait with bated breath and poised eyebrows.

'Both are about preparing yourself to go on stage. However much you might feel like the wrath of God, you have to forget it *the moment* your public comes in.'

The only response to such an attitude is 'Bravo!' As you may have guessed, Mr Selbie once 'trod the boards' himself and now runs the elegant Austins Hotel in Aldeburgh with partner and chef Julian Alexander-Worster.

It's a promising First Act. Sitting in the womb-like Theatre Bar filled with original paintings, posters and signed photographs –including one of Maureen Lipman taken a very long time ago – the show goes on as Mr Selbie meticulously mixes drinks and gossips some more. 'When we arrived, this place was called The Granville,' he confides. 'What a state it was in. We had to send most of the furniture to auction...and *we* ended up owing *them* £2.07.'

From the dinner menu I choose a Dover sole: 'Plain grilled, no butter please.' Shortly afterwards Mr Julian Alexander-Worster bounds in from the nether regions with an 'anyone for tennis' look on his face. 'Just a touch of hazelnut oil perhaps? I want to cook it the way *you* want,' he explains.

How very cosseting. So far, then, Act Two's going well. The candlelit dining room has pale grey walls and yellow curtains. Toplit modern paintings are hung in strategic positions. At the centre table a trio of elderly mother, doting son and glaring pregnant daughter-in-law engage our interest, as do the pair of earnest young musicians rattling on about the New York Philharmonic and something by Janacek. 'I just *love* that piece,' sighs the even-more-intense one.

For starters we have gnocchi al pesto (with lots of garlic) and a cheese soufflé with a tomato and herb sauce, both of which taste pretty good, ditto the Dover sole Julian.

Puddings include an excellent crême brulée, a favourite of mine, and delicious cherry apples flambéed in pastry. If only I'd remembered to enquire exactly what cherry apples are – they don't have them in Sainsbury's you see.

Afterwards we drink good strong coffee in the pale grey lounge and peer over the heads of the earnest musicians at the signed black-and-white photographs struggling for space with exquisite flower arrangements on top of the grand piano.

Now for the Third Act. After the opulence downstairs – the huge portrait of Robert Selbie's great-grandfather dominating the reception area, the collection of oriental china crammed into a glass-fronted cupboard – our bedroom by contrast is awfully boring. Plain cream walls, rosy frieze, rosy curtains, two paeony limited edition prints. True, there's a video to liven things up and now we must pause for a story by Julian Alexander-Worster: 'We had this Iranian bodyguard staying, you see, who demanded "gentlemen's" videos at 4 am. He was not happy when offered *Amadeus* and *The Marriage of Figaro.'*

During the interval, beds are discovered to be comfortable, lighting just right, tea-and coffee-making equipment in good working order and – a bonus – a conveniently placed socket to plug in the kettle.

Alas, Act Four does not have the panache of Act Two. Naively we assume the freshly squeezed orange juice is just that – it isn't – while cereals in packets let the side down. Yes, I know they remain crisp that way, but...

Yet all in all, it's an excellent performance. As we depart, we encounter Julian Alexander-Worster and four gambolling King Charles spaniels. 'Last night I nearly got arrested on the beach. The police were having a drugs raid. They thought I was a drug smuggler... "But I'm walking my *dogs*," I explained with dignity.'

Richard Selbie writes: 'Having been taken to task, we have seen the error of our ways and now serve freshly squeezed orange juice at breakfast and, when ordered, in the bar. But we do take a stance on the small cereal packets. We offer a range of ten cereals and, if they were all in large packets, they would be so stale after a few days no one would be interested. As it is, we have had to give several packets of Coco Pops to the kitchen assistant's son, and then suddenly had a rush on them. You can't win!'

Austins Hotel and Restaurant,

243 High Street,
Aldeburgh,
Suffolk IP15 5DN.
Tel: (01728) 453932.
Fax: (01728) 453668.
Robert Selbie and Julian Alexander-Worster.
Location: close to the beach.
Open: all year.
Rooms: 7. 1 single (£47.75), 6 twin/ double (£70), all ensuite. Single in double (£47.75).
Restaurant: dinner is served 7.30–9.30.
Chef: Julian Alexander-Worster.Table d'hôte £19.75. Cooked breakfast £7.50.
Wine List: short, sharp, affordable, from £7.50.
Children: small babies and over-12s.
Dogs: Welcome.
Smoking: no cigars or pipes in restaurant.
And Also: The Snape Maltings Concert Hall, nearby bird sanctuaries, Framlingham and Orford Castles.

At seven-thirty on a rainy Saturday evening it's all go at Crouchers Bottom Hotel near Chichester. In the crowded car park a couple leap merrily from a red open-top Morgan hitched to a trailer carrying windsurfing gear, another from a bright blue Lotus Esprit.

Inside, the reception area is teeming. Baggage litters the floor. From the adjoining sitting room comes a hubbub of voices. No wonder the owner, Pam Foden, looks faintly bemused.

Signing the book at last, we are escorted to a room in a recently converted coach house a few steps from the main building. Here we find pale yellow walls, country pine furniture, yellow striped duvet, toning flowery curtains, and a door leading to a brick-paved terrace where the owners' young son is whizzing round on his bike. A notice politely requests us not to smoke.

The first thing my husband does is inspect the bathroom. 'The shower looks promising,' he reports, trying not to get over-excited – showers that look promising, let alone work properly, are a rarity. But he emerges disappointed. 'Should've guessed. More impressive in appearance than in performance.'

Now we saunter into the sitting room for a drink. The place is packed. Nowhere to sit. Would we like to take our seats in the dining room now? we're asked. No thanks, it's too early, we'll wait. Disappointed, we slope back to our room.

But soon there's a telephone call: 'There's room in the lounge now...' an anxious-to-please voice informs us. Well, how friendly. Fancy bothering to phone.

In fact, the Crouchers Bottom crowd seem to bother about everything, giving us the distinct impression that guests really count – something it would be nice to take for granted everywhere we go.

Contentedly knocking back stiff Camparis, we study the proffered menu, make our choice and listen in on a riveting argument over the bill between seven people who appear to have been less-than-joyously 'reunited' after a great many years. This room is comfortable in an unremarkable kind of way. Sink-into sofas and armchairs are neatly arranged. There's a piano. White-painted walls with a swirly plaster finish are emphasized by lighting that's on the bright side.

Arriving at our table, we find the Lotus–Morgan conglomerate sitting behind us, unfortunately not quite out of earshot.

Food is simple and very good. There's a choice of starters: melon, goat's cheese and tomato salad; smoked turkey and mango salad for the main course; the roast beef is supposed to cost £1.50 extra, though we aren't charged for this.

Now Pam Foden comes bustling in with puddings on a trolley. 'All homemade,' she says. When my husband looks faint at the sight of so much cream, she offers him a dish of summer fruits instead. 'You are so boring,' I remark, tucking into a pavlova.

Once again there's trouble during the night. No, nothing to do with the pavlova. It's the hot, thick duvet. Why are hotels addicted to these fat sleep preventers? Perhaps it's a cunning method of ensuring that guests totter into breakfast whey-faced and bleary-eyed.

But what a treat breakfast turns out to be: a picture-postcard alcove window, blue-and-white napkins, a help-yourself table of juices and fresh fruit that includes pineapple and strawberries, perfectly cooked eggs, couples reading the Sunday papers, parents and happily chomping model children.

As we leave, we encounter the blue-shirted Mr Foden. 'Good morning.' As we try to engage him in conversation, his wife appears and he gratefully, I suspect, melts away. Perhaps he doesn't like crowds.

'The shower in Room 2 is working well at the moment,' says Pam Foden, crossing her fingers firmly.

Crouchers Bottom Country Hotel,

Birdham Road,
Apuldram,
Chichester,
West Sussex PO20 7EH.
Tel: (01243) 784995.
Fax: (01243) 539797.
Ron and Pam Foden.
Location: half a mile from Chichester Yacht Basin.
Open: all year except 1 week Christmas.
Rooms: 6. 6 twin/double (£63–£75), mostly ensuite. Single in double (£49). 1 ground-floor room specially adapted for the disabled.
Restaurant: open for dinner from 6–9pm.
Chef: Pam Foden. Table d'hôte £18.50.
Wine List: good range, from £8.
Children: yes.
Dogs: by arrangement.
Smoking: not in restaurant or bedrooms.
And Also: Chichester Cathedral, Goodwood and South Downs.

Madame takes us upstairs to a bedroom so typically Gallic that we suspect the plumbing at once. Look, there's even a shed in the corner complete with douche. Our spirits droop.

Downstairs it's just as Gallic but much more fun. The large beamed room, lit with stained-glass lamps, has a smoky corner bar where four men are earnestly conversing in a foreign language. 'Allo, 'allo, Germans,' whispers my husband. 'Belgians, bet you,' I whisper back.

In the dining area adorned by an ancient French stove, vases of tulips stand on tables covered with pink checked cloths and couples seriously munch. We sit ourselves down in the sitting-about bit furnished with tables and armchairs. There's even a little black poodle for company.

'Got lost, did you?' smiles the very English madame who bustles towards us. 'How did you know?'

'Because everyone does,' she laments. Off she trots to fetch us the menu and wine list.

No, we are not in France but in The Old Coach House, a 19th-century country auberge on the A2 near Dover and the chef/patron's name is Jean Claude. 'She must be his wife,' says my husband. 'Probably. Sssh. Here she comes.'

Mme Jean Claude brings over menus. One, leatherbound, the other written on a blackboard. She props the blackboard on a chair. Mmm, the menu offers three courses at £14.95 and includes meat dishes, but we are more excited by the fishy blackboard offerings at £4.25 extra. 'Our food's not just decoration,' she assures us. 'We *really* feed you here.'

Well, who would imagine it could be quite so pleasant sitting at a table overlooking a main road with lorries hurtling past? We sip French Chardonnay, eat French bread spread with butter from little brown pots and enjoy delicious grilled sardines and moules à la marinière, followed by grilled bream and halibut accompanied by lightly cooked vegetables and crisp sauté potatoes. Thank you, Jean Claude.

'So where is he?' I ask the waitress. 'At the bar,' she says, pointing. Sure enough, there he is, in a blue shirt, smoking and chatting to some punters.

Later, Mme Jean Claude introduces us officially to the little black dog. 'She is half poodle, half King Charles.'

'Ah, half French, half English, how *very* appropriate,' we smile. Then she reminds us that breakfast is served between seven and nine o'clock and please would we order now? Oh, but how do we know whether we will be hungry? When in doubt, do nowt. 'Continental, please.' On our way up to bed, we find a copy of The European to take with us.

There's no traffic noise and, after sleeping well, we're delighted to find that the shower offers not a dribble but an avalanche. Down we saunter to the dining room where Jean Claude sits

reading the paper. Up he jumps. '
Are we driving you away from your
breakfast?'

'No, my breakfast is coffee and a
cee-garette.'

Offering us his paper, he brings us a
jug of fresh orange juice, strong coffee
and a basket of hot bread, croissants
and a couple of *petits pains au chocolat*.

'Dinner was a treat. Do you do all
the cooking?' I ask. 'Yes, and zee
washing-up too,' he says mournfully
and, looking out of the window
moments later, we see him, wreathed
in smoke, surveying the traffic from
beneath his flagpole.

As we settle up, we discover that
most of his travellers come from The
Other Side. 'The only problem is,
because our postal address is in the
village of Barham, everyone goes to
Barham, and zen zey get lost,' he says.
We know, we know.

*Mme Jean Claude, now revealing
herself as Angela, tells me they have
redecorated all their bedrooms –
'we've even acquired some Burgundy
hand-made quilts' – while the newly
decorated restaurant now boasts pale
pink linen cloths, white slips and
napkins.*

The Old Coach House,

(A2), Barham,
Kent CT4 6SA.
Tel: (01227) 831218.
Fax: (01227) 831932.
Jean Claude and Angela Rozard.
Location: On the A2
London–Dover road.
Open: all year.
Rooms: 6. 1 single (£42), 4
twin/double (£48), 1 family room
(£55 – up to 4 people), all ensuite.
Single in double (£42).
Restaurant: dinner is served from
7.30–9.30 pm.
Chef: Jean Claude Rozard. Table
d'hôte £15.
Wine List: from £10. (Connoisseurs
should ask for Jean Claude's 'other'
list). Continental breakfast £4.50,
cooked breakfast £6.50.
Children: yes.
Dogs: no.
Smoking: not in bedrooms.
And Also: Gastronomic House
Party Weekends, minimum 10
people – please enquire.
Convenient for an early ferry or the
orchards of Kent.

*B*arwick, *Somerset*
LITTLE BARWICK HOUSE

At Yeovil, you take the A37 towards Dorchester. Turn left at The Red House pub and drive through a sandstone cutting to Little Barwick House, country house restaurant with rooms, view of trees, fields, cows...and not a lot else.

We had booked in that morning, and a small room with shower is the only one of six rooms left. Parking the car in the nearly full car park, we make our way hopefully across a gravelled drive to an elegant, white-painted, 18th-century house with steps leading up to double front doors. Inside, rugs cover ancient polished boards and the muzak-free hush is enlivened by a babble of voices off.

Here's a place to please those who crave comfort of the homely kind. The sitting room at Little Barwick House is furnished with deep sofas, armchairs, lamps, framed Hockney posters, knick-knacks, a blazing fire...and Mr Christopher Colley.

What could be more comforting than the sight of the pinnied and nimble Mr Colley racing round keeping guests happy. As he hands out menus and wine lists, snatches of merry little phrases like 'A hint of vanilla...' drift across the room. Now he surpasses surely even himself. When the chap who's the spitting image of Douglas Hurd (upright stance, jacket with two vents, *that* voice) announces he's left his reading glasses behind, Mr Colley with ears at the back of his head does a graceful arabesque in the direction of the mantelpiece and produces a

communal pair. A resourceful host.

Helping him is a proliferation of smiling ladies with short memories.

'Can I get you a drink?' asks one.

'We've ordered, thank you.'

'Would you like drinks?' enquires another. Now the first one returns:

'Can I get you a drink?'

The wine list is imaginatively, not to mention colourfully phrased. We are so intrigued we take ages reading it. Mr Colley hovers. 'Is it safe to take your order now?' We choose the one with the, I think, herbaceous explosion – a palatable New Zealand Sauvignon at £13.90.

Although this isn't the kind of hotel where you have to dress up, in deference to Veronica Colley's excellent cooking and the graceful, high-ceilinged, red-painted dining room next door, you'll wish you'd made the effort.

Dishes are tempting, for example a starter called Popeye Pancake, with cream cheese and spinach. Too filling, advises Mr Colley, looking nervously at two slim-to-middling people. I choose Rack of Lamb. 'Pink or cooked through?' he asks, showing beyond all reasonable doubt they're on the right (t)rack here.

So we eat. A wonderfully flavoursome chicken tikka salad, followed by pink and perfect lamb for me, wild duck for him with legs grilled (and served) separately. The waitress brings them almost as an afterthought. 'Your legs, sir.' Almost the best bit is the sight of Mr Colley himself giving a splendid performance of duck slicing at a nearby small table. The man should get an award.

No awards for our room, though, which doesn't pretend to be anything but fairly basic in spite of the unusual armchair that should carry a whoopee warning. And if a hotel is going to provide only a shower, then it should be a good one. Even on tiptoe I cannot reach the showerhead to adjust it, nor is there anywhere to put the soap.

These niggles vanish along with breakfast and the information that Mrs Colley had cooked forty-two main courses the night before. 'We ran a restaurant in Bristol for ten years,' Mr Colley says. 'When we came here, my wife told me that, if I insisted on having hotel rooms, then *I* must take charge of breakfast.' Although recommending his scrambled egg and basket of mixed toasts and croissants, we wish we'd met the *real* cook.

'There's a new shower in Number One complete with step ladder!' chortles Christopher Colley (how thoughtful), adding modestly they've just been awarded an AA red star.

Little Barwick House,

Barwick Village,
nr Yeovil,
Somerset BA22 9TD.
Tel: (01935) 23902.
Fax: (01935) 20908.
Christopher and Veronica Colley.
Location: on the edge of village.
Open: all year except 3 weeks January.
Rooms: 6. 6 twin/double (£76), all ensuite. Single in double (£48).
Restaurant: dinner served 7–9pm.
Chef: Veronica Colley. Table . d'hôte £17.50–£24.90.
Wine List: reasonably priced, from £9.20.
Children: yes.
Dogs: yes.
Smoking: not in dining rooms or at breakfast.
And Also: Folly Hunting: using local guides (Dobermans Amy and Poppy), visit the three Barwick Park Follies (DB&B £57 per person).

Bosham, Sussex
THE MILLSTREAM HOTEL

'I'd appreciate your views on The Millstream,' writes a reader, mentioning he stays there from time to time.

Approaching the pristine sailing village of Bosham, we find The Millstream at once, with white tables and chairs on its front lawn. The car park's full – no lonely dinner for us tonight – and we're greeted by an ultra-polite receptionist who asks what time we'd like to eat before she directs us to a pleasant 'hotelish' room. 'You mean inoffensive,' suggests my husband.

On the dressing table – complete with stool, not always the case I assure you – they've forgotten to remove the card written out for the previous occupant. In fact, the foreign-sounding gentleman was here till this morning and, apart from his spectre, everything's ten out of ten: trouser press, the right kind of lighting, plenty of towels.

In the bar, the tall, bespectacled barman asks what we'd like to drink. My husband mutters something unintelligible and the poor chap looks bewildered. 'Don't worry about him, he's talking to himself again,' I explain.

'Oh really?' Now the barman looks *really* alarmed.

Drifting into the long, low-ceilinged sitting room next door, we find a sofa. In a corner a lady pianist is earnestly playing 'Rustle of Spring' music and we enjoy the convivial Friday night atmosphere. Then the head waiter appears before us brandishing menus. 'Pork tenderloin's off,' he cheerfully announces. I glance at my watch.

'At *eight* o'clock?'

'They all eat early round here,' he grins.

When he reappears, I ask for the 'grilled whole witch'. 'Complete with broomstick,' adds my husband. The head waiter ignores this sally. 'You're lucky,' he exclaims. 'it's the last witch.'

'What *is* a witch?' I ask, displaying my ignorance.

'Fish,' he says. Yes, I'd guessed that.

'What sort of fish?'

'A bit like lemon sole,' he comes up with at last.

Although the wine list includes house wines at around £10, many others cost substantially more than those in recently-visited hotels. On the other hand, dinner at £16.75 sounds reasonable – depending on what it tastes like of course.

Disconcertingly, our table is right next to a mirrored wall. I'd rather look at *us*, though, than at the cross-looking man blowing his nose the other side. 'When he's not blowing, he's tuning in to everything we say,' I whisper indignantly.

'You do that all the time,' my husband reminds me.

But we soon shut up as first courses arrive, served by lots of friendly people. I'm in the mood for plain melon with stem ginger: 'Nice, juicy, unmolested melon,' I comment. My husband complains mildly about his *un*molested salad: 'A touch of some dressing would be nice.'

My whole witch is thick and juicy – much tastier than lemon sole. My husband *quite* likes his chicken Provençal, 'though a few herbs and touch of garlic wouldn't come amiss.' The vegetables are crisp and delicious – if only they'd leave them, and the wine, on the table so we could help ourselves. Our verdict: the food is like our room, pleasant but predictable.

Afterwards we adjourn to the lounge for coffee and peer hopefully into the magazine rack. 'Is there a *Spectator* or *Harpers*?' I ask. My husband holds aloft *Yachting* and *Autocar*. 'All out of date,' sniff the couple next to us. But much better than reading magazines is the awesome sight of four elderly people getting worked up over their game of bridge. 'She's going to hit him with her stick, I think!'

Now I often receive letters complaining that the hotels I stay in are too expensive. The Millstream's rates aren't the cheapest...but at breakfast next morning – guess what? – the dining room's full of *Telegraph* readers. Our nose-blowing friend is even reading 'Room Service'. Nasty thought: is he the one who suggested I visit here?

This piece provoked a waspish letter from a female reader saying how ridiculous of me to describe the bedroom as 'hotelish'...but that I always made stupid comments anyway!

The Millstream Hotel,

Bosham Lane,
Bosham,
Chichester,
West Sussex PO18 8HL.
Tel: (01243) 573234.
Fax: (01243) 573459.
General Manager: Jeremy Rodericks.
Location: close to old Bosham church.
Open: all year.
Rooms: 29. 5 single (£59–£69), 23 twin/double (£89–£99), 1 four-poster (£109), all ensuite. Single in double (£79).
Restaurant: open for dinner 7–9.30 pm.
Chef: Bev Boakes. Table d'hôte £17.25.
Wine List: extensive, from £9.15.
Children: yes.
Dogs: yes.
Smoking: not in restaurant and some bedrooms.
And Also gardens, stream, walking. Special bridge, walking, sailing and flower arranging weekends – please enquire.

There's nothing pale and uninteresting about the timbered 17th-century Bradfield House. Good heavens no. They've gone for the can't-miss effect: Suffolk pink exterior, bright blue hall, dark green and pink restaurant, coral and turquoise breakfast room.

Our room's got to be the *pièce de résistance*: giant cabbage roses rampage across its walls, enhanced by shocking pink woodwork. 'The house was mostly cream when we arrived five years ago,' explains owner Sally Ghÿben. 'We thought it needed livening up.' Nice Mrs Ghÿben, in her top and leggings, pales into insignificance beside her paintwork.

In fact, she's so laid back, we're not 100 per cent sure she's boss. 'She *is*,' decides my husband, ensconced in a pink squashy armchair in our wild, wild room. There is – hmm – one over-wild touch: a large gold bobbly lampshade diverted from the centre of the room by a length of flex attached to a hook in the ceiling. 'A temporary arrangement perhaps,' is my charitable comment.

Arriving early, we try out the tea-making equipment. 'Fresh milk can be ordered from reception,' announces a card. We'll have some of that. How civilized to sip tea in such comfort.

Over drinks in the drawing room, we encounter an elderly stand-offish couple and a pair of honeymooners. The elderly husband seems quite taken by *them*. The honeymooners politely respond.

We peruse the 'early summer' menu: it looks good. Decisions, decisions. Right, let's indulge in pea, mint and lettuce soup. My husband's ravenous: 'I'm having wild boar pie casseroled with bacon, mushrooms and rich Guinness gravy, nice and filling,' he says, smacking his lips. The rather more prosaic me chooses fillet of lamb with tartlets.

In the dining room, all the tables are occupied – yes, if *I* lived locally, I'd come and eat here too. 'Hang on,' says Hub, 'we don't know what the food's like yet.' Meanwhile, we enjoy the ambience, the windows that overlook the gardens and the archway leading to the blue hall and grand piano.

We ask the chap who brings our wine if he's going to entertain us on the piano after dinner. 'I don't play,' he says, looking alarmed. 'The owners' daughter is the only one who does, and she'd be *much* too shy.'

The food, served by a pretty waitress, doesn't disappoint. My lamb arrives neatly sliced in a pool of pan juices – I just *know* I'll drop a potato in those juices and splatter my jacket. But I carp: it's all wonderful. 'You haven't asked me what mine's like,' complains the wild boar expert. Tell me then. '*I* think wild boar should always be cooked with Guinness,' he pronounces. As for my crême brulée, it's got to be the *creamiest* I've ever had.

When we go upstairs, the scene's been set: beds turned down, voile blinds pulled, curtains drawn, bedside lamps switched on. But there's trouble in t'night. It's the duvet. In my view, most normal people can sleep beneath a duvet, even if they prefer sheets and blankets. Not so some people. One duvet cover is eventually removed, duvet tossed to the floor, the cover used as a sheet...and it isn't *mine.*

At breakfast we sidle towards the table with the best note-taking position. 'Are you all right tucked away in that dark corner?' asks Mrs Ghÿben. 'Oh yes, I just love dark corners.'

From our vantage point we spy a half-constructed building at the end of the garden. 'It's going to be a summer-house,' says Mrs G. 'My husband (he's also the chef) is never happier than when he's building something. In fact, we've just contracted the children to move a load of bricks...' At that moment, the bearded master-builder-chef himself appears. 'It was a lovely dinner...thank you.'

'Thank *you,*' he bows.

Writes Sally Ghÿben: 'I'll be armed with sheets and blankets ready for your husband next time!'

Bradfield House Hotel and Restaurant,
Bradfield Combust,
Bury St Edmunds,
Suffolk IP30 0LR.
Tel/Fax: (01284) 386301.
Roy and Sally Ghÿben.
Location: 4 miles south of Bury St Edmunds on A134.
Open: all year except 1 week Christmas/2 weeks August.
Rooms: 4. 1 single (£45), 2 twin/double (£70), 1 four-poster (£85), all ensuite. Single in double (£50).
Restaurant: dinner is from 7–9pm.
Chef: Roy Ghÿben. Table d'hôte £16.50.
Wine List: international, from £7.50.
Children: yes.
Dogs: no.
Smoking: not in dining room.
And Also: large garden with scented yew hedges and fully fledged summer house. Convenient for Lavenham, Long Melford, Newmarket and Cambridge.

*B*rampton, Cumbria
TARN END HOUSE HOTEL

'Don't worry if you hear a few creaks and bangs...they're all friendly,' says Mrs Ball, escorting us to a rather strange room at Tarn End House Hotel in remotest Cumbria.

Now I'm a sucker for creaky houses that come with clichés like 19th century, friendly, family-run, log fires, lakeside, idyllic...et al. Tarn End's got the lot. *But:* the barns are still barns; the forlorn old rowboat's upside down; the drawing room's a mess. And our room beneath the eaves, whose curtains and wallpaper are pure *Homes and Garden*, has junkshop armchairs and a candlewick bedspread that *almost* covers the bed.

There are reasons for these oddities. The Balls arrived at Tarn End only recently, from a hotel down on Merseyside. And they have Plans. (Note: take above comments with pinch of salt. Tarn End could be quite different in six months' time.)

For example. Sipping our drinks in the bar with 'blazing log fire', Mr Ball expresses reservations about his dining-room wallpaper. What do *we* think, he asks? Hold on, haven't seen it yet – may we tell you later? And while we're studying the vaguely Franglais menu and all the other guests, he reveals he's got Plans for the bar as well. Oh good. 'Throw out all these chairs. Put in a completely new bar and...' says Mr Ball with a reckless glint in his eye.

He mentions they've just done up the hall and landing. The doors are painted a pretty duck-egg blue. 'We got

someone in to advise us,' he confesses. *I* hope they're going to restore the antiques and patchwork look I'd read about in the guidebook.

A smartly dressed waitress trips in. 'Your table's ready,' she tells us. Off we saunter. Yes, that dark stripy wallpaper *is* a touch can't-miss. At a window table we spot a mother and son: 'And those two over there, they've got to be mother and daughter...' It seems this place is not just family run but family patronized. In the corner a party of six chortles loudly. Uncurtained windows overlook the tarn.

Tables are as smartly dressed as the waitress, with white starched cloths and napkins. Rudely I speculate on the food being pretentious and somehow wrong – but it's not.

Scoffing a basketful of delectable bread with the prawns in garlic butter, I realize I've drawn the short straw. Messy and garlicky though the prawns are, my husband's spaghetti carbonara starter with mushrooms and chunks of ham from the bone comes under the heading 'memorable'. Grilled trout with almonds and chicken breast with Madeira sauce are accompanied by two side plates of eight different vegetables.

Easy to tell the stuff on the trolley's homemade – the sponges have crooked edges and they're not mean with the cream. By now, our hosts are also having dinner. Mr Ball hospitably offers us some of the German wine from his table. 'Nice with your puddings?' he suggests, pouring us generous glasses. How kind. And it is. Now the chef emerges, making a beeline for the chortling ones. Old friends we presume.

We make *new* friends over coffee. Mother and son, both from Northumberland. They've moved up from the South. 'And I'd never go back,' says rather-grand Mother in the most determined of voices.

Later, what a surprise. Whipping off the horrid candlewick bedspread, we find maroon blankets and an old fashioned pink eiderdown. Just right for remotest Cumbria. After breakfast – perfect poached egg and more starched napkins – we set out for a brisk walk around the tarn. There's only one cliché: idyllic.

I hope Tarn End stays that way. Here's a lovely house with potential. Give it the wrong treatment and it'll be spoiled. Of course Mr and Mrs Ball know that. I wish them well.

'Who's the sneaky one then?' asks David Ball. 'Anyway, we felt you set the scene and ambience of Tarn End just right – exactly as we plan to keep it, with tasteful improvements. And you'll be pleased to know that our little bird table by the dining-room window continues to attract many new and varied guests.'

Tarn End House Hotel,

Talkin Tarn,
Brampton,
Cumbria CA8 1LS.
Tel: (016977) 2340.
Fax: (016977) 2089.
David and Vivienne Ball.
Location: on Talkin Tarn.
Open: all year.
Rooms: 7. 1 single (£29.50–£39.50), 6 twin/double (£62–£118), some ensuite. Single in double (£29.50–£39.50). 1 ground-floor room.
Restaurant: open for dinner from 7–8.30pm (but not written in stone).
Chef: Kevin Bull (in liaison with the Balls). Table d'hôte from £13.50.
Wine List: good quality, to suit all pockets, from £7.95.
Children: no
Dogs: yes
Smoking: not in dining room
And Also: Hadrian's Wall, Roman Army museum, coarse fishing, golf and...red squirrels.

'Let *me* take your bags,' says Dick Tudhope, grabbing them as we come through the door of his snug little bar. 'It doesn't matter if *I* get a bad back – that's an industrial injury – but if *you* do, it'll ruin your weekend.' Your back's safe Mr Tudhope. Our bags are feather-light.

We've just arrived at Tŷ Mawr, a small 16th-century country hotel and restaurant with an away-from-it-all concept. In fact, the brochure verges on the poetic: 'a quiet haven, far removed from stressful pursuits. The purest of air to promote a sharp appetite.'

Alas, we never get to stay anywhere long enough to sniff the pure air. What we do sniff, though, are enticing aromas coming from the Tŷ Mawr kitchen. 'Is your wife the chef?' I ask. 'She's not called the wife, she's the chef,' replies Mr Tudhope enigmatically. Oh? I wouldn't dare argue.

Bags now firmly grabbed, he takes us up to a flowery cottagey room with a spare bed and lots of magazines. *Not* a room to set the world alight, but I guess decorative stimulation is not part of the Tŷ Mawr concept.

After a quick change, we're down in the bar again discussing the merits of this or that drink. Mr T directs us towards the lounge: 'I'll bring them through.'

Wandering into a room with stone walls, deep sofas, armchairs and a flint-lock gun slung over the fireplace, I choose the chair draped with a Welsh blanket. Now Mr Tudhope's bustling in with drinks and titbits and menus tucked under his arm. 'Gentlemen are always served first in this valley,' he announces gravely, 'but tonight I'll reverse the process...'

'How kind – I'm honoured.' He hands me my drink, smiling that enigmatic smile.

This is an inviting menu. Apart from those wonderful kitchen smells, we just *know* – famous last words – it'll be good. As for the wine list, it's classy (if pricey): 'We have selected the very best wines each region has to offer,' says the blurb.

In the low-ceilinged, quarry-tiled restaurant, the tables are covered with white lace cloths. The herb bread's freshly made – very more-ish. So what else do we eat? Well, my starter's called 'twice-baked cheese soufflé' and it's: 'crisp on the outside, gooey inside, delicious,' I sigh.

My husband's Carmarthen ham and papaya salad is equally memorable. 'How would you like your garlic lamb?' Mr Tudhope had asked. 'Pinko, please.' And it *is*. My husband has one word for his 'duck with orange, honey and thyme': 'Mouthwatering'. Meanwhile, Mr Tudhope provides running entertainment with remarks like: 'It's 100 percent Celtic round here – most wives don't even sit at the same table as their husbands.'

But I mustn't let him distract me from our yummy puddings: elderflower jelly with yogurt and honey cream (me) and chocolate bombe (him). 'Coffee will await you in the lounge,' announces Mr Tudhope, appearing suddenly. 'Unless we beat you to it!' we giggle. 'You won't,' he says. We do. *And* get in conversation with a couple of Welsh ex-pats here to visit their mothers.

A few niggles, though: there's a duvet – admittedly feather-filled but still hot and we don't all like duvets, you know; a shower that runs hot and cold; and oh – that wonderful dinner is let down by indifferent breakfast orange juice. In a place like this, surely it should be freshly squeezed?

PS: In spite of Mr Tudhope's naughty sexist jokes, I'm delighted to note the Resident Proprietors are listed as 'Beryl and Dick Tudhope (in partnership)'. He *was* winding me up.

Ho ho. Mr Tudhope's quick to point out that the Paddy Burt room was just awaiting refurbishment: 'What a pity you did not see the others already done,' he laments. The room, he declares, is now 'transformed' with a notice urging guests to request sheets and blankets if preferred. Great. But there's more: fresh orange juice, he says, is now 'available on request at breakfast olé', and I think he's apologizing for his sexist remarks. 'A little winding up sometimes breaks down barriers between guest and host – we always hope it is taken with good humour.' Loved it, Mr T.

Tŷ Mawr Country Hotel,

Brechfa,
Dyfed SA32 7RA.
Tel: (01267) 202332.
Fax: (01267) 202437.
Beryl and Dick Tudhope.
Location: 7 miles from junction of A40 and B4310 at Nantgaredig.
Open: all year except Christmas week, end January/end November.
Rooms: 5. 4 twin/double (£68–£84), all ensuite. 1 double with private bathroom (£68). Single in double (£44).
Restaurant: open for dinner from 7–9.30pm.
Chef: Beryl Tudhope. Table d'hôte £16–£19.50.
Wine List: all tastes catered for, from £8.25.
Children: yes.
Dogs: yes.
Smoking: not in restaurant or bedrooms.
And Also: river valley of broadleaf, oak and conifer. Walking, fishing, riding. Castles galore. Television and newspapers only for those who're desperate.

$\mathcal{B}$righton, East Sussex
TOPPS HOTEL

The dirty weekend may be an outdated concept, but it's good to know that, in Brighton, it flourishes still. Take the couple holding hands at the table next to ours in the restaurant of Topps Hotel in Regency Square: a middle-aged blonde decked out in gold sporting a diamond the size of a Malteser, whose companion has a grey-streaked Rod Stewart haircut and Jack the Lad shoulders. They are married, we decide – but not to each other.

We've no such wicked speculation about Topps Hotel itself, which offers value of the good, old-fashioned kind. What it lacks in style, it makes up with hospitality. In our room on this wet Friday evening, the gas coal fire has been lit and there are fresh flowers and 'welcome' chocolates on the table. As for the mini bar, it's the alcoholic equivalent of a toy cupboard with a selection of hard and soft drinks, lemon slices, chocolate bars and the sort of price list you might expect to find in a supermarket.

'As you are doing all the work,' explains the amiable owner Paul Collins, 'we feel that prices should be less than in a bar.'

Which is just as well. Topps Hotel doesn't have a bar, nor a proper sitting room (unless you count the reception area), though our room, described as a standard double, is obviously intended to make up for this lack – the furnishings include a sofa, a chair and Topps monogrammed carpet.

I wish I could say that the conversion of these two adjacent Regency houses is as successful as the general welcoming atmosphere and comfort of the place. We enter our standard double via a small lobby, with the bedroom to the right and bathroom to the left. Off the bathroom is a large cupboard containing hanging space, trouser press, iron and board, extra pillows and blankets. All very nice, but how much more convenient if it led off the lobby. It seems to me all this lovely space is wasted and might have benefited from a designer's touch.

For example, you could get lost in our bathroom where there is an abundance of bathtime goodies, including bathrobes, his and hers slippers, two wash basins, piles of towels and a hair dryer. There's even an antique Captain's chair, a bidet and a pouffe(!). Yet in this space large enough to hold a party in, there's only a shower of the hand-held variety attached to the bath.

A brisk walk along the windy seafront sharpens our appetites for the unpretentious dinner cooked by owner Pauline Collins and served by her husband. I start with herb noodles with mushroom and garlic; my husband with a hot bubbling concoction of Brie, apple and almonds. 'Extremely good,' he says. I follow with a plain Dover sole, accompanied by nice crunchy vegetables, while he tucks into a beef Stroganoff he pronounces excellent.

'If Pauline takes an evening off, we close the restaurant,' says her husband. Clearly no one else has her touch. And I certainly approve of her Atholl Brose pudding – a cream, honey, whisky and oatmeal concoction. 'A classic Scottish dish,' comments Paul Collins helpfully.

Settling the bill next morning, I spot a white convertible Jag with customized number plate parked outside. 'Does that belong to er...?'

'Who else?' replies Mr Collins, hiding a smile. But that Jag is far too conspicuous for a getaway car. Perhaps Jack the Lad brought his own wife after all.

'We now have showers and baths in all rooms,' writes the imperturbable Mr Collins.

Topps Hotel,

17 Regency Square,
Brighton,
East Sussex BN1 2FG.
Tel: (01273) 729334.
Fax: (01273) 203679.
Paul and Pauline Collins.
Location: off the seafront, opposite West Pier.
Open: all year: restaurant closed January.
Rooms: 14. 1 single (£45), 12 double (£79–£89), 1 four-poster with balcony (£99), all ensuite. Single in double (£69–£79).
Restaurant: open for dinner from 7–9pm.
Chef: Pauline Collins. Table d'hôte £18.95.
Wine List: good house wine, from £7.50, including selection of half bottles.
Children: yes.
Dogs: no.
Smoking: feel free.
And Also: 100 yards from sea. 5 minutes main shopping areas. Parking in Topps garage or NCP car park opposite.

THE TWENTY ONE

A Brighton taxi driver enlightens us: 'Charlotte Street? Just off Marine Parade.' Whizzing round the corner, we find The Twenty One, a tall, terraced Victorian house in a nondescript street full of hotels. There's a No Vacancies sign in the window.

Pressing the bell, I'm greeted by a middle-aged, lugubrious looking man in a white shirt. 'We've booked a room ...but we can't park here, can we?'

'Too true,' he says, launching himself in the direction of the car and my husband.

While all this is going on, I fill in a booking form. 'I'm afraid the room you asked for isn't available. This one at £46 is cheaper,' announces owner Mrs Power kindly but firmly, no explanation given. Hmmmm. Maybe we should inspect Room Five, two flights up, *before* having a moan.

But it's all right. The brown and cream patterned curtains match the wallpaper exactly, the pictures are carefully chosen, the effect is warm. Suddenly I remember her words: 'Please come down to dinner as soon as you can.'

In the dining room, there's classical music and a couple from Amsterdam who announce they're staying here for two weeks: 'Arrived today.' The penny drops. *They* got our room.

Our melancholy host with twinkle-in-eye shows us an unpretentious wine list. My husband asks for a half bottle of house red. 'And nothing for me...'

'But you must have a little something,' he exclaims. 'Oh, all right then'

– I succumb to a glass of white.

Next, he's tenderly placing bowls of carrot and orange soup in front of us: 'Madame – *M'sieur.'* We dive in – it tastes of both those things. 'Very good indeed.'

He executes a little bow. 'Prepared with my own fair hands.'

'Oh, really?'

'Here I am, chef, waiter, London cabbie...' he intones.

'*And* part- time Maurice Chevalier,' my husband quips.

'Waiter!' calls his wife from the kitchen. Leaping to attention, he seizes a white napkin, drapes it theatrically over his arm and winks at us before vanishing behind the scenes. No one told us free entertainment would be thrown in as well.

Along with smoked salmon pâté accompanied by prawns and salad, he reveals that he's not often down in Brighton. 'I work at night. Alas, Madame – *M'sieur,* this evening the waitress couldn't come, so you got *me.*'

Classical music is his passion, he confides, over slices of tender pink breast of wild duck. 'Shot it yourself this afternoon?' we ask. 'But of course.' A faint smile crosses his face. The Dutch couple are looking bewildered. We are amused. How curious, in a small hotel in a seedy looking Brighton street, to find a London cabbie with a penchant for Beethoven and a wife who cooks like a dream.

Further gems of a revelatory nature arrive along with the crêpes and lemon and brandy sauce. 'We learned hotel-keeping the hard way in Torquay. But the place didn't suit me, it was dead at six o'clock.'

I'm dead at eleven. It's been a long, hard day. We wake up to sunshine and agree that, yes, the mattress was a bit lumpy wasn't it. The shower's efficient though. Mrs Power has thought of everything.

She *certainly* has at breakfast. There are linen napkins, big jars of Elsenham jams and marmalade and flowers on each table. The extensive menu even includes a low-calorie, high-fibre breakfast. And the little restaurant is full.

Here comes our waiter. 'Good morning, Madame – *M'sieur.*' He pours orange juice and tries to persuade me to have fresh grapefruit. 'No? You must have more juice then.'

'You're worrying about her,' teases my husband. 'But she's not eating anything,' is the stern reply. I hope they will forgive me if they read this piece. The astute Mrs Power may be embarrassed, but I don't think she'll be entirely surprised.

'I was rung that Saturday by a friend who said: "You'd better go out and buy The Telegraph." *Then of course it clicked: I knew exactly who you were. My husband, who you may have gathered is a bit of an extrovert, was most flattered.'*

The Twenty One,

21 Charlotte Street,
Brighton,
East Sussex BN2 1AG.
Tel: (01273) 686450.
Janet and David Power.
Location: off Marine Parade, close to sea front.
Open: all year.
Rooms: 6. 6 twin/double (£46–£68), 1 with private bathroom, otherwise ensuite. Single in double (£35–£50).
Restaurant: dinner served at 8pm.
Chef: Janet Power. Table d'hôte £15.95.
Wine List: good selection, from £7.50.
Children: over 10.
Dogs: no.
Smoking: feel free.
And Also 10 percent discount off full room rate for stays of 2 or more nights on production of this book.

THE MALT HOUSE

At The Malt House, Mr Nick Brown is in hot water or should I say cold. 'The plumber's on his way. I'll soon get it fixed,' he says, looking dreadfully worried. And he does. But at breakfast time he's *still* worrying. 'I woke up in a cold sweat at two-thirty this morning thinking about the hot water,' he confesses.

Yet it's not disasters that matter so much, it's how they're handled. Does the average hotel rush to fix the hot water/faulty heater/on-the-blink TV? Do they say: 'I'm so sorry, Madam, I'll reduce the bill.' Not often enough they don't. Mr Brown may lack experience in this game – he only took over The Malt House recently – but he has the right ideas.

His wife had told me when I rang to book that we could have a double room at the special price of £70 (normally £85). After mentioning their son Julian was the chef, she then threw me by asking what we'd like for dinner. 'Chicken, duck...or there might be salmon.' Not having a clue what I would want to eat in twenty-four hours' time, I suggested they surprise us: 'though perhaps we could each have different things.'

Because of thick fog, we fear other guests may have cancelled. How nice then to meet in the elegant drawing room a Bath couple who have escaped from their children for the night and to knock back G and T's into which gin has been poured with reckless abandon.

Meanwhile Julian in chef's apron asks us what wine we'd like, dropping into the conversation the information that he runs a B&B in Stow on the Wold. We are now treated to a riveting discussion between father and son as to whether The Malt House is guest house or hotel. The result is a draw. 'Oh, by the way supper is ready,' says Julian.

The low-ceilinged, softly lit dining room with painted beams is as attractive as the drawing room. The meal is served by Julian and his friend Matthew at one large table. As Matthew seems somewhat ill at ease when handing round the French onion soup, we quiz him about his day job. 'Guess,' says Matthew. We all have a go: student, solicitor, computer programmer. He does not care for that last suggestion. 'I am an art dealer,' he says with dignity. *Touché.*

Julian's food is on the homely side, with piles of crisply cooked vegetables. I get salmon; my husband half a duck. 'Where's the other half?' he asks.

'We're just fighting over that in the kitchen,' replies Julian.

A few salient facts about The Malt House, which describes itself in its brochure as 'exclusive.' It consists of three 17th-century cottages cleverly knocked into one so that all bedrooms look out on a wonderful garden with orchard beyond. It is filled with unusual antique furniture, and now Mr Brown admits to a secret vice: 'I'm a saleroom addict.'

Our room has some lovely pieces, but amenities get only five out of ten: the TV has no remote, the clock thoughtfully provided is not plugged in, the shower is of the hand-held variety and there's an inappropriate fringed pink lampshade hanging from a beam – though I must add that, on a cold night, it is blissfully warm in here.

This may be the exclusive Cotswolds but, even so, The Malt House seems a touch expensive for what we actually get. And if you're wondering about the absent Mrs Brown, she's speechless. 'Lost my voice,' she croaks.

The Malt House has now received a Michelin Red House rating, a four Q rating from the AA and Johansens' awards for quality of service. All rooms have been upgraded and...
'Do you want that pink lampshade?' asks Nick Brown (who signs himself 'Action Man'). 'I've kept it in the hope that one day you'll come back and claim it.'

' No thanks, Action Man, but I'm glad to hear it's been dispensed with!

The Malt House,

Broad Campden,
Chipping Campden,
Gloucestershire GL55 6UU.
Tel: (0386) 840295.
Fax: (0386) 841334.
Nick and Jean Brown.
Location: near The Baker's pub in Broad Campden.
Open: all year except Christmas.
Rooms: 7. 1 single (£45–£55), 4 twin/double (£69.50–£87.50), 1 four-poster (£69.50–£87.50), all ensuite, 1 family room with private bathroom (£69-50–£105). Single in double (£55).
Restaurant: dinner served at 8.15 pm.
Chef: Julian Brown. Table d'hôte £21.50.
Wine List: small, sensibly priced, from £7.75.
Children: yes.
Dogs: yes.
Smoking: not in lounge or dining room.
And Also: large tranquil garden with croquet lawn, stream and orchard. Cheltenham Gold Cup breaks, with transport organized to and from racecourse – please enquire.

FROGG MANOR HOTEL & RESTAURANT

When visiting Frogg Manor near Chester, a liking for frogs, though not imperative, is desirable. The first encounter of the amphibian kind is at the hotel entrance where a larger-than-life Jeremy Fisher-type doffs his hat and points the way. The second intimation of a devotion to the species is a notice that urges you to 'Drive carefully, frogs crossing'.

But it is not until we open the front door of this elegant Georgian manor house hotel and are greeted by an urbane man in a frock coat who says 'I am Chief Frog' that we begin to wonder whether we've come to the right place. But everyone needs a gimmick after all, and Chief Frog, alias John E. Sykes, is no exception.

Now let's forget frogs (though it's hard) and concentrate on first impressions, such as the hall where we come face to face with a fire, a cheerfully crowded desk, a delightful old English sheep dog and the sort of background music Edward VIII and Mrs Simpson might have danced to.

Mr Sykes grabs our bags and frog marches us (sorry) up the staircase to a creatively decorated room that stuns with its wealth of accoutrements: chandelier, gleamingly modern brass bed, chaise longue, table laid with bone china cups and a liberal jug of milk, an abundance of elegant drapes, trouser press, wash basin (in addition to the one in the bathroom), even an iron and ironing board. It is impossible not to detect a warming generosity of spirit overall. 'You should be comfortable in here – if not, let me know,' says Chief Frog.

Pre-dinner drinks are served in a vast upstairs sitting room, where great care has been lavished on getting the lighting just right: lamps, uplighters and spots enhance large numbers of subtly lit oil paintings of the sort I wouldn't mind having at home. On a table is a wind-up gramophone with brass horn and, on a sideboard, a tray of cafetière coffee and cups is waiting for people to help themselves.

There is also an impressive collection of comfortable Victorian chairs of the nursery variety, sink-into sofas, tables decorated with lacy cloths covered with collections of – you've guessed – frogs, a roaring fire and a number of Friday-night diners relaxing over coffee and liqueurs as they swop horse stories. Of course we earwig on all these tales of Cheshire life.

Rarely have I visited a hotel so full of 'things'. Beneath the stairs, for example, is a corner where a table with chessboard is set out. Do frogs play chess?

The dining room has yet more splendid antique furniture and leads onto a conservatory where tables are laid with pink cloths. What with Edward and Mrs S, the lighting and floodlit garden beyond dominated by a marble Aphrodite, the effect is unreal.

Dinner – served by the host himself – lacks his *joie de vivre*. While I fare better with my carrot soup and lamb, my husband's crab is swamped by rice and he pronounces his beef (also with rice) as 'really rather dull'. Except *nothing's* dull when Mr Sykes is around. As each course arrives, he ceremoniously adjusts the dimmer switches and how we love it when he terrorizes with a glance the man who's had the temerity to light a cigar. 'This is a *non*-smoking dining room,' he intones.

And why are you called Frogg Manor, I ask? 'Ah, because there is a big frog pond here.'

'Oh, simple as that then?' I confess to being disappointed.

'Well, perhaps the *real* reason was because my girl friend at that time was called Frog...'

That's more like it. 'And now,' adds Mr Sykes, croaking slightly, 'I just can't *stop* people giving me frogs.' A fact which is more than evident.

'Nothing changes at Frogg Manor – all rooms are continually being upgraded,' says John E. Sykes. 'I also thought you'd like to know I've now got over 300 frogs... signed Froggards.'

A joke's a joke, Mr Sykes. Will there still be room for guests?

Frogg Manor Hotel and Restaurant,

Fullers Moor,
Nantwich Road,
Broxton,
Chester,
Cheshire CH3 9JH.
Tel: (01829) 782629.
Fax: (01829) 782238.
John E. Sykes.
Location: off the A534 Wrexham-Nantwich road.
Open: all year.
Rooms: 6. 6 double (£48–£95.50), all ensuite. Single in double (£40–£80). (One room, the Wellington Suite, is entered via a bookcase in the sitting room.)
Restaurant: open for dinner from 7–9.30pm.
Chef: John E. Sykes. Table d'hôte 18 guineas or £22.21 (sic). Also à la carte, average £25. Continental breakfast £3 (orange juice extra), English breakfast £7.50.
Wine List: eclectic, from £11.
Children: yes.
Dogs: yes.
Smoking: not in one part of the restaurant.
And Also: 10-acre garden with frog pond.

*B*urnham Market, Norfolk
THE HOSTE ARMS

Outside the back door of the 17th-century Hoste Arms in Burnham Market lurks Basil the chow. 'He's hungry,' confides a small girl, putting loving arms round Basil's hairy neck.

And outside the front door, a notice informs potential guests that all its bedrooms are 'on suite' (sic), while a quick recce of first-floor windows reveals further refurbishment in the form of what's known in impolite circles as knicker blinds.

Knicker blinds notwithstanding, The Hoste Arms seems a homely sort of place with a bar teeming with locals knocking back bitter and a small adjoining restaurant crammed with jolly people. We search in vain for a reception desk and end up at the bar. This place has an identity problem. Is it pub or is it hotel?

Eventually a girl leads us away from the crowd and up a quiet staircase carpeted with thick, good quality carpet to a large knicker-blinded room at the front, with four-poster, blue armchair and sofa.

How comfortable it looks. The radiators are on full blast. But isn't there some . mistake? I did not book this lovely four-poster room. The girl gazes at us blankly. Does she think we're complaining?

We're not. When she's gone, we have a quick nose around. Behind a door there's a walk-in wardrobe and, in the bathroom, one of those devices for which the correct term is masticator.

But now for mastication of a different kind. Sautéed strips of beef fillet with chilli, mushroom and red peppers makes a warming start, as does thick pumpkin soup. A disappointment, however, to be told that lamb stuffed with spinach and pine nuts is off the menu and how hard not to glare at the man who gets the last serving. I concentrate instead on the fascinating love scene being enacted in one corner involving the blowing of many tiny kisses. Goodness, he's old enough to be her grandfather.

Puddings include Bakewell and treacle tarts and bread and butter pudding. Cheese and biscuits means lots of butter, three different cheeses and half an apple. If you have one course it costs you £8.75, two £11.75 and three £13.75. This strikes me as an eminently sensible arrangement.

Now owner Paul Whittome does the rounds. 'Was everything all right?'

'Yes, thank you.' And so on. While it's good to have such a caring host, this sort of earnest concern *can* be overdone. We retire to the still-crowded bar to drink our coffee.

Meanwhile we have learned from the menu that The Hoste Arms was named after Captain Hoste, a protégé of Nelson. On Monday evenings at eight-fifteen there's jazz ('no electrified instruments') and on Wednesdays classical music, with piano or string quartets played by a selection of musicians 'chosen' by nearby resident, Lady Margaret Douglas-Home.

Glancing around, we realize everyone in here seems to know each other.

But at ten-thirty, as if at some unseen signal, they exit leaving just seven regulars cackling among themselves.

Our room, which was so inviting after dark, is even better in the morning with those blinds pulled up to reveal a view across the village green. My only niggle, once more, is about hot duvets – though I have been scolded by one reader who says these things should be called quilts.

We collar Mr Whittome who tells us that he, personally, has been in charge of the restoration and refurbishment of his pub/hotel. Why don't you have jazz and classical music at weekends as well, we want to know? 'We're always full at weekends. The music is for the benefit of the locals,' he explains. Oh, very well then. Next question: why did you give us such a posh room and only charge us the normal rate? Now the smiley Mr W becomes very smiley-wiley indeed. 'It just happened to be vacant...and we do like to show our hotel off.' Point taken.

'We've spent several enjoyable weekends here,' says a Cambridge reader. 'The owner claims to have the best bedrooms in North Norfolk, and we quite believe him.'

The Hoste Arms,

The Green,
Burnham Market,
Kings Lynn,
Norfolk PE31 8HD.
Tel: (01328) 738257.
Fax: (01328) 730103.
Paul Whittome.
Location: overlooking village green.
Open: all year.
Rooms: 15. 13 twin/double (£64–£76), 2 four-posters (£82), most ensuite. Single in double (£47). 2 ground-floor rooms.
Restaurant: open for dinner from 7pm.
Chef: Peter Howard/James Patterson. A la carte, average £13.50.
Wine List: to suit all tastes/pockets, from £7.
Children: yes.
Dogs: yes.
Smoking: feel free except in new no-smoking restaurant.
And Also: live jazz every Monday and Friday, art gallery. Hotel open all day for breakfast, morning coffee, lunch, afternoon teas, evening meals.

*C*ambridge
PANOS HOTEL-RESTAURANT

This week I'm sent a copy of *Best Loved Hotels of the World*, a new guide stuffed with quotes of the 'we arrived as guests and left as friends' ilk. If only. Inside its glossy pages, I discover the Panos Hotel in Cambridge and I don't have to be Sherlock to guess it's Greek.

Except the girl who says hello as we hurtle in from the rain is Scottish. And then we are welcomed by Madame, only she turns out to be French. Clearly a cosmopolitan sort of place.

'Follow me,' says the Scots girl, inviting us up the narrow staircase where she opens the door of a room with a brown executive air. 'Thank you,' we smile. 'We'll be down for dinner shortly...'

Looking around, we decide this little room could teach some other hotel rooms a thing or two. The effect may be brown, but the furniture is matching, there are two stylish bedside lights, a clock radio, a mini bar, a well positioned TV and well stocked bathroom. There isn't much they can do about the view, alas – this is a town hotel after all.

Deciding it's a sweater and jeans sort of night, we waltz downstairs looking forward to the action. The two dining rooms on either side of the narrow entrance hall are buzzing. 'Ees everything all right upstairs?' enquires Madame, popping out of a back room.

'Yes, thank you.'

'Thank *you*,' she says.

'Perhaps you'd like a drink in the conservatory while looking at the menu?' suggests the Scottish waitress. Indeed we would.

The conservatory – built out onto the street – is filled with wicker furniture, plants and – an unusual touch – Christmas tree lights. 'Anything goes as long as it's done with panache,' my husband, in banal mood, remarks. 'You mean *Pan os*.'

Panos offers a residents' special set dinner at £12 – not bad considering some of its à la carte dishes cost nearly as much. Suddenly it's all very Greek. We choose from the set dinner: Greek sausages, hummous, grilled entrecôte steak and lamb souvlaki – all served with Greek salad. To drink? Retzina of course.

In the main restaurant there are round tables and curved red banquette seats along one wall. Our table is the other side, but that doesn't stop us from eavesdropping on the group of four arguing about the merits of various New York art galleries or watching, faintly appalled, as a woman fondly pats her partner's *embonpoint*.

Phew. The food's very nice – typically Greek – but the portions aren't small. So what on earth makes me say yes to homemade baklava? Well, it's all part of the job, isn't it. 'Rubbish,' says my husband. 'It's greed.'

Staggering out afterwards we collapse in a small sitting room where a giant solitaire board sits on the coffee table. Madame, whose name is Geneviève, shows us how to play. 'See, it's easy.' For her, perhaps.

Eventually we give up and go to bed. After discovering how efficient the shower is, it's no surprise to find the bed is comfortable too.

When we come down to breakfast the restaurant is empty, our table is laid and classical music plays. 'A newspaper?' asks Geneviève. 'Yes, please – ' and she nips outside to buy one. 'Thank you,' we say. 'Thank *you*,' she replies.

Suddenly I'm curious. 'Why – when you're French – are you running a Greek restaurant?' I ask.

'Ah, but Greek food tastes so much better in England,' she explains. 'You have such wonderful meat here.'

Er yes: but I still don't *quite* understand:

'Panos, he's my ex-husband, is a Greek Cypriot. I've been on my own for two years now...and I *love it*,' says Geneviève with a big grin.

'When I opened The Telegraph *that morning I felt great elation,' says Geneviève. 'It was an unexpected reward for me after many months of efforts.'*

Panos Hotel-Restaurant,
154–156 Hills Road,
Cambridge CB2 2PB.
Tel: (01223) 212958.
Fax: (01223) 210980.
Geneviève Antoniou.
Location: 10 minutes city centre.
Open: all year except 1 week Christmas.
Rooms: 7. 4 single (£45), 3 double (£60), all ensuite. Single in double (£45).
Restaurant: open for dinner from 7–10pm.
Chef: Hossein Vojdanpak. Residents' menu £12, table d'hôte £16.50.
Wine List: Mostly French, from £7.95.
Children: yes.
Dogs: no.
Smoking: in one restaurant only.
And Also: residents' sauna.

Castle Cary, Somerset
BOND'S HOTEL AND RESTAURANT

'And do you have a restaurant?' I inno-cently ask Mr Bond of Bond's Hotel when booking. 'I'm not modest...our restaurant's *renowned*,' he replies.

I'll confess. A year ago Mr Bond wrote suggesting a visit to Bond's Hotel: 'Your dry – nay, sick – humour can only be fully appreciated by someone of similar ilk. The chance of publicity from your column far outweighs the fear of your critical pen...'

Bond's is an attractive listed Georgian house with a Thought for the Day placard outside: 'Start with break-fast and finish with dinner – does a better day exist?' Equally uplifting is the Christmas-red front door and, beyond, the sight of Mr Bond leaping out from behind his antique desk. 'I'm Kevin Bond. Which morning newspaper would you like?' he asks. 'Good heavens, haven't a clue. Oh, *The* – ' I add, hastily denying my interest in newspapers that begin with T.

As I sign the book, he gestures towards an attractive member of staff: 'She's a big strapping girl, she'll take your bags up,' he says. Now I'd bop him one for that, but perhaps I've no sense of humour. *She* carries on smiling as she shows us into a front bedroom where, after a quick change act, we beetle down to the bar.

Mr Bond now apologizes for cata-pulting us into decision-making the minute we arrive. 'As I get older, I forget to ask people what paper they want. My wife gets cross, you know

what women are like?' Yes, Mr Bond – you're speaking to one.

He mixes us drinks: Scotch for my husband; Angosturas and tonic for me, only I think he just ran out of Angosturas and isn't telling. As we peruse the menus, cooked by his wife Yvonne, he tells us how he observed Fergie squeezing Andy's bottom when the couple had dinner here in '87. 'I liked her, she was warm and friendly,' he comments.

The 'renowned' restaurant is small and unpretentious looking. Two uniformed waitresses flit in and out. I'm not in the mood for drinking, so deli-cately sip a glass of Australian Fumé Blanc while my husband quaffs a modest half bottle of Chianti.

And, oh, the food. It's superlatives all the way. My Red Lancaster and Gorgonzola soufflé is terrific. A dish of sardine fillets marinaded in olive oil, accompanied by salad and dollop of aubergine casserole is wonderful. Ditto my roast saddle of lamb served pink and tender – not a sliver of fat to be seen –and his stuffed leg of duck that's crispy round the outside. It's the veg, though, that deserve special mention: courgette stuffed with grated celeriac; green beans with onion and flaked almonds; fennel stuffed with olives; dauphinoise potatoes. Such care and attention. As for the puddings...

By now the Bonds are settling down to dinner and invite the couple at the next table to join them for a glass of something. Feeling faintly *de trop*, we retreat to the bar where we are joined by a talkative fellow guest who's staying here on a Special Offer. 'Are *you?*' she asks me eagerly.

Upstairs, grey marks to: a bedroom door that won't lock; a shower that squirts out sideways with no curtain to stop it saturating the nice pink carpet, nor even a bathmat to soak it up; a wardrobe that involves moving the television first. Yes, I know it's a small room but...

And a *black* mark to the tea-maker. Opening it, what do we find? A used, dried-up herb tea bag...Yuk. If you had been around, Mr Bond, when we paid the bill, I might, just, have mentioned it.

This man is not called Bond for nothing. Not only does he send me a sporting letter after the piece appeared, it also seems he has been busy: 'The shower screen has now been replaced in Room 1,' he says, 'there are notices to all rooms asking guests to put tea bag in cup, not machine (!), a new housekeeper has just started, having first attended a training course on tea-making machines...and the lock on Room 1 does work (he forgot to add 'so there').

Hmmmm. We did try it several times – is it a coded lock perhaps?

Bond's Hotel and Restaurant,

Ansford Hill,
Ansford,
Castle Cary,
Somerset BA7 7JP.
Tel/Fax: (01963) 350464.
Kevin and Yvonne Bond.
Location: on the A371 in the village of Ansford.
Open: all year, except Christmas week.
Rooms: 7. 6 twin/double (£60–£80), all ensuite. 1 double with separate private bathroom (£64). Single in double (£38–£51).
Restaurant: dinner served from 7–9.30pm.
Chef: Yvonne Bond. Table d'hôte £12.50, also à la carte.
Wine List: international, with New World emphasis, from £8.50.
Children: babies and over 8s.
Dogs: no.
Smoking: ask if in doubt.
And Also: special breaks according to season – please enquire.

Cawston, Norfolk
GREY GABLES COUNTRY HOUSE HOTEL

Brrrrming along north Norfolk country lanes guaranteed to drive you round the bend, we find Grey Gables – *pow!* – just like that. What luck. And what an appealing small country house this former rectory is, not smart, not run down, but just-right looking.

When booking, I remember making promises about arriving at seven-thirty for dinner but, judging from the hubbub coming from the dining room, I bet they're glad we haven't turned up bang on time and starving.

A young woman takes us up to a room that reminds us of an attic. Presenting us with menus and a vast wine list, she suggests we ring our order down straight away. Perhaps she just *assumes* we're gannets? 'No, thanks,' we say, feeling pressured. 'We'll be down for a drink first and then we'll order.' Besides, there's a phone call to make: I've left the iron on at home.

This is a dear little eyrie, we decide, before glancing, astonished, at the wine list which has a section taken presumably from some ancient Book of Physick. There are wines for the relief of *Constipation, Diarrhée, Trouble de la Menopause* and other ailments too delicate to mention. As for the menu, we're totally confused. Should we have the cold platter, salad and pudding for £10? The residents' dinner (£15.50)? Or maybe splash out on three courses (£17), four courses (£19) or – help – five courses (£21)?

Undecided, we wander down to the sitting room. Here's a nice family place,

painted in cool, calm grey with antique furniture, a handsome fireplace, pictures and shelves filled with books, groups of teapots and Staffordshire dogs.

Now we meet the owner – Mr Snaith, we presume? – yes, yes, of course it's him. 'Are you ready to order?' he asks, with great charm and a touch of shyness that I reckon wouldn't be hard to turn into a blush. 'W-e-l-l, almost....' We decide to put him to the test over the wine. 'What do you recommend?'

He isn't blushing, but he does seem a mite embarrassed. 'It depends on how much you want to spend.' Eventually he suggests a white Burgundy with no particular curative properties. 'I think you'll like this.'

Returning, he pours some in a glass for me to taste – always a winning touch as far as I'm concerned. 'I *do* like it...' We quiz him about the room. 'Are all these family things or did you go out and choose them?' 'A bit of a mixture really, but you're right, a lot of it *is* family stuff...we all use this as our room, you see...when we have time.

Soon he reappears. 'You may as well go and join the fun,' he grins. We follow him into an inviting dining room which has polished mahogany tables, decorative wall plates and candles.

Yes, we *did* choose. My husband's having the local crab with salad and I the humus (sic) with fresh herb and tomato sauce and date chutney. We're bowled over. Now for something entirely different: deep, steaming bowls of lovage soup. 'This is the most interesting, delicious soup I've *ever* tasted,' declares my husband extravagantly. 'Lovage is very easy to grow,' says Mr Snaith appearing obligingly from nowhere and gesturing in the general direction of the garden.

The rest of dinner – trout, sautéed turkey in a green peppercorn sauce – is just as good. Declining coffee, we nip up to bed where we debate whether to have an argument about the *one* bedside light.

In the morning, we do almost come to blows – over the shower. I can't get it to work, so decide to have it cold. 'Don't be such a martyr,' snarls my husband, wrenching at the controls. Oh dear. Not the best shower in the world, and as for those three small, mismatching towels...

Mr Snaith becomes almost chatty over the bill-paying ritual. 'You didn't meet my wife, did you?' 'No.' 'She's a bit shy,' he says, giving us a rather shy smile himself.

How impossible not to warm to all this diffidence and, indeed, to modest Grey Gables...

'Actually we're not shy,' say the Snaiths – diffidently.

Grey Gables Country House Hotel,

Norwich Road,
Cawston,
Norfolk NR10 4EY.
Tel: (01603) 871259.
James and Rosalind Snaith.
Location: 1 mile south of Cawston village.
Open: all year.
Rooms: 8. 2 single (£20),. 6 double (£56), mostly ensuite. Single in double (£40).
Restaurant: open for dinner from 7pm.
Chef: Rosalind Snaith. Table d'hôte from £15.50.
Wine List: extensive, from £7.50.
Children: yes.
Dogs: yes.
Smoking: not in dining room.
And Also: lawn tennis court at hotel; Norwich, the Broads, the North Norfolk coast.

BROCKENCOTE HALL

The perfect hotel? Does it exist? Yes, raves 'Room Service' reader, Mrs R of Leeds, who went there and penned me two pages of purple prose: 'At this country house hotel, you'll have no complaints about the shower, lack of towels, bedside lamps and...' she purrs.

How nice to have my foibles so carefully monitored. *I'm* not purring, though, when we miss the M42 west turn-off and head north instead. By the time we bowl up Brockencote Hall's sweeping drive, it's 8.40pm and I'm wondering why we always arrive early at the uncomfortable places and are late for the perfect one.

In the hall, a pile of logs nudges the ceiling. 'We like to keep the place warm,' explains the pretty owner Alison Petitjean, mistress of understatement. *Warm?* It's wonderful. She whisks us upstairs.

Enjoying the quarter bottle of Harveys Bristol Cream provided, we contemplate a room of discreet luxury: old-fashioned radiators, elegant repro furniture, French wallpaper, chandeliers with frosted-glass shades, fashionably distressed picture frames.

I particularly appreciate the wardrobe's *cachet* of gentleman's-club wooden hangers – these really do add to that cosseted feeling, even though some of us prefer to drape our clothes across the backs of chairs – though not tonight Josephine.

Soon we're skipping downstairs in best bibs and tuckers and arranging ourselves expectantly in a grand conservatory with tented ceiling. By now, sated diners are staggering in to relax over coffee, but I'm delighted to see a jolly family party including baby, who, like us, haven't yet eaten.

A man in black glides purposefully towards us, proffering wine list and menus. Oh lord, *he* looks forbidding, I think, as we devour nibbles and peruse the three gourmet French menus priced at £21.50, £28 and £35.50. No prob: we pick the £21.50.

Now our man in black permits himself a smile – just a small one, mind. He would like – er – to suggest a different wine – 'better' in his view – than the one we've chosen. 'If you don't like it, we'll change it...'

'But it will have been opened!'

'I'll think of something to do with it.'

'Like drink it, you mean.' Forbidding? Head waiter Trevor's a *hoot*.

The restaurant consists of three interconnecting rooms, one of which – ours – is panelled. Although the white, damask covered tables are well spaced, we can hear all that's being said next door: 'I interviewed Roger Moore, Cubby Broccoli and Topol,' booms one Pebble Mill type. 'Gosh, that must have been *a long time ago*,' I hiss and I'm sure my husband would have agreed if only he hadn't been so busy earwigging too.

It's not even our birthdays! The perfect dinner is served by meticulously trained boy waiters. The Trevor-wine is light and crisp. Just to stop things getting too reverential round here, Trev chucks in the odd po-faced joke between the carrot and leek soup, gravalux (sic), light fish medley on a Provençal vegetable ragôut and roast noisette of Barbary duck breast.

Just when we're too full for words, he conjures up mini crême brulées: 'Pre-puddings!' he announces maliciously. Oh, what? I'm ashamed to say we sample the real puddings too and can report they're works of art.

Everyone's so nice to us here at Brockencote Hall. Nothing's too much trouble. I'm not surprised in the morning to find the breakfast room full. As we leave, we meet the unassuming Mr Petitjean on duty at reception – only hands-on owners in this hotel. When I suggest he's a perfectionist, he quickly changes the subject and tells us about his young children. 'Our eldest was so jealous when his brother arrived that he fell downstairs and needed 12 stitches...' In spite of the grandeur, this is a proper family hotel.

'Trevor is as helpful and witty as ever,' writes Alison Petitjean, *'and was "astonished, pleased and proud" – his own words – at his sudden fame. Incidentally, Trevor-wine is a typical example of country wines from France which we have recently introduced.'*

Brockencote Hall,

Chaddesley Corbett,
nr Kidderminster,
Hereford and Worcester
DY10 4PY.
Tel: (01562) 777876.
Fax: (01562) 777872.
Alison and Joseph Petitjean.
Location: on edge of village.
Open: all year.
Rooms: 17. 17 twin/double (£90–£115), all ensuite. Single in double (£75). 1 ground-floor room adapted for wheelchair users, with stair lift.
Restaurant: open for dinner from 7pm.
Chef: Eric Borchet. Dinner £21.50–£35.50.
Wine List: Mainly French, with some New World, from £9.40.
Children: yes.
Dogs: no.
Smoking: not in dining room.
And Also: bird watching in grounds, Severn Valley Railway, walking in Malvern Hills and Long Mynd.

*C*heltenham, Gloucestershire
ABBEY HOTEL

Hoteliers bombard me with letters extolling the virtues of their hotels. Come and visit us and you will not be disappointed, they purr. Mr Jacques Lorraine of the Abbey Hotel in Cheltenham adopts a more pragmatic approach: 'Cast thy bread upon the waters and you may get back a sandwich, which is the reason for this invitation,' he says. Accompanying his letter is a modest brochure: 'It's an accurate description of what my wife and I have to offer.'

Assuming that *Telegraph* readers nourish a burning desire to know about inexpensive hotels in the centre of Cheltenham, I book a room – incognito – leap into the car and zoom down the M4. We discover the Abbey to be a small Regency hotel of the two-houses-knocked-into-one variety. There's a parking space right outside and a car park at the end of the street.

Mrs Lorraine, looking fetching in leggings, comes dashing up the hall making chirruping sounds. In fact, so warm is her welcome that at first we think we must be the only guests. But no – in the sitting/dining room we encounter a shy couple holding hands on the sofa.

This room is painted a tasteful blue-grey and has some good paintings and antiques. Sadly, there is only one upholstered chair, the rest of the sitting apparatus being cane. A gas coal fire burns invitingly in the fireplace.

The shy couple are now summoned to dinner and Mrs Lorraine presents us with the menu. 'I'll get my husband to tell you about the wine.'

We had presumed that Mr Lorraine was slaving over the hot stove. 'Oh no – I'm the cook. It's my hobby,' says Mrs Lorraine very firmly indeed, the perfect unflustered hostess.

Jacques Lorraine, enigmatic letter writer, now ambles towards us – how disappointing to discover that, in spite of the name, he's so frightfully English. After a certain amount of waffle, he mentions he has a very good house white at £6: 'A Californian, really excellent, and I've tasted *a lot* of wines, particularly in South Africa where we come from.'

'But what else do you have?' After a great display of charm on his part unaccompanied by further offerings, we are obliged to settle for his Californian house white and are reminded of that famous quote of Henry Ford when the Model T was first introduced: 'You can have any colour you like so long as it's black.'

Mr Lorraine's Gallo house white is the opposite of full-bodied, but Mrs Lorraine's food is unpretentious, full of flavour and quite delicious: the two-course table d'hôte menu at £12.50 consists of chicken Kiev accompanied by red cabbage and apple, boiled parsley potatoes and celeriac *rémoulade*, followed by apple strüdel and cream.

We opt for coffee in the sitting room, which the shy couple have deserted in favour of a wander round Cheltenham.

Mr Lorraine tells us that in South Africa Mrs Lorraine was in Arts Administration and he in advertising and marketing. Hence the rather clever letter – of *course.* 'We have two sons who're being educated over here now. I retired once and then bought this hotel a year ago...'

Now we ask about the music. 'Is it Prokofiev?' Mrs Lorraine turns up the volume of her cherished new CD player situated in the office behind the dining room and puts on some Rachmaninov. Shortly afterwards one of her large sons lollops in. His opinion of Rachmaninov is crystal clear. Aiming himself at the CD, he turns the sound right down. We take the hint and decide on a wander round Cheltenham too.

A word about Room 2. Amenities are not up to scratch. There shouldn't be a shower as inefficient as this one when there's no bath to compensate. The creepy thing is that I only have to *look* at the plastic towel holders and they fall off. Such inconveniences should, however, be taken in conjunction with the bill: in these expensive days, £78.30 for dinner, bed and breakfast for two is not extortionate.

This piece prompted a reproachful letter from Don Rogers of The Belvedere Guest House, who said: 'I would be extremely upset if my showers did not work or if my non-plastic towel holders fell off the wall. If one offers a service, however cheaply, the customer is entitled to receive what he is paying for.'

Abbey Hotel,
16 Bath Parade,
Cheltenham,
Gloucestershire GL53 7HN.
Tel: (01242) 516053
Fax: (01242) 513034.
Jacques and Miggi Lorraine.
Location: in the centre of town.
Open: all year.
Rooms: 13. 6 single (£30–£35), 7 twin/double (£52–£58), mostly ensuite. Single in double (£40).
Restaurant: open for dinner 7–9pm.
Chef: Dania Chirnside. Table d'hôte £9.50–£12.50.
Wine List: 2 whites, 2 reds, from £7.
Children: yes.
Dogs: yes.
Smoking: feel free.
And Also a collection of etchings and watercolours by Cotswold artist Edward Payne, a garden with apple trees.

He's right of course. Meanwhile, there have been changes at the Abbey. Cooking is no longer Mrs Lorraine's hobby: 'Our new addition is a willowy blonde South African, Dania Chirnside, who is blessed with superb culinary skills.' The house is now Suffolk pink, the sitting/dining room a deep maroon. As for that cane furniture, it's been banished to the large son's flat, together with Nirvana CDs. The other good news? Showers have been 'improved' and those plastic towel rails replaced..

*C*helwood, Avon
CHELWOOD HOUSE

No sooner are we drifting down the grand staircase of Chelwood House Hotel, *circa* 1681, and into the smaller of its two drawing rooms than Mr Rudi Birk, our host, is rushing towards us bearing glasses of mulled wine. 'Our compliments – and welcome,' he cries.

We're quite overcome. 'How nice. Thank you...' but Mr Birk has already scurried away – as chef, he has a nagging stove to tend. Meanwhile, his smiling wife, Jill, wearing a fetching blue waistcoat and matching dirndl skirt, flutters daintily in and out with menus and small talk.

But why the folksy outfit? It seems that Friday night is Bavarian Night at Chelwood House, converted by the Birk family from a private house into a hotel ten years ago. There's a £13.50 Taste of Bavaria menu, a preponderance of German labels on the wine list and jolly Bavarian muzak tinkling away in the background.

The next hospitable gesture is when my husband requests a Campari and tonic. Mrs Birk returns with an apologetic air. 'I'm afraid we've almost run out of Campari. Please have what we've got left with our compliments.' That's nice. Between them, they're making us feel that, as guests, we matter.

Dinner is served in an elaborately furnished and decorated conservatory. At one end there's a view of the garden and, down each side, trellis pelmets and lacy curtains encompass murals of enticing pastoral scenes. Some of the tables – ours included –have pink curved sofas to sit on.

Our bottle of Frankonian white in fancy bottle, chosen because it's more appropriate than Australian Chardonnay and also because it's 'the proprietor's favourite', is not as dry as we'd hoped...but what the hell. By now, we've entered into the Bavarian spirit.

The other tables are occupied by a plethora of well behaved young couples murmuring to each other across such freshly prepared dishes as Flädle Suppe – clear chicken soup with shredded herb pancake – and Pikanter Wurstsalat – sausages, apples and gherkins with mayonnaise.

I can't resist something with a name like Flädle Suppe – though it turns out to be rather tasteless – followed by Schweinegoulasch mit Semmel Knödel – pork in a yummy paprika sauce with bread dumplings. My husband has the strips of fillet of beef with mushrooms, gherkins, tomatoes and cream with fresh herbs, otherwise known as Herrentopf. Both dishes, if not quite *haute cuisine,* are splendidly flavoursome. Mrs Birk, meanwhile, trips merrily to and fro in her rustling dirndl, attending to all needs.

Upstairs we're not surprised to find the bed's been turned down and the curtains drawn. The room – indeed the whole house – is generously supplied with radiators and is wonderfully warm. The colour scheme has a tendency towards pinks and blues of the distinctly pastel variety and there's even a little sofa for us to watch the telly on.

'Huh, those bedside lamps are just like dirndl skirts,' mutters my husband – though his tone's affectionate. The bathroom is well appointed too, down to spare loo roll in a dear little pink crochet case – Mrs Birk's handiwork? must remember to ask – and a brilliantly efficient shower as well as bath.

Perhaps almost the best bit of our stay is breakfast, when the conservatory is bathed in sunlight and there's fresh orange juice, grapefruit halves, scrambled egg with smoked salmon, pancakes and maple sauce, black pudding, fresh croissants, homemade marmalade and jam, a choice of teas and a selection of newspapers, including *The Daily Telegraph*, to read. Like the reader who wrote suggesting Chelwood House – to whom thank you –we also leave feeling that a few stresses and strains have miraculously disappeared.

The sad news is...Mrs Birk no longer dazzles with her dirndl on Bavarian Nights. Why? Bavarian Nights are now off the menu. But the glad news is that Mr Birk is still cooking dishes such as Herrentopf and Griesknödel, a regular part of dinner at Chelwood, along with that Bavarian feeling.

Chelwood House,

Chelwood,
Bristol,
Avon BS18 4NH.
Tel/Fax: (01761) 490730.
Jill and Rudi Birk.
Location: between Bristol, Bath and Wells.
Open: all year except first 2 weeks January.
Rooms: 11. 3 single (£49–£65), 8 double (£69–£95), all ensuite. Single in double (£59.50). 2 ground-floor rooms.
Restaurant: open for dinner from 7.30–9pm.
Chef: Rudi Birk. A la carte, average £20.
Wine List: choice of 70 – French, German, New World, from £9.50.
Children: yes, over 10.
Dogs: no.
Smoking: not in dining room.
And Also: golf, trout fishing, walking in the Mendips.

Chirk, Clwyd
STARLINGS CASTLE HOTEL

The road leading to remote Starlings Castle – just over the border into Wales – is paved with good intentions...and potholes. What's more, it isn't a Welsh castle at all but an Englishman's home.

Opening the door of this 18th-century farmhouse, we ring a bell in the flagstoned hall and out dashes the aproned Englishman himself (though no doubt he'll now write accusingly and tell me he's Scottish, Welsh or Double Dutch). As for Starlings Castle, it's on the borders of Shropshire and Wales. Whose side is it on? The map says Wales, the hotel brochure Shropshire.

Mr Antony Pitt is bearded and charming in a reserved kind of way. He conducts us up to a plain white-painted room furnished with mahogany antique furniture and lots of magazines. 'I'll just go and get milk for your tea,' he says, returning two ticks later with a jug.

After all his trouble, we forget to make the tea. Drifting downstairs to the bar, we encounter his glamorous wife Jools ('everyone expects me to be a man') who tells the story of how they met in a restaurant in Bath. 'When we got married, we bought this place from my uncle and aunt. We opened as a hotel right away, it was an impulsive thing.'

'Goodness, that was brave.'

'Well, you've got to have a challenge in life, haven't you...'

Reading the brochure, it wasn't such a challenge. 'The Chef Patron has gained a reputation and twenty years' experience in leading hotels and restaurants in the West Country.'

'He has no help in the kitchen,' says Jools proudly. 'He does *everything.*'

So we look forward to dinner. Meanwhile how comfortable to be in the bar with its wood-burning stove, deep blue-green painted ceiling, brave red walls, patterned curtains, books, dried flowers, squashy settees and sleeping cat.

Now other guests arrive, including a distraught lady who's quickly ushered to the upper regions followed by soothing room service tray. A well-brought-up small boy scurries through to private quarters the other end. 'Good evening,' he mutters, head well down. 'Our two boys go to the school in the village,' explains Antony Pitt, shoving logs on the fire.

Apparently six of the eight rooms are booked. The couple from Stafford are definitely on matey terms with Jools. A party of diners arrive from nearby Chester, together with an elderly mother who declines to remove her fur hat.

A huge pine dresser dominates the centre of the long, white-painted dining room. The menu is exotic but not manically so. For starters we opt for Cumbrian air-dried ham with fresh figs and pigeon breast, walnut and mixed leaf salad. All the tables are now occupied and Jools is dashing to and fro like a dervish, with the help of just one waitress. Catering for eighteen is no mean feat for a team of three, but they make it look easy.

Next we have fillet of brill with a leek and mussel sauce and monkfish with tomato coconut and coriander. Our plates are scraped clean. 'What does that tell the chef?'

'Either it was extremely good or you were extremely hungry.' says Madam.

'It's both.'

The eight bedrooms share two bathrooms. Amazingly, there's no queue. We don't even fret when the shower's useless because we can have a bath instead. But if only we'd all been given keys. At 1.30am someone stumbles into our room. 'Made a mistake. Terribly sorry.'

By morning it's extremely cold and the room isn't quite warm enough. In front of the wash basin, my husband is on his knees – it's the only way he can see in the mirror to shave. Downstairs, breakfast scrambled egg is clearly prepared by someone who understands scrambled egg. The toast is made from homemade bread. The coffee, served in a pottery jug, is good and strong. Outside the latticed windows, snowflakes are whirling.

'Our new barn conversion seats parties of up to 50 and gives the place much more of a castle feel – very atmospheric,' say the Pitts.

Starlings Castle Hotel,

Bronygarth,
Oswestry,
Shropshire SY10 7NU.
Tel/Fax: (01691) 718464.
Antony and Jools Pitt.

Location: only just in Wales. Ask for directions.

Open: all year.

Rooms: 8. 2 single (£20), 6 twin/double (£40), none ensuite, 2 public bathrooms. Single in double (£30).

Restaurant: open for dinner from 7.30–10pm.

Chef: Antony Pitt. A la carte, average £18–£20. Cooked breakfast £3.

Wine List: supplied by Adnams of Southwold, from £9.50.

Children: yes.

Dogs: yes.

Smoking: feel free.

And Also: next-door pottery studio with items for sale. Fishing, walking, pony trekking. Jazz and wine-tasting evenings, 4-day cookery courses where Antony teaches some of the secrets he's spent 25 years learning – please enquire.

MOORS FARM & COUNTRY RESTAURANT

In narrow lanes reminiscent of Devon rather than Codsall near Wolverhampton, we discover Moors Farm and Country Restaurant. Zapping merrily into the yard, we blink in the ferocious glare of a welcoming(?) searchlight and then blink again. Call this a *farm?*

Townies like us have stupidly romantic ideas about farms that offer 'superior farmhouse accommodation'. Sorry, but we naively look forward to thatch, quaintness and old Windsor chairs.

So much for great expectations. Here's a real working farmyard with a good sprinkling of rural-looking objects, old sheds, friendly dog and a farmhouse built, at a guess, in the fifties.

Entering the small hall we are greeted by Mrs Moreton. 'I don't want to hassle you, but could you choose from the menu *now.*' What? We have booked dinner for eight-thirty and for once we're not late. 'Oh, all right then.' Putting down our bags we peruse the leather-jacketed menu thrust in front of us.

We're in for a surprise. This one has as many vegetarian as meat dishes. Even vegans are catered for. But time is of the essence. Our hostess hovers. So we make up our minds fast and afterwards wish we hadn't. Who knows, if the pressure had been off, we might have plumped for chestnut roast or nut round with sherry, sultanas and onion, both of which sound delicious.

Yet what, I wonder, do vegetarians make of the wall decorations in bar and dining room: all those jolly little stuffed animals, squirrels, an owl and a peacock (thankfully not a pussycat), not to mention the fox posing on what looks suspiciously like a loo seat.

If it's quaintness we're after – pseudo or otherwise – the bar has it. Behind the counter, a cheerful bespectacled lady mixes drinks and dashes to and from the adjoining kitchen. After a couple of drinks we are summoned to the dining room.

Now we twig that all food is being cooked to order. We also discover the regular waitress is off and that the proprietor's sister is deputizing. She places Pyrex-type bowls of homemade beef and veg soup on our hunting scene table mats. 'Who's the cook then?'

'Oh, my sister. She's lovely. She does everything herself.'

The soup's good, as is lemon sole with prawns and turkey and tarragon casserole. Vegetables, I regret to say, are overdone and potatoes positively naked.

Our lovely deputy waitress is now urging my husband to try the alcoholic passion cake. 'Have it, go on. You've got all night,' she chides. How churlish to refuse. When she brings it to table she giggles: 'The cook says she won't be responsible for your actions after this.'

By this time couples are arriving at twenty-minute intervals. Do we want coffee? 'We'll have it in the sitting room, please.'

This is a comfortable room, if on the brightly lit side, with a carpet more effusive than the one in the dining room. Orange velvet curtains with bobbles shut the darkness outside. Furnishings tend towards the tan, complementing the quarry-tiled skirting. An unusual clock, made from a polished brass horseshoe, has pride of place over the coal-effect fire. A dresser holds a collection of Evesham pottery and varying sizes of pottery horses.

Upstairs to bed. Our clean, tidy and functional room has two singles and one double bed, and an electrically operated shower that seems reluctant to part with hot water.

We are awakened in the morning by the country sounds of geese. Rushing to the window, we even spot the Wellington-booted farmer himself. Over breakfast and a view of grazing sheep, we learn about our hostess's vegetarian sympathies: 'I realized all I could offer vegetarians was an omelette. I knew that if *I* were a vegetarian and had gone out for a meal, I wouldn't want an omelette. So I decided to do something about it.'

'I am old-fashioned enough to happen to prefer my vegetables plain and not under-cooked,' writes Mrs Moreton. 'Townies have an odd sense of humour - but we're all different. You came on Valentine's night, didn't you? I remember distinctly because the restaurant was fully booked and I hardly had any help. Hope to meet you again one day.'

Moors Farm and Country Restaurant,

Chillington Lane,
Codsall,
Wolverhampton,
Staffordshire WV8 1QF.
Tel/Fax: (01902) 842330.
Mr and Mrs W. Moreton.
Location: between Codsall and Codsall Wood villages, on Shropshire border.
Open: all year.
Rooms: 6. 6 twin/double (from £40–£48), 3 ensuite. Single in double (from £24–£29).
Restaurant: open for dinner from 7-8.30pm.
Chef: Mrs Moreton. Table d'hôte from £10.
Wine List: good general list, from £6.00.
Children: yes, over 4.
Dogs: no.
Smoking: not in dining room.
And Also: Ironbridge Gorge, Gosford Aerospace Museum, Black Country Museum.

Cranbrook, Kent
KENNEL HOLT HOTEL

Some readers seem to think I'm a shower-fetishist. It's an unusual accolade. This week, though, no mention of showers. With good reason. Our bathroom at Kennel Holt Hotel hasn't got one.

On arrival, we make a rainy dash through delightful country gardens to the front door – suddenly it opens. We don't *quite* fall in but it's a close thing.

The proprietor, it seems, saw us coming. Dreadful weather, we agree, shaking ourselves in the hall. Now she hovers. 'We've got a party of nine tonight. A ruby wedding. We've put you the other side of the room, away from them. The restaurant's so *small*,' she laments, metaphorically wringing her hands.

'Sounds fine.' I'm busy looking around the hall which has a pleasant lived-in look. There's a desk as untidy as mine; an antique wood frame sofa, piled with papers; a mournful dog called Clovis.

Upstairs we go. Books spill from shelves and lurk in alcoves. On the landing is a dolls' house. There may be ten bedrooms here, it may call itself a hotel...but it's more like home. Our room has a four-poster bed and pink velvet chairs arranged in front of mullioned windows.

Going down again, where's everyone, we wonder? After peering into the empty restaurant, we wander into a sitting room with a log fire. Still no sign of life. Back to the hall. Now I spot a man in chef's clothes. 'Where can we get a drink?'

'In the room over there, round the corner,' he says, pointing. 'Pour yourselves what you want and write it down.' Oh my God. The sitting room we'd briefly sat in has got Private on the door. Well, it *was* open...

Finding the 'room over there' – an oak-panelled and heavily beamed library – we pour ourselves drinks from a collection of bottles on a corner table. The ruby wedding party's in full swing. Now a waitress approaches us: 'You're welcome to go back to the private room,' she offers. 'No, we're very happy here.'

'Are you *sure*?'

Dinner consists of simple and unpretentious food. For starters we have nectarine and walnut salad, and avocado, mozzarella and tomato salad, then tender lamb fillet with mint, rosemary and garlic for me and *coq au vin* for him. We finish with Tarte Tatin. Couldn't be nicer.

Coffee is brought to us in the library, where we play some opera on the record player and browse through a collection of old children's books. Then the ruby wedding party returns. The children's concern for their parents is touching. A cake is produced. 'Thank you,' says the daughter to the waitress, 'you've all been *so* kind.'

In the morning we look out onto a tranquil mass of trees and a croquet lawn. We get spoiled rotten at breakfast, with fresh orange juice and pink grapefruit cut up specially for me.

On leaving, we chat with our host, whose name is Neil Chalmers. 'Was that your daughter who gave us our breakfast?' we ask. 'No. *Our* children are still in bed,' he grins. He tells us that, until recently, he was in advertising but had always wanted to cook. 'In fact, Sally's the cordon bleu lady,' he says. 'I'm just the amateur, but I love it...'

There's much to love about Kennel Holt. The food; the laid-back, welcoming attitude; the beautiful old house, the gardens and topiary that are quite special. *But*...when you pay £98 for your room, you get picky. You reckon the bathroom should be – well – a bit more luxurious. You expect it to have carpet that's not patched and a shower along with the bath...and you *certainly* expect water that doesn't take five minutes to get hot.

'Quite correctly,' writes Neil Chalmers, 'you pointed out that your bathroom was not up to the standard of the rest of the hotel nor in line with the room rate. Since then we have created two new rooms with high quality bathrooms and, where necessary, replaced baths and other fittings. Now we are happy about our bathrooms!'

Kennel Holt Hotel,

Goudhurst Road,
Cranbrook,
Kent TN17 2PT.
Tel: (01580) 712032.
Fax: (01580) 715495.
Neil and Sally Chalmers.
Location: between Goudhurst and Cranbrook.
Open: all year.
Rooms: 9. 9 twin/double (£85–£105), all ensuite. Single in double (£85).
Restaurant: open for dinner from 7.30–9pm.
Chef: Neil Chalmers. Table d'hôte £17.50–£20.
Wine List: comprehensive, from £8.50.
Children: yes.
Dogs: no.
Smoking: not in restaurant.
And Also: the gardens of Sissinghurst and Great Dixter. Scotney, Leeds and Hever Castles. Fishing and water sports.

Crudwell, Wiltshire
CRUDWELL COURT HOTEL

'We're *so-oo* impressed with Crudwell Court Hotel we'd like your comments,' writes Mr Grey of Truro. 'Room 4's very comfortable!' he adds. Now *there's* a recommendation. But I've news for Impressed of Truro. Crudwell Court, a 17th-century rectory in the Cotswolds, is already on my list.

And, yes, I *am* impressed by the response to my one-night booking: first, the helpful chap on the end of the phone, followed by a letter of confirmation with directions and potted history of Crudwell Court. Quite unlike some hoteliers who give me the strong feeling they can't be bothered with one-nighters who may never be seen again. That's short-sighted I'd say.

No, we're not offered the 'comfortable' Room 4. Instead we're propelled from the flagstoned hall up various staircases and round corners to Room 7 by a welcoming young woman who tries to snatch both our bags: 'But mine's got magazines in it *and* the kitchen sink!' I cry, alarmed.

Our large and inviting attic room has a view of the church, a huge bed, a couple of armchairs and the sort of lighting that caresses rather than dazzles. Better still, there are separate switches for each light: it's very irritating to flick a switch and find you've triggered the Blackpool illuminations.

Upon arrival, we'd noticed that the drawing room was heaving with people. Where are they all now? The dining room, silly, says my husband. Huh – no one to eavesdrop on. Never

mind. Riffling through luxurious heaps of *Tatlers* and *Harpers*, we order drinks and peruse the menu, the whole meal priced according to which main course we have.

The panelled dining room has a reverent air. White starched cloths and napkins convey to us that serious food is served here. We start with pear and watercress soup – very nice too – and a salad consisting of avocado cubes, orange, chestnuts and crispy green bits.

'Where are you from?' asks the waitress in a sudden *non sequitur* as she removes my soup plate. London, I tell her, surprised – but how kind of her to enquire. Our main courses are poached turbot on a bed of herbs served in its own juices: 'Just wonderful!' I exclaim. 'Ditto,' says my husband of his sliced breast of duck in an orange and lime sauce. I can't help feeling, though, that such scrumptious food deserves better than a standard side dish of vegetables, especially as these include a strong tasting ratatouille at odds with the delicately flavoured food. Finishing with sticky toffee pudding and cream, we crash out in front of the drawing room fire where a cat called Lister allows me to play with him.

A wild wind blows in the night – bad news because the casement catch is missing and the window is dragged wide open. As for that church clock, it doesn't allow *anyone* to forget the time.

Leaning out in the morning, we admire the formal walled gardens: geometric flower beds, lawns, lily ponds, majestic trees. The bathroom's all it should be, and so down to breakfast where yoghurt, prunes, dried fruit and homemade muesli are laid out on a side table. A grumble: if dinner has been indifferent the night before, I'm resigned to indifferent breakfast orange juice. If dinner has been good, as in this case, I'm not. I expect the best. Some readers may think I'm being obsessive but, honestly, you can get better quality orange juice than this from almost any supermarket.

Having said that, the bacon and scrambled egg are fine and our contented fellow noshers, not as pernickety as I, all seem to be reading *The Sunday Telegraph.* Very appropriate.

'We have upgraded our orange juice!' chorus Nick Bristow and Iain Maclaren.

'Huh, how pernickety can Paddy Burt get,' grumbles one Telegraph *reader. 'Fancy complaining about a faulty window catch...'*

Crudwell Court Hotel,

Crudwell,
nr Malmesbury,
Wiltshire SN16 9EP.
Tel: (01666) 577194.
Fax: (01666) 577853.
Nick Bristow and Iain Maclaren.
Location: on the edge of Crudwell village.
Open: all year.
Rooms: 15. 2 single (£55–£85), 13 twin/double (£95–£120) all ensuite. Single in double (£60).
Restaurant: open for dinner from 7.30–9.30pm.
Chef: Chris Amor. Table d'hôte, from £19.50.
Wine List: wide-ranging, from £9.50.
Children: yes.
Dogs: yes.
Smoking: not in dining room.
And Also: croquet, heated outdoor pool (Easter–September), wonderful gardens. Special Church Architecture and Wine Appreciation weekends – please enquire.

$\mathcal{D}$ittisham, South Devon
FINGALS

If you want, say, to stand on your head in the dining room or slide down the banisters at Fingals Hotel no one is likely to stop and stare. Doing your own thing, however dotty, is what this hotel is all about.

Hotel, however, is too strong a word. The brochure issues subtle hints to this effect: 'Fingals is a special place'; 'not straightforward'; 'an abundance of personality'; 'an *experience*' – though in *my* experience, anything described as an experience should usually be avoided at all costs.

The 17th-century manor house called Fingals sits tranquilly among fields, winding lanes and the nearby River Dart. An amiable Australian member of staff speaks in tones of awe: 'You step outside at night and it's utterly dark and silent,' he says. 'All you hear is the occasional sheep.'

One's experience of the Fingals experience is immediate. It's getting in: not as easy as it sounds because the front door isn't the front door at all. Entrance is via French doors at the side, two sets of them, with just a narrow space between. Negotiating bags and baggage requires slimness, a touch of ingenuity, not to mention nerve: are we *really* coming in the right way?

Yes. All's well. Here's a small, cheerful bar, with stools and a settle and smiling Antipodean girl in charge. 'What's your names?' she asks in friendly fashion. She means first names of course – this place is not stuffy, heaven forbid – though the lady who wrote to me recently, saying how much she hated the unending muzak churned out by most hotels, would, I suspect, be deeply unhappy: 'Wake Up Little Susie' is followed by more of the same and it's loud.

I had a particular reason for wanting to visit Fingals, having often passed a restaurant of the same name in London's Fulham Road which offered enticing glimpses of a verdant conservatory inside. I never did get around to eating there and now it's no more, though the Devon experience *is* – same owner, same style.

There's a rather charming indifference to time here. Impossible not to notice the sign that says Good Morning (it's 6.30pm), the menu that's dated 12 March (it's 12 April) while, upstairs in the bedroom, the electric clock is forty minutes slow.

Then, when booking by phone, I'd been asked what time we'd like dinner. 'Nine o'clock?' enquired the Antipodean voice. What a joke. They are just *pretending* to be like other hotels – you cannot be in Fingals five minutes before you realize that dinner will be served when it is ready.

What's more, we will dining *en famille*. This particular evening there are just two other guests besides ourselves, the rest of the crowd being made up of owner Richard Johnston's family and friends, including several small children. The dining room (as opposed to the panelled restaurant) is laid for nine at one long table. 'Richard can be mischievous,' explains his girl-friend over drinks in the bar later. 'He tends not to tell people they'll be eating together. Of course, if anyone wants to eat privately, they've only got to say...'

Dinner is excellent and, better still, light: turbot soup, Dover sole garnished with Oriental vegetables, an imaginative cheeseboard, a choice of light puddings. We order our own wine and get on famously with our neighbours.

We do not get on quite as famously in the tiny bedroom, described in the brochure as an ND – normal double. The bed takes up most of the space and, as everything we need is the other side of it, we create constant traffic jams. There's a bath, but no shower. Only one bedside light. Not a room to hang about in, in spite of its wonderful view of the garden. But the rest of the house is such fun – pictures every-where, snooker room, library, TV room and, outside, a stream, summer house and pool. What more, I ask myself, could anyone want? Pedantic souls might disagree.

'You probably got us in our most relaxed mood,' growls Richard Johnston. 'Because of friends and family, you unfortunately had the twin room unsuitably converted to a double. If only you had told me you were a journalist... Anyway I thought you'd like to know that dinner is more punctual nowadays – especially when journalists are present!'

Fingals,

Old Coombe Manor Farm,
Dittisham,
Dartmouth,
Devon TQ6 0JA.
Tel: (01803) 722398.
Fax: (01803) 722401.
Richard Johnston.
Location: Old Coombe, Dittisham, near River Dart.
Open: all year except January–Easter.
Rooms: 10. 9 double (£65–£90), 1 family suite (£125–£130), all ensuite. Single in double (£55–£60). 1 downstairs room.
Restaurant: open for dinner when-ever it is ready.
Chef: Richard Johnston. Table d'hôte £25.
Wine List: international, with half from the New World, from £9.
Children: yes.
Dogs: yes.
Smoking: one smoke-free dining room.
And Also: conservatory with heated pool, real countryside, Dartmouth and the sea. Opera and music weekends during the summer – please enquire

*D*ulverton, Somerset
ASHWICK HOUSE

Leaving my husband to bring in our bags, I creep guiltily into Ashwick House. Why? We're late. I mean how *could* we have imagined zizzing down to Exmoor on a Friday in three hours flat?

Over the phone, Mr Sherwood, the owner, had said: 'Don't worry, I serve dinner till nine-thirty.'

'Oh, we'll be there long before,' I'd confidently replied.

What a joke. 'Are we the only guests?' I ask. 'Actually, yes,' he replies. Funny – when I've tried to book previously, I've always got the 'I'm sorry, we're full' treatment. Gosh, the poor man has lit the fire specially in the galleried hall, prepared dinner, turned the heating up to full and is making us feel like honoured guests as well.

He shows us to a delightful room. Alas, no time to nose around. Dashing smartly down the majestic, red-carpeted staircase to the dining room, we find a handwritten, violet-embossed card on our table that says: 'The - - - - Party'. 'Party?' I ask. 'Um, well, some ladies object to being called by their husband's name, it's safer this way.' he says.

'In that case,' I retort, 'why have you just poured the wine in my husband's glass for *him* to taste?'

'Ah, I get into trouble for that too,' Mr Sherwood replies equably, 'but you can't help the way you've been brought up, can you?' You certainly can't.

This cool, calm character now proceeds to bring us a scrumptious four-course dinner, cooked by himself. Yes, he *does* employ a waitress and a washer-upper on busy nights – that's all right then. First, it's olde Somerset parsnip and apple soup and light Roquefort mousse with melba toast. Then melon and parma ham, followed by fresh Barbary duck breast with orange and vermouth sauce and lovely crisp veg. Oh... *no* pudding for me, thanks.' My husband, whose eyes are bigger-than, wants chocolate hazelnut slice, mutters 'Wonderful' and complains he's too full to move. I drag him off to bed, where we find two bunny rabbit hotwater bottles have beaten us to it.

After a blissfully comfortable night, we belatedly discover two glasses of Italian vermouth on the mantelpiece, accompanied by a handwritten 'welcome' note. No, we *don't* drink up – just wish we had. In the bathroom I test the highly efficient power shower and step on a weighing machine that tells me the worst and warbles: 'Have a good day.'

Talk about a crowded room: dressing gowns, heaps of towels, a Bull-worker (honest), fruit, magazines, books, clock radio, cassette player with a pile of classical tapes, and handwritten epistles everywhere: 'If you find you've left something behind, we have a small stock of chemist items in reception, toothbrush, razor, flannel...and *condoms*.' Gee, thank you Mr Sherwood. Now listen to this: 'For a holiday with complete privacy, ask for a VIP residential suite with private entrance...we regret we are not able to accommodate armed security personnel, though a security system can be set up if required.' Perhaps the *Queen* comes here? Mr Sherwood's not telling, discretion is his middle name. From our window, I spy grass with rabbits scampering about, trees, a lake. Ashwick House is miles from anywhere. Peace, perfect peace.

Over breakfast, Mr Sherwood explains why guests are in short supply. 'They all want to book Friday *and* Saturday, and tonight I've got a full house and a rather grand house party to organize.' Gliding into the kitchen, he returns and plonks down tumblers of amber liquid. 'Freshly pressed apple juice,' he murmurs. There's homemade muesli too, served with slices of banana, and perfect poached egg. I'm totally unwound.

As we pay the bill, he remarks *en passant* that his grand house was built in 1901 by a Bristol businessman as a retreat. 'Don't you find it lonely?'

'No, because the world comes to *me*,' declares Mr Sherwood. The cost of this treat? £48.50 each, plus bottle of wine, total £112.25.

'As it's become a tradition for guests to breakfast outside during the summer,' writes Richard Sherwood, 'we have just enlarged the south-facing terrace...now more people can sit and watch the wildlife overlooking the wooded Barle valley. And since your article, everyone looks forward to their bunny hotwater bottles at night – the guests call them "Paddy Burt's bunnies"!'

Ashwick House,

Dulverton,
Somerset TA22 9QD.
Tel: (01398) 23868.
Richard Sherwood.
Location: on the southern slopes of Exmoor.
Open: all year.
Rooms: 6. 6 twin/double (£102–£130) – prices include dinner. Single in double – when available (£61–£75).
Restaurant: open for dinner from 7.15–8.30 pm.
Chef: Richard Sherwood. Table d'hôte £21.75 (included in room rate).
Wine List: international, from £8.50.
Children: yes, over 8.
Dogs: yes, but not in hotel.
And Also: Sweeping lawns, water gardens, wildlife, views. No credit cards.

DUNSLEY HALL

When Dunsley Hall comes with a 'recommended' tag from another hotelier, I wonder if there's a conspiracy afoot. I need not have worried. There's no red carpet laid out for me in remote North Yorkshire.

For here's a turn-of-the-century stone pile that's a one off. It boasts masses of oak panelling in perfect condition, a billiard room with full size 'Matchplay' table and stained glass windows and a delectable heated indoor pool.

Arriving just before six, we park as stipulated behind the wall next to the putting green. The heavy oak front door opens into a thickly carpeted hall and a hostess who spells out the rules as she escorts us on a brisk guided tour.

When booking, she had pointed out that: 'We serve plain food here and, being small, we are restricted on choice.' Small is not a word I would immediately apply to an edifice as grand and comfortable as Dunsley Hall, though maybe she's referring to the fact there are only seven rooms, the rest being self-catering flatlets.

Seven rooms, though, doesn't seem *that* small to me and most similar size establishments I've visited certainly do not make a point of offering a restricted choice.

'Dinner is seven-thirty,' instructs Mrs Rosalie Buckle, indicating the parquet-floored dining room. 'Your table number is the same as your room number. I'll take your orders now.

She produces a business-like pre-printed list divided up into sections.

On it there are spaces for four starters, two second courses and two main courses. As we choose, she ticks the requisite squares. 'The vegetables are put on to cook as you sit down,' she explains.

After dumping our bags in our small-ish room at the back of the house, we hurry down for a swim in the pool converted by the Buckles from a series of falling-down greenhouses. Bliss. As Mrs Buckle had said, 'It's the pool that keeps us going in winter when other places are empty.' (Yet how disappointing when breakfast is served between eight-thirty and nine-fifteen and the pool isn't opened until 9am unless by special request.)

In the downstairs lounge with bar in corner, we meet our fellow guests, an eclectic bunch of young couples. There seems to be some difficulty getting a drink. Eventually the amiable Mr Buckle ambles towards the bar. He seems confused when I ask for a Campari and orange juice. 'Don't think we've got that. I'm not very experienced at all this,' he confides.

Seven-thirty finds all guests seated in the dining room and, on the dot, first courses are brought by a nervous-looking waitress. The pâté served with toast is all right, but peach halves piled with heaps of mayonnaise and decorated with bits of salad remind me of that Dylan Thomas story of his aunt pressing her carefully hoarded tinned peaches onto the mother of his best friend Jack.

'Could we have the wine list please?' The nice Mr Buckle seems far too bewildered to hear us. Perhaps we should rephrase: 'Do you *have* a wine list?' How unkind. They do. Meanwhile second courses arrive: thick, nourishing cauliflower soup – phew – and a somewhat incongruous sorbet.

Our bottle of Sancerre – not cheap at £15.95 when it isn't the best I've tasted – comes with indifferent main courses of chicken à la King and pork fillet with mustard sauce. And the freshly cooked veg? They've been freshly cooked for too long.

On a brighter note, our room is warm, our bed comfortable. After a breakfast accompanied by packet butter and ketchups, Mr Buckle reveals after a bit of persuasion that he's been a farmer for most of his life. 'After that we ran a caravan park for eight years. When I bought Dunsley Hall we started off as B and B ...'

Dunsley Hall's new menu, introduced by new chef Wendy Parkin, sounds much more interesting and dinner is now served at eight!

Mrs Buckle writes: 'Your article infers I'm the grotty, old-fashioned seaside landlady (a tag my husband has never let me forget!), when all we're trying to do is show consideration to our guests. If you are this way again, try us – be ill, have a car breakdown (and borrow mine), ask if I'll go present shopping for you – we've done it all for guests...it's all about CARING.'

Dunsley Hall,

Dunsley,
Whitby,
North Yorkshire YO21 3TL.
Tel: (01947) 893437.
Fax: (01947) 893505.
Ian and Rosalie Buckle.
Location: just outside the village.
Open: all year except 25/26 December.
Rooms: 7. 5 twin/double (£73), 2 four-poster (£83), all ensuite. Single in double (from £36.50).
Restaurant: dinner served at 8pm.
Chef: Mrs Wendy Parkin. Table d'hôte £15.
Wine List: choice of 7 red, 7 white, plus house wine, from £5.95.
Children: yes.
Dogs: yes.
Smoking: not in dining room or lounge.
And Also: heather-clad moors, Pickering's Steam Railway, ruined abbeys, priories and castles.

Duns Tew, Oxfordshire
THE WHITE HORSE INN

'We are unique,' announces the manager of The White Horse Inn in a letter to *The Daily Telegraph*. 'Come and see for yourself.'

In hot pursuit of uniqueness, we zoom up the M40 straight into the White Horse bar. 'Sorry,' apologizes the barman, scratching his head. 'We've lost the key to your room.' Looking bewildered, he vanishes.

Cheerfully hanging about in this laid-back country pub, we watch gossiping locals and a woman rocking her baby on her hip. *Laid-back*? When booking, I hadn't even been asked for a telephone number, let alone other credentials. At the back of the brick and timbered room, we catch an inviting glimpse of a restaurant with pale blue cloths. At last the barman returns, triumphant, with key. 'It had been dropped between here and the cleaning shed,' he says.

Following him out into the driving rain, we pass a smart motel-like building. But what's this? A forlorn Rapunzel is leaning out of an upstairs window: 'Excuse me, I'm locked in,' she wails. Is The White Horse Inn always so entertaining? 'That's Friday for you, isn't it,' growls our harassed barman.

Promising to rescue her when he's disposed of us (he didn't put it quite like that), he marches us up a steep iron outside staircase and into a small cottagey room. After he's pointed out its amenities – brrrm – he's off to the rescue.

'It's bit basic,' comments my husband, looking around. I disagree:

'No, simple's a better word.' But that's before I spy the elaborate gold-edged mirror, the fussy fringed lampshades and wardrobe festooned with gilt Adam bows. But ah. Here *is* a unique touch: it's air-conditioned.

Down in the bar they're discussing Maastricht: 'I'm totally agin it,' bellows a grey-haired gentleman whose lavish moustache is edged with froth. Listening in to at least four conversations at once, we take our drinks over to a table separated from the kitchen by a glass wall. Now this deserves an award for courage. *I* wouldn't like to prepare dinner in front of an audience.

More punters are drifting in. We wander over to take a look at the £14.95 menu, chalked up on a blackboard. 'Ready to order?' asks the amiable blonde waitress, waving a wine list in our direction.

'Yes. We'll have the homemade soup and crusty bread, one trout and one grilled chicken *without* the sauce.'

'No problem,' she grins.

'And a bottle of the Mâcon 'packed with fruit'.'

The restaurant's as pleasant as the bar: walls are decorated with horse brasses and collars; there's a flagstoned floor and huge fireplace. Our wine's plonked on the table – the 'would you like to taste the wine, sir?' routine would be inappropriate here.

Food is just as described, though no one mentioned the vegetables would include tasty potato dauphinoise and *samphire.* We just about manage pudding: something chocolatey for him, an alcoholic lemon syllabub for me.

Draping ourselves in the sitting room afterwards, we find ourselves opposite a famous horsey lady (no, not Princess Anne): 'Love it, *love it,*' she says repeatedly, slapping her thigh.

Can't say the same of our one bedside light, use of which involves either switching the television off, or plugging it elsewhere and leaving it on the floor. But the tiny bathroom's OK, all dark green tiles and brass fittings – though what a pity about the broken bath-plug chain and discoloured bath.

'Golf widows, eh?' sympathizes the breakfast waiter next morning to the party of wives whose husbands have decamped for the day. Now we uncover The White Horse Inn's true claim to 'uniquity'. Just up the road they have their own private golf club for residents.

'We like being laid-back and unpretentious here...but we have purchased a double adapter for the TV!' chuckles Eddie Sinclair.

The White Horse Inn,
Duns Tew,
Oxfordshire OX6 4JS.
Tel: (01869) 340272.
Fax: (01869) 347732.
Manager: Eddie Sinclair.
Location: in centre of village.
Open: all year.
Rooms: 13. 13 twin/double (£45), all ensuite. Single in double (£29).
Restaurant: open for dinner from 7.30–9.30 pm.
Chef: Eddie Sinclair. Table d'hôte £14.95.
Wine List: over 100, from £7.95.
Children: yes.
Dogs: yes.
Smoking: feel free.
And Also: Golfing Special: 3 nights' dinner, B&B and golf, £95 per person.

'We have just the one single room left,' says the receptionist at Edinburgh's Howard Hotel on the phone. 'What sort of room?' I ask. 'It's the one we have left.'

The first thing I notice about The Howard – three Georgian houses made into one – is its emerald front door. As it doesn't want to open, I ring the bell. A red-headed chap flings it wide, grinning. 'It needs a hefty poosh,' he explains.

After I've signed in, he shows me my room. 'You'd better hurry if you want to catch the shops,' he urges. Taking his advice, I shoot out at once.

On my way back – The Howard isn't far from the centre – there he is again, going off duty. 'Did you treat y'self to something?' he asks, eyeing my French Connection bag.

'Oh, yes.'

'And did you go to Jenners? Now, there's a splendid shop...' We chat for a couple of minutes. Back at the hotel I ask the receptionist where the restaurant is. 'Downstairs.'

My room is small, stylish and luxuriously kitted out with desk, armchair, narrow high single bed and a wardrobe with pink taffeta curtains behind glass doors. And so it should be, at £110. There's just one problem. Can I get the TV to work? No, I can't.

I ring reception. 'I'm afraid our maintenance people have gone off for the day.'

'But there's a particular programme I want to watch,' I wail. 'I might have

been able to change it for you except the hotel's full,' says the receptionist smoothly. Oh, thanks a lot.

As I sit on the bed and fulminate, there's a knock at the door. 'Room Service,' says a voice. For a moment I wonder: has this column been rumbled? But no. At my 'Come in', a wee Scottish lady bustles through the door and spots the rebel TV. I tell her the story of how the maintenance men have gone home.

'Och dear,' she says, most · concerned, launching into an elaborate spiel of a film she had watched the night before which had ended in a stabbing. One story leads to the next – perhaps being a 'single' guest isn't so lonely after all? 'I'll get someone from the kitchen to look at your telly, dear,' she says at last.

Moments later a chap in white shirt and waistcoat appears along with the room service lady. 'Ah, there's nae *aerial*,' he says. 'I'll go and find one.' Maybe he swipes one from another room – see if I care. Anyway, back he comes, aerial in hand, and spends five minutes grovelling on the floor. 'Why didn't the receptionist think of asking you?' I wonder aloud. 'She never does,' he says sadly.

The rain vanishes and a picture appears on the screen. 'Thank you so much.'

'Nae trouble,' he replies.

By now there's not much time to fit in dinner before the programme. In the spacious basement restaurant with luxurious dark green carpet, the bringer of TV aerials turns out to be one of the waiters. My table's laid ostentatiously for one with white starched cloth over flowing tartan. Across the room a couple of Americans discuss the Royal family. 'Margaret Rose?' enquires the husband. 'Sister of the Queen dear,' his wife replies.

I start with soup. 'Like your soup?' asks the head waiter. 'Yes, thank you.' Now I have lamb cutlets. 'Enjoy your meal?' he asks. 'Very much.'

Looking at my watch, I explain there's a television programme I particularly want to watch. 'So perhaps I could return afterwards for my pudding?' The head waiter has a better idea. 'Why don't we bring it to your room?'

As the credits roll, in he sails with a tray laid with a white cloth, immaculate fruit salad and the rest of my half bottle of wine. Settling back in the armchair, I reflect that The Howard Hotel has come up trumps and that it's really rather nice being a single guest.

'We think the only thing to point out is the departure of the less than helpful receptionist!' says The Howard Hotel sweetly.

'Our team now is extremely helpful, as you will see from these recent guest comments...' Thank you Howard Hotel. They make good reading.

The Howard Hotel,

32–36 Great King Street,
Edinburgh,
Lothian EH3 6QH.
Tel: (0131) 557 3500.
Fax: (0131) 557 6515.
General Manager: Gillian Thompson.
Location: in street parallel with Princes Street.
Open: all year, except after New Year.
Rooms: 16. 4 single (£110), 10 twin/double (£180), 2 suites (£255). Single in double (£140).
Restaurant: open for dinner from 7.30pm.
Chef: Gordon Inglis. Table d'hôte £18.95.
Wine List: international, from £11.50.
Children: yes.
Dogs: by arrangement.
Smoking: not in restaurant.
And Also: A city centre hotel offering unashamed luxury.

*E*ton, *Berkshire*
THE CHRISTOPHER HOTEL

When telephoning the Christopher Hotel I'm told they have two kinds of room: 'A standard in the courtyard at £65, an executive in the main house £73,' chirrups a female voice. 'The executive please.' Who wants to be stuck in a courtyard when the best bits – bar and restaurant – are in the main building? Not I. Anyway, it might be pouring with rain.

And it *is*. By contrast, the lights of The Christopher in the High Street are yellow and inviting. Zooming through the covered street entrance, we park in a courtyard surrounded by creeper-clad, mews-style bungalows. These look much more attractive than that 'standard in the courtyard' description. Wonder what they're like *in*side.

Much better to be in-*house*, though. Trotting back to reception via the High Street, we announce ourselves. 'Pity. If you'd booked a courtyard room, I'd probably have upgraded you, we aren't full tonight,' says the receptionist cheerfully, adding they prefer to keep people in one place instead of scattered here and there. *Now* she tells us. Handing over a key, she leaves us to find the way up to the second floor.

Being 'Executive', our room boasts a trouser press, in this case inconveniently positioned through lack of space. What swear words do executives use, I idly wonder, if, like me, they stub their big toe on it when squeezing towards the bed? My husband, with a sudden and baffling desire to press his trousers, approaches it confidently.

Trousers are inserted but nothing happens. 'The damn thing doesn't work.' He wrestles with it. A leg falls off. 'For God's sake leave it alone...'

To clear the air, I suggest a drink. Whizzing down to the bar, we discover it cleverly retains the ambience of a local while jazzed up with smart accessories such as whirring fans, built-in wooden settles, brass fittings, lots of stained glass. Over the other side of the room, people are tucking into what looks like tasty shepherd's pie and chips. It's a nice place to be.

But *we* are eating in the next-door Christopher's Brasserie – also a nice place to be: a large, airy, warm room decorated with slatted wooden blinds, posters, tiled floor and wooden tables with wrought-iron bottom bits. Although humming with punters, there are just two waiters: a chap with an engaging grin and the girl who'd greeted us in reception earlier.

The menu is – well – brasserie-ish. Thumbs up to shellfish Provençal and grilled sardines, though thumbs down to lamb cutlets doused in dark brown, very salty gravy. What does our waiter recommend for pudding? 'Oh, the crêpes,' he says, flashing his grin. Crêpes it is.

But have we strayed into Fawlty Towers? From where we're sitting, we have a good view of the open-plan outer kitchen. And if the phone hadn't rung at that precise moment, our waiter would never have been spotted rushing to answer it clutching a long thin box to his bosom marked 'Crêpes Suzette'. How we giggle at this exposé of kitchen secrets. Nothing wrong with packet crêpes of course. Depends how they taste.

And they're *much* nicer than the leathery efforts we had a couple of weeks ago in a grand French château hotel, served and cooked with pomp and circumstance at table. 'Did you like them?' our waiter asks eagerly, as he rushes breathlessly past. 'Excellent. Really lemony and buttery.'

So what else do I like about Eton's Christopher Hotel? The view from our bedroom window of Eton's playing fields. The waiter. The rest's OK. Though I don't *much* like the way our mention of the recalcitrant trouser press is greeted. Indifferent I'd say. Good thing we're not top execs.

'Corby rather took your comments to heart,' writes proprietor Carol Martin, 'so much so, they have now checked over all our trouser presses! Perhaps you'd also like to know that we now have some beautiful Turkish carpets and tablecloths in the restaurant and that we choose our food very carefully – for example, our meat comes from a butcher who has his own farm, and I personally collect whole lambs from the Wiltshire Downs...'

The Christopher Hotel,
110 High Street,
Eton,
Windsor,
Berkshire SL4 6AN.
Tel: (01753) 852359.
Fax: (01753) 830914.
Proprietor: Carol Martin.
Location: 5 minutes across the bridge from Windsor.
Open: all year.
Rooms: 34. 8 single (£60), 23 twin/double (£68–£77), 3 family rooms (£73.50), all ensuite. Single in double (£68).
Restaurant: open for dinner from 7pm.
Chef: Christian Dalla Costa. Table d'hôte £12.50.
Wine List: international, from £8.75.
Children: yes.
Dogs: yes.
Smoking: currently under review.
And Also: special theatre and racing weekends – please enquire.

A reader writes to me about The Evesham Hotel. No, he hasn't stayed there himself – his daughter has. He adds mysteriously: 'The problem is, you might need more column inches than usual to cover the owner's idiosyncracies.'

In the car park it's hard even to find *car* inches. 'Yes, we're full – all forty rooms,' beams the receptionist. This causes a bespectacled man apparently minding his own business to spring like Jack in the box from a nearby sofa. 'Best hotel in the world, that's why!' he cries. 'I promise I didn't pay him to say that,' smiles the receptionist, handing us a key attached to a teddy bear.

The owner, it seems, has a penchant for bears. Bears hang from hooks. A row of bears sits on the reception counter. 'They're made specially for us,' the receptionist explains.

She takes us to a room that's the last word in comfort if not designer elegance. Everything – and more – is here: iron and board, hairdryer, radio, alarm clock, clothes brush, bottles of washing liquid, bath bubble and shampoo, plus large jars of coffee and chocolate. A teddy sits on one of the two squashy chairs. There's a rubber duck in the bathroom.

On our way downstairs again, we pass two small boys amusing themselves with the vast selection of games and toys. In the crowded bar a tall, thin man wearing a Dennis the Menace tie hurries towards me. 'Can I sell you a menu?' he asks, black brows bristling.

'Ah,' I retort, 'I've already had a *free* look at the menu left in our room.'

'Free? That's what *you* think. It'll appear on the bill. Now can I interest you in the grey soup?'

Grey soup? He means mushroom (I think). The menu is a work of art all right, dotted with exclamation marks and jokes of the 'Fresh Salads (we re-iron the lettuce daily)' kind. The wine list is embellished with photographs, comments and more jokes. French wine? He hasn't stocked it for fourteen years. Good heavens no. Far too expensive.

Dennis dashes back. 'Booze?' he enquires. We ask for an Australian Chardonnay. 'Only £14 – we run a charity here,' says Dennis, aka John Jenkinson, idiosyncratic owner.

Nipping across the room he addresses two men: 'I wouldn't sit by that door,' he advises. 'Someone might open it and you'd look even more silly than you do now.' After a moment's stunned silence, the chaps laugh. Titters follow Dennis wherever he goes.

In the Cedar Restaurant, we sit by the Georgian bay window and admire the 180-year-old Cedar of Lebanon tree in the garden outside and the glittering chandelier inside. The food and service are just right. My husband has a fillet of cold poached trout to start and then some rather good pinkish lamb on a tomato and basil sauce. For me it's tasty grey soup followed by my favourite Dover sole. Vegetables are crisp. The only thing I don't like is the Apricot and

Rose Water Sorbet – flakes of flavoured ice, *I'd* call it.

Coffee is served in the sitting room. Everyone's playing games: Scrabble in one corner; Mastermind in another; cards over there. Dennis strides among his contented guests flogging liqueurs. We shake our heads. 'You're not taking me seriously,' he scolds.

Back upstairs, the water's hot and the shower works a treat. In the information leaflet, I discover a note suggesting that complaints (if any) should be sent to 'The watchdogs of industry. This helps to keep us (or any hotel/restaurant) on our toes.' There's even a list of addresses to write to. Bully for Dennis.

Driving home, though, we unkindly wonder if the charms of the ebullient owner might wear thin if one were staying for longer than a single night. We shall never know. But, as promised, The Evesham Hotel is an enjoyable and unusual experience.

John Jenkinson put pen to postcard the minute the piece appeared: 'Many thanks for most bearable write-up! Slight apologies if I sometimes do go a bit OTT, but English hotels are so pinstriped and po-faced that one has virtually to force the English to relax in them! Anyway, I enjoy myself and your description will certainly scare off anyone without a sense of humour. My wife thinks you're colour blind, as she says my brows are going the colour of the soup! Best wishes, Dennis.'

The Evesham Hotel,

Coopers Lane,
Off Waterside,
Evesham,
Hereford and Worcester
WR11 6DA.
Tel: (01386) 765566.
Fax: (01386) 765443.
The Jenkinson family.
Location: just off Waterside – River Avon.
Open: all year, except 25 and 26 December.
Rooms: 40. 6 single (£53–£59), 33 double/twin (£70–£82), 1 family suite (£105), all ensuite. Single in double (£59). 10 ground-floor rooms.
Restaurant: dinner served from 7.30–9pm.
Chef: Ian Mann. A la carte, average £18.50.
Wine List: wines from 40 countries, but not France or Germany, from £9.
Children: yes.
Dogs: yes, but not in public rooms.
Smoking: no cigars/pipes in restaurant.
And Also: croquet, table tennis, heated indoor swimming pool, wheelchair access to public areas and restaurant.

Exminster, South Devon
THE TURF HOTEL

Anyone thinking of bringing their race-horse to the Turf Hotel, known locally as 'the Turf', should think again. Here's a place for twitchers and sailing types. Horses? The very idea.

The name is confusing enough – finding it even more so. The Turf sits at the point where the Exeter canal joins the Exe estuary. You drive along a bumpy dirt road with fields on either side until you come to a narrow lock bridge. Suddenly there's the hotel, in splendid isolation, surrounded on three sides by water, with its own canal boat, the *Water Mongoose,* moored up ready to take people on trips – 'BBQ parties a speciality'.

Owners Clive and Ginny Redfern have worked hard to repair, paint and polish their watery home. 'We've been here four years,' Clive, an ex-estate agent, explains. 'And there's still more to do.'

The second confusing thing about the Turf is that it isn't – well – exactly a hotel. The downstairs area is open-plan, consisting of bar, tables, chairs, old wooden pews and an expanse of beautifully polished floorboards. 'I prefer to call us a pub with rooms,' grins Clive.

Now he propels us through a door marked Private and up a secret staircase. Then down another smaller one with a trick step at the bottom – 'It's deeper than the others – be careful,' he warns.

Our room is decidedly basic. No television, a creaky window. Moving the lamp to a bedside position is just not possible – the only way to read one's new Edna O'Brien is from the wrong end of the bed. Towels, duvet cover, sheets and pillowcases, however, are brand new. Yet in spite of its smashing view across lock and fields beyond, somehow this little den holds few charms.

Emerging, we get a glimpse of the other rooms – sadly, both taken – which are larger and much more inviting, furnished with nice pieces of simple antique furniture.

Downstairs, log fires are cheerfully burning. We buy drinks and take a pew. Suddenly an onslaught of merry, guernsey-clad people bundles in. There has been a local regatta and the cry has gone up: 'Let's go to the Turf!' Everyone clamours for drinks at once. Soon there's a queue at the pine counter above which the substantial bar menu is chalked up.

'Bottle of house white please,' I ask Clive at the bar. He plucks a bottle from the shelf. '*I* think this one's great,' he says enthusiastically, carefully polishing both glasses before handing them over.

We tuck into homemade tomato and lentil soup, tuna bake and garlic bread – all meals in themselves – and join in the conversation at our table. They're into weddings. One couple has recently married, another is just about to. At the other end, a discussion's going on about meditation and the merits of contemplating one's navel. An entertaining evening.

At breakfast, there's just a group of four men – and us. The group's about to go sailing. 'Are you a fit crew?' Clive asks briskly. They shake their heads blearily. It's the morning after the night before.

Cereal, fruit juice and muesli are attractively laid out. We help ourselves. Then Clive brings toast to accompany the scrambled egg – and vanishes, forgetting the butter. Coming back he's mortified: 'I'm terribly sorry, I'll bring you fresh toast.'

'What a waste,' we chorus.

'No problem. The kids, or Scooter, can have it.' Scooter is the family Jack Russell.

When we comment on the plethora of handsome pews, assuming they'd come from some ancient church or other, Clive admits: 'They're from a mental hospital.' Not the same thing at all!

Settling the bill, we meet Clive's wife Ginny. What nice people. And have we enjoyed the Turf experience? Yes, though it's not really our sort of place. But then, we're neither sailing types nor twitchers.

'Did you know that our pasta is made by an Italian living across the estuary, that our beef comes from Dartmoor and that our ice cream is made by a farm Ginny's parents once owned?' asks Clive. No, I confess I didn't. 'Oh, and we've finished refurbishing the pub. It looks great.'

The Turf Hotel,

Exminster,
Exeter,
Devon EX6 8EE.
Tel: (01392) 833128.
Clive and Ginny Redfern.
Location: where estuary meets canal – ask for directions.
Open: March–November.
Rooms: 3. 1 twin (£35), 2 double (£45), none ensuite.
Restaurant: open for dinner Fridays and Saturdays only, from 7pm, average £15. Otherwise excellent home-made bar food available. Outdoor barbecues in summer.
Chef: Ginny Redfern.
Wine List: inexpensive and 'improving with age', from £7.75.
Children: yes.
Dogs: yes.
Smoking: not in dining room please.
And Also: watery pursuits, bird watching. No credit cards.

THE BISHOP'S TABLE HOTEL

The street outside The Bishop's Table Hotel in Farnham, Surrey, is all double yellow lines. Shooting in, we ask about parking arrangements. *Are there any?* The owner smiles and gesticulates. 'We have an agreement with the Library Car Park next door for guests to park after eight, though we'd be grateful if you moved your car by nine tomorrow morning,' he says.

It's a deal. Now Mr Kass K. Verjee (for that's his name) takes us through a conservatory and along an unenticing passageway to our room, one of several created from what looks like an old stable block. 'Is it warm enough for you? Would you like me to turn the heating up?' he fusses.

'No, thanks.' But we appreciate his concern, remembering places where no one's bothered to switch the heating on at all. 'Then let me show you how to do it,' he insists. And he does.

He may be lovely, but our small room *isn't.* There's a faint reminder of smoke, giving the strong impression it's designed for businessmen. Cheering up, we remind ourselves that it's colour co-ordinated – even the blanket matches the decor – and that the new-looking furniture's a good quality oak. 'My fault,' I say to my husband. 'I should have asked for a room in the house.'

We wash in the smallest wash basin in the world, so close to the floor that even I have to curtsey to use it. Gosh, those mixer taps stick out. Mind your nose there.

All spruced up, we march forth down that cheerless passage. In the cosy red bar, framed documents record the various dates on which this Georgian house has been sold at auction over the years. 'It was a mess,' recalls our host. 'A week before we took over, eight years ago, we came for a meal and a fox walked into the restaurant.'

Over in the corner, a family group sip their drinks. Bet we know why *they're* here. Bet it's the interesting-sounding vegetarian menu and bet their teenage daughter regards meat as dead animal. 'Artichoke please,' I hear her say. Alas, the waiter returns with regrets: 'I'm *reliably informed* there's no artichoke today,' he says, bowing.

Being curious, *I* order artichoke too. This time he's got it off pat: 'Artichoke's out of season.' I'm tempted to query why it's still on the (printed) menu, but desist. Instead I ask for mushroom risotto (with woodland mushrooms, bamboo shoots and water chestnut with Thai spices), followed by pesto parcels.

There are lots of people in the inviting restaurant with its spanking white cloths. Our waitress confides it's her first week. You'd never know. 'She sure knows her silver service,' whispers my husband admiringly.

His spinach, potato and lentil soup is delicious. (I *know*, because I taste.) So's my risotto. Now Mr Verjee appears, like a conjuror, producing sorbets: 'To refresh the palate. An old English custom,' he grins.

Accompanied by a bottle of excellent Mâcon Villages, we enjoy noisettes of lamb with red wine and peppercorn sauce and dinky little cabbage parcels that, when opened, reveal goat's cheese and pine kernels. Bread's good, and so are the crisp vegetables.

Come breakfast time, it's Mariam Verjee, sister and co-owner, who's taking the orders. Now, if I were hungry, I could have herb omelette, grilled grapefruit or scrambled egg and smoked salmon. My husband doesn't let the side down. *He* has scrambled egg. 'And?' I enquire. 'Very good indeed.'

Later, in the hall, people are coming and going. 'You *are* busy,' we comment. 'I hope that hasn't spoiled your stay?' asks Mr Verjee anxiously. 'No, no.'

'That's good. Being a host means treating your clients as guests, *never* as customers...'

'Since I went into the hotel business,' says Kass Verjee, 'it's always been my ambition to be reviewed in a quality newspaper... and now we've achieved it!'

The Bishop's Table Hotel,

27 West Street,
Farnham,
Surrey GU9 7DR.
Tel: (01252) 715545.
Fax: (01252) 733494.
Kass and Mariam Vergee.

Location: in the centre of town.
Rooms: 18. 7 single (£70), 11 twin/double (£85), all ensuite. Single in double (£76.50).
Restaurant: open for dinner from 7–9.45pm.
Chef: Paul Hackett. Table d'hôte £16.50–£19.
Wine List: small, with good balance of French and New World, from £9.65.
Children: yes.
Dogs: no.
Smoking: guests are asked not to.
And Also: Farnham's antique shops. Special golf weekends – £120 per night for two, DB&B with 18 holes on nearby golf course.

$\mathcal{F}$ishguard, Dyfed
TREGYNON COUNTRY FARMHOUSE HOTEL

The 16th-century Tregynon Country Farmhouse Hotel describes itself as being 'in the heart of Pembrokeshire Coast National Park in a forgotten ice-age valley rich in wildlife'. What could be more romantic?

'We try and steer people into arriving between four-thirty and six, so that we can discuss the dinner menu with them,' owner Peter Heard stresses over the phone. Assuming this to be one of his funny little ways, I promise not to be late. 'I'll fax you directions,' he offers. 'No, no, we'll find you...' I'm sure he doesn't believe me.

Polishing our halos, we turn into the yard of the pretty stone farmhouse perched on the edge of the valley at 5pm. Mr Heard welcomes us warmly and saunters us across the yard to a row of converted stone cottages. There follows a conducted tour of the small (blissfully warm) room and an account of how £7,000-worth of technology pumps spring water through his highly efficient shower.

Peering at us over half-moon specs, he earnestly explains that wholefood and vegetarian meals are a speciality: 'But we have plenty of traditional dishes too.' He delivers the menu verbally and stands by for decisions. Actually I'd much rather clasp the menu in my hot little hand and choose at leisure, but maybe there's something about this unusual technique that keeps the prices down?

As soon as he's gone, we're off exploring the woodland and legging it down to the valley and stream below. Magic. We return to our room feeling ten times healthier and come across a leather-bound folder that tells us all we need to know about Tregynon. We decide *not* to wear jeans for dinner.

The beamed 'mind your head' sitting room is milling with people and our urbane host is whisking around bringing drinks, wine lists and good cheer. Dinner is a smart affair with royal blue napkins, soft lights and a mixture of young and old diners. We tune in to the next table where Grandfather is entertaining his family with Second World War stories. 'Did you really meet Hitler?' asks a small girl wide-eyed, but I don't think she believes him any more than I do.

As Mr Heard's made such a point of vegetarian dishes, I just have to try one but, at £2.50 extra, the wholemeal stuffed crêpe topped with cheese and baked in a Moscatel sauce (whatever that is) is somewhat over-hyped, as is my husband's rack of lamb. The mange-touts are just as they should be, but mushrooms and apricots do not a happy marriage make.

Talking of happy marriages, after dinner we find yet another leather-bound volume. The Story of Tregynon describes and illustrates with photographs the development of the hotel from a derelict building, interwoven with the development of the Heard family from wife number one to the present Mrs H. There's a picture of Peter and Jane and assorted children on their wedding day in 1991 – there's even one of Mr Heard as a young Bank of England executive wearing, I suspect, flares.

The bed *would* have been comfortable except for lumpy pillows and the restrictive thought that Sunday breakfast is between eight-thirty and nine. We make it – just – and I'm unlucky enough to get a runny boiled egg. Mr Heard notices and is appalled. 'You must have another.'

'No, thanks, I'm into toast and marmalade now...'

'Well, then, I insist on deducting £5 because it has spoiled what should have been an enjoyable experience.' How exemplary. Of course things sometimes go wrong, but when they're managed with this much charm, it's the charm that will be remembered.

PS As we settle up, his deputy confides there's been an inquest in the kitchen. The verdict? It's the new egg timer's fault!

Sniffs one reader: 'I'm amazed that any hotel proprietor would be fool enough to deduct £5 for a supposedly "runny egg". He would obviously cook another egg and give it to the customer. But I suppose he was afraid you would complain in your weekly bleat re hotels...' (Pity this reader didn't give her name and address.)

Peter Heard is of a more positive ilk: 'All the pillows have been replaced and that faulty egg timer thrown away,' he says.

Tregynon Country Farmhouse Hotel,

Gwaun Valley,
Fishguard,
Pembrokeshire SA65 9TU.
Tel: (01239) 820531.
Fax: (01239) 820808.
Peter and Jane Heard.
Location: in the Pembrokeshire Coast National Park.
Rooms: 8. 3 twin/double (£46–£53), 4 cottage rooms twin/double/family (£59.90), 1 cottage four-poster (£64), all ensuite. Special arrangement for singles – please enquire.
Restaurant: open for dinner 7.30–8.30pm.
Chef: Jane Heard. Table d'hôte £14.75.
Wine List: wide range, from £7.60.
Children: yes.
Dogs: yes, but not in the building.
Smoking: not in dining room or bedrooms.
And Also: Wonderful scenery, walking, utter peace, listed EC beach 5 miles.

Frinton on Sea, Essex
THE MAPLIN HOTEL

Time for a hotel expedition to deepest Essex. 'I can offer you one of our best rooms, overlooking the famous greensward. *Pole* position,' urges Nigel Turner, owner of The Maplin. '*What?* You *don't know* Frinton on Sea? Then we must make your visit a memorable one.'

And in spite of being Don't Knows, we find our way like lemmings to the seafront – straight down the main street and turn right. *There's* The Maplin, a white-painted Edwardian house facing the sea. *There's* the greensward and people walking their dogs. A few Porsches, Rolls and Mercs swoosh past. Ah. The penny drops. This place must be seaside to London's East End and all those car-dealers.

In the Maplin front garden, the lawn's so perfect we know it's come straight from the carpet warehouse to complement the neat rows of daffodils planted in oblong beds. Inside, the real carpet's red-patterned and the oak panelling original. When we press the bell, a man scurries down the hall towards us. Mr Turner? "Fraid not. Proprietor's out. I'm the maitre'd.' Snatching our bags, he rushes us up to a first-floor front. 'Please ring if you want anything,' he says. Then he rushes off again.

Wow. We are in a huge room with wall-to-wall beige floral carpet, thick and luxurious. Yards of red flowery curtains adorn curved bay windows complete with sea view. Plump ruby-red velvety fringed armchairs just beg

to be sat in. The radiator's on full blast – no mean spiritedness here. And over in the corner, the original tiled fireplace boasts a gas fire that works.

Downstairs, we snatch a quick drink in the equally elaborate Cocktail Bar before being whisked off to eat. As we walk into the dining room, other diners turn and stare. Hang on, we're not *that* odd. And what a mixed bunch they are: a young chap on his own, a trio of very senior citizens, a bright blonde woman and her beau, two couples of indeterminate age but undoubted devotion.

Maitre'd and waitress have donned black and white uniforms, and I hope they don't think I'm being picky when I decline the first and second courses. But I can rely on my husband not to let the side down. Diving into the home-made chicken soup with alacrity, he declares it to be made with 'proper chicken stock. Have some,' he offers. Tasting it, I agree. His second course has a funny name, Salamagundy, and consists of iceberg lettuce and warm chicken livers. Tasting this too, it's what I call a 'rather you than me' dish.

Now we're into Dover sole and wing of skate with mustard sauce – both go down a treat. While he tucks into chocolate pudding, I marvel at the various period pieces: the imposing oak fireplace, fringed lamps, silver candelabra and dumb waiter with green felt cubbyholes.

No point in sitting in the lounge afterwards – it reminds me of an old folks' home. The bar's empty. Up we trot to our flowery room. Sitting on one of the twin beds, I discover a brass knob with cord attached, which I tug. To my amazement, via a Heath Robinson arrangement of pulleys, it operates a heavy brass bolt which opens the door...and I only wanted to switch the light on.

The beds are comfortable – something to do with real cotton sheets? – and our breakfast is 'Aga cooked'. The dining room's full with two family parties and we catch glimpses of the ebullient Mr Turner charging in and out of the kitchen.

As we pay the bill, he expounds on Frinton: 'The nice thing is that we get no problems with drunks. No pubs in Frinton, you see.' He laughs at his joke – the *real* joke being he's an ex-publican himself – and charges us £97.50 for bed, breakfast and dinner including service charge and VAT, plus bottle of wine at £12.85.

Somehow, The Maplin fulfils all expectations of what a seaside hotel in Frinton should be...

'Actually my name's Nick, as in 'old',' sighs Mr Turner.

The Maplin Hotel,

Esplanade,
Frinton on Sea,
Essex CO13 9EL.
Tel: (01255) 673832.
Nick and Sue Turner.
Location: sea front.
Open: all year, except January.
Rooms: 12. 2 single (£26.25–£39.50), 10 twin/double (£70–£90), all ensuite. Single in double (£42.50).
Restaurant: open for dinner from 7–9pm.
Chef: Nick Turner. Table d'hôte, £15.95–£18.95. Also vegetarian menu.
Wine List: varied, from £8.50.
Children: yes.
Dogs: yes.
Smoking: not in dining room.
And Also: heated outdoor swimming pool, use of beach hut, close to Frinton golf links and tennis club.

Glasgow
BABBITY BOWSTER

I book a room at Babbity Bowster – café/bar/restaurant/pension – and then forget which street it's in. No problem. Everyone in Glasgow's heard of Babbity Bowster.

Arriving at last in narrow Blackfriars Street, we drive the car gingerly along – it's not a car sort of street. Babbity Bowster is the attractive three-storey building (reputedly designed by Robert Adam) just across the cobblestones.

Plunging through the front door, we find ourselves in a large, stylishly decorated café/bar. Spirits rise. BB looks fun – the opposite of staid. A friendly chap in T-shirt and earring greets us. 'Did ya have a good journey?'

Don't mention the journey. But it's great to be here. 'How do we get the car into your car park?' we ask – we can only think of carrying it in, through the bar. He points us kindly to a separate entrance, just round the corner.

Soon we're back. Our host takes our bags and sprints us up to the second floor. Opening a door, he says: 'Here you are.' The room's basic – but it's *clean.* And womblike. The beds have pale blue duvets and pillows; the modern furniture is pine and pale blue. Adjoining is a small shower room.

Off we go for a scamper round Glasgow. Around the corner is the elegant Italian Centre, a few streets away all the big shops.

Later, over a drink in the small paved garden, we enquire about dinner in Schottische, their upstairs restaurant.

But there's a hitch: 'You haven't booked you see.'

'I was told on the phone there was no need.' The manager scratches his head. 'Saturday's are so busy,' he laments. Eventually he squeezes us in at seven-thirty, warning he will need our table by nine. 'Will that do?' Fine. It's better than no table.

Like the bar, the restaurant is painted pale grey and has a wooden floor and sandblasted fireplace. At the next table there's a couple who look like one half of Abba. There are other Scandinavian voices. Suddenly I click. These are delegates from The International Whaling Conference held in Glasgow this week.

A waitress tells us we may choose from both the written menu and the blackboard. 'We've already chosen, thank you.'

'Oh, I won't be able to give you my recital then.' She sounds so disappointed and has such gorgeous red hair that we relent. It's an Oscar performance.

My dinner is very good indeed, especially the *poussin a l'ail*, though my husband isn't ecstatic about his monkfish, declaring the sauce too rich for his taste. 'Actually it's made me feel queasy,' he confesses – not too queasy, though, to consider the possibilities of *soufflé du jour*, made to order in twenty minutes. Fortunately there isn't time – we have to vacate our table. So we go for a walk, falling back later into Babbity's jam-packed and well-behaved bar.

In the morning the bar – where breakfast is served – has a sleepy air. 'We usually have freshly squeezed orange juice,' says the waitress apologetically, 'but today there isn't any.'

Oh, if only all hotels were so honest. Skipping the OJ, we indulge in porridge and cream and a Babbity Traditional Breakfast Special. Over the cappuccino – alas, the cafetières remain firmly in the restaurant upstairs – we ponder on the meaning of Babbity Bowster.

The brochure has the answer – it's not just an 18th-century Scottish name, but also an 18th-century Scottish dance. What's more: 'the proprietor has a keen interest in music, theatre and painting and a regular monthly poetry and music event provides a platform for established poets and new young writers.'

Settling the bill, we ask who the proprietor is. 'Oh, haven't you seen him? You'd certainly know if you had. His name is Fraser Laurie, he wears an eye patch and he looks like a pirate...' Congratulations to the pirate. He runs a tight ship.

'Aye, I insist on a well behaved bar,' says Fraser Laurie. 'It's the product of nine years' hard slog. I see it as a place for people to communicate, to have conversations with each other. Although we sell alcohol, we don't sell alcohol without responsibility. We have just built our own boules court adjacent to the hotel – boules helps to encourage conversation I find. We drink, then play, or play, then drink...it's not a boozy activity.'

Babbity Bowster,

16–18 Blackfriars Street,
Glasgow G11 1PE.
Tel: (0141) 552 5055.
Fax: (0141) 552 5215.
Fraser Laurie.
Location: in the city centre.
Open: all year.
Rooms: 6. 1 single (£36), 5 twin/double (£56), all ensuite. Single in double (£40).
Restaurant: open for dinner 6.30pm–late.
Chef: Fraser Laurie and Mairi Sutherland. A la carte average £17.50. A la carte breakfast in bar is extra.
Wine List: small, well chosen, from £7.75.
Children: yes.
Dogs: no.
Smoking: feel free.
And Also: boules court and private car park.

THE STARR

'Hah! You're staying!' roars Brian Jones, our host at The Starr, slapping his hand on the reception counter as he watches us totter across his threshold clutching newspapers, magazines and bulging bags. 'How did you guess?' I smile.

My little sally is greeted with hoots of laughter. 'See you later,' he shouts as a member of staff arrives to escort us to our room in the converted stableblock across the courtyard.

The Pine Room's not *quite* as characterful as its owner – it would be hard – though it's just the sort of neat and tastefully kitted out room I'd expect to find in a smart Essex restaurant with rooms. But wait: can some of these pretty pine pieces of furniture be original antiques? Yes. Being so highly polished, they just *look* new.

Looking around our temporary abode, I pick up an information card: 'Dinner Mon–Fri from £13' it says. 'Gosh, dinner's reasonable,' I say. We also discover filter coffee, bottles of mineral water and puzzle over why the posh, brass-festooned bathroom has two wash basins, bidet, large corner bath but only a hand-held shower. Why not a proper power shower, I wonder, instead of a bidet? Do people *really* use them?

Arriving in the bar, we discover inflation has struck even as we crossed the courtyard. Blackboard menus announce Dinner and Supper menus that cost £21.50 and £32.50 respectively. 'There's always a catch,' I murmur sadly.

Food's clearly the thing at The Starr – and the glamorous Mrs Jones, dressed in red, is an actress at heart. Her menu recital is a virtuoso performance. 'Phew, I feel I've eaten already,' teases my husband. 'So shall I bring coffee now?' she answers back, quick as a flash.

Now the bar is filling up. I choose melon and ham followed by Dover sole. My husband's unsure. 'Tell me about the red mullet again,' he asks. This time Brian obliges: 'Fillet of red mullet with a rosemary sauce on a bed of puréed leek,' he says, smacking his lips.

'Yes, I'll have that.'

''Ope you like it,' he adds in mock concern, raising his eyes heavenwards. 'Double canapés, I'm starvin',' yells a burly chap at the next table.

The pretty, low-ceilinged restaurant is as posh as our bathroom, only greener. The oak beams are reputedly 15th century. Wall lights are concealed by shades in the shape of maple leaves. The waitresses are smartly dressed in black and white, the plates monogrammed, the white cloths starchy. Offstage, Brian's shouting 'Wakey wakey' to someone – otherwise an air of calm prevails.

I enjoy my dinner, except for the steamed apricot pudding which is disappointingly banal. Mine host sensibly doesn't follow up his concern over the artistically arranged red mullet. If he had, my husband might have told him (rather than me) that he would have much preferred it without all that buttery creamy sauce. Sssh. I'm riveted by the group at the next table: "'E frew my burfday cake up the garden, I'll never forgive 'im for that...' How we laugh.

No wonder it was obvious we were staying. We're the only ones. Our breakfast waitress explains this particular Friday night was 'unusual, we're always full as a rule'. Yes, dear. She also explains that 'continental breakfast only' is included in the room rate: 'But you could pay the supplementary and have cooked breakfast,' she suggests brightly. No, thank you, The Starr's literature doesn't reveal how much a cooked breakfast costs, but I suspect it may not be a bargain.

After settling the bill and proffering £10 gratuity for the restaurant staff, I'm cross afterwards to find that a 10 percent service charge has already been added to our separate restaurant bill. Yes, *of course* I should have noticed – but it would have been nice if they'd said.

'Well!' says Brian Jones. 'We have removed all the old price cards that our new chamberlady found at the back of a drawer (first printed 1986) and replaced them with current ones indicating that service is added and showing current restaurant prices.'

Thank you, Brian. But my price card wasn't at the back of a drawer, it was on the bedside table. Honest!

The Starr,

Restaurant with Rooms,
Market Place,
Great Dunmow,
Essex CM6 1AX.
Tel: (01371) 874321.
Fax: (01371) 876337.
Brian and Vanessa Jones.
Location: in centre of Great Dunmow.
Open: all year except first week January.
Rooms: 8. 7 twin/double (£75), 1 four-poster (£100), all ensuite. Single in double (£50). 2 ground-floor rooms.
Restaurant: open for dinner 7–9.30pm.
Chef: Mark Fisher. Table d'hôte Mon–Fri £21.50 or £32.50, Sat £35. Cooked breakfast extra.
Wine List: from Lay & Wheeler, French/New World, from £10.95.
Children: yes.
Dogs: yes.
Smoking: not in bedrooms or dining room.
And Also: guests can go punting in Cambridge, just 40 minutes' drive, and be back for dinner.

*H*arnham, Wiltshire
THE OLD MILL HOTEL AND RESTAURANT

Beware of Ducks says the sign in the village street. But the ducks have legged it to the nearby Old Mill Hotel where someone's throwing them bread: fat ducks, thin ducks, mother ducks, *fortunate* ducks.

Some would count The Old Mill fortunate too. Own river frontage and own feathered friends. Also river backage, sideage and underneathage. View of Salisbury Cathedral thrown in.

The Old Mill Hotel is, in fact, two buildings joined by an ancient stone passageway. The mill, dating from 1135, is now a restaurant with a difference – beneath its floor, the River Nadder hurtles. The tall warehouse, added in the 18th century, is the hotel and pub.

A couple of Americans beat us to reception, complaining they've had difficulty finding the place. Haven't they even noticed how idyllic The Old Mill is? The young owner, Roy, deals calmly with the sudden influx. After booking us in and gently disposing of the Americans on the first floor, he gallops us up to the top, assuring us this room has the *best* view over the millpool and river. Well, he would wouldn't he. He has a nice line in chat.

The room is newly and unpretentiously done with a genuine old beam, a double and single bed, pleasant repro furniture and a large bathroom. There's even a clock radio. Although the whole effect is pristine, pictures and a TV set would add considerably to its charm. Perhaps we're supposed to view the view.

Downstairs, the bar crowd – mostly locals – is spilling out onto the towpath outside. Inside, they're all scoffing dressed crabs and thatched pies from the bar menu. We wander into the restaurant which, disappointingly, isn't very different from the bar except for the sounds of rushing river water.

And the food's not unlike the bar food either. After gi-normous starters of delicious garlicky Mediterranean prawns and mussels, we're too full to move. Now if we were sensible, we'd be off there and then. But no – we order main courses from a selection that doesn't include duck. 'Out of respect for our many dear feathered friends who happily share Harnham Mill with us, DUCK IS NOT SERVED HERE.' Hooray.

There is, however, a choice of fillet steak, lamb and apricot pie, seafood special, saffron rabbit and something called salmon koulibiac – poached fillet of salmon wrapped in spinach, then pancake, then brioche pastry. 'Bit complicated to cook,' I murmur to the waitress, who hesitates before saying she's not sure whether it's made in the kitchen or not. Puddings are equally substantial. Who's for a brisk walk along the towpath?

Coming back, we fancy watching the news quiz programme on Channel 4. Could we take our coffee up to the 'television lounge' on the first floor? All right then, says the waitress, surprised. No softly-lit little den, this. I do hate rooms with bright overhead lights. 'I'm having an early night...'

Our bed has no truck with too-hot duvets, it has real sheets and blankets. Bliss. Peering out of the window in the morning, I can see ducks but no duck-lings.

'Who eats them? Rats? Swans?' I ask. '*Crows,*' says Roy. If he weren't so pleasant, I might have a moan about his breakfast. Oh, for some decent orange juice, a choice of decent cereals and creamy – not crumbly – scrambled egg.

The attraction of The Old Mill is undoubtedly its wateriness and the fact that Salisbury city centre is only a ten-minute walk along the towpath. No wonder Salisbury-bound businessmen have discovered it. Roy puts it this way: 'They don't want to pay corporate prices any more.'

PS It seems rude calling him *just* Roy. On the pretext of writing, I ring to check his surname. 'Is the letter personal?' he asks.

'No.'

'Then address it to the manager,' he snaps.

'Following your article, we have made the lounge more comfortable, increased the selection of breakfast cereals, and now specialize in scram-bled eggs,' says Roy Thwaites. 'But we still have no televisions in the bed-rooms – this is a conscious decision.'

And he apologizes for snapping – it seems he thought I might be trying to sell him insurance!

The Old Mill Hotel and Restaurant,

Town Path,
Harnham,
Salisbury,
Wiltshire SP2 8EU.
Tel: (01722) 322364.
Fax: (01722) 333367.
Roy and Lois Thwaites.
Location: just across the water meadows from Salisbury city centre.
Open: all year.
Rooms: 11. 2 single (£40), 7 twin/double (£50–£65), 2 family rooms (£65–£85) all ensuite. Single in double (£50).
Restaurant: open from 6–10pm.
Chef: Roy Thwaites. A la carte, average £17. Also bar meals.
Wine List: inexpensive, from £8.75.
Children: yes.
Dogs: no.
Smoking: in public areas only.
And Also: riverside gardens shared with dippers, wagtails, kingfishers, mallards and swans.

*H*assop, *Derbyshire*
HASSOP HALL HOTEL

'That's lovely,' says the receptionist when I telephone to book a room on Friday night at Hassop Hall in Derbyshire. 'We look forward to seeing you...'

Driving along the road towards the village of Hassop, the first pair of gates marked Hassop Hall are closed. A sign directs potential visitors to the next turning on the left. Wonderful. What seem like miles of estate wall later, we discover a lodge and majestic drive leading to a stately pile. If I hadn't got a letter from the owner that morning that ended 'I am, dear Madam, yours sincerely, Tom Chapman', I might have thought I'd stumbled on Buck House in the Dales.

There's certainly a royal welcome from a vigilant member of kitchen staff. As he spots us debating which way to go, he dashes from his kitchen in his white apron. 'The entrance is round the front,' he says, pointing the way. 'Why don't I take your bags and meet you at reception?'

The front door is massive, reminding us that Hassop Hall was mentioned in the Domesday Book and rebuilt around 1600. In the hall, a sad-looking pianist bashes out 'Unforgetti-bul' in a manner that suggests he's done it many times before. At reception a smiling woman says, 'You've had a long journey – bet you're ready for your dinner. There's no hurry now.'

Unused to such genuine niceness when arriving late, we follow our white-aproned friend up a grand stair-case to a room that strikes us as engagingly eccentric – more of which later. Right now we're hungry.

In the bar, the owner's brother-in-law introduces himself: 'I'm just helping out.' Then – whoosh – in strides Clark Gable. Welcome! He pumps my husband's hand and sweeps *mine* to his lips. 'Haven't I seen you here before?'

'No. 'Fraid not.' My eyelids flutter. It's my first hotel kiss.

The packed dining room is lit with chandeliers and the mumsy waitresses bustle about in black dresses and white pinnies. Clark Gable bounces over and says why don't we visit Chatsworth Fair the next day? Why not, we say.

The food is what I'd call typical middle-of-the-road hotel fare accompanied by slightly over-cooked vegetables. I choose grapefruit cocktail. Even Clark Gable's eyebrows are raised at this choice. 'I *like* tinned grapefruit,' I murmur. I also like nourishing French onion soup and whole filleted Dover sole. Puddings you have to be in the mood for. The sweet trolley consists of mounds of sherry trifle and other confections of similar calibre.

Back upstairs, someone has left a note saying that breakfast is served in the rooms. What? No option? Seems not. Other minor idiosyncracies include having to crawl under the dressing table to plug in the kettle; a carved bedhead that bangs against the wall when leant against; and a novel dressing table swivel mirror from which the best place to view yourself is sitting on the floor.

Funny goings-on in the bathroom too. Lots of towels but no rail to drape them over. The bidet's not happy either – the towelling dressing gowns are in it. On the floor, cold lino.

We wake to the sound of squawking peacocks and make a major decision. We don't fancy eating breakfast up here. My husband goes in search of Clark Gable. 'Of course. Whatever you like,' he says, looking slightly amazed.

Now for the best bit. A proper Room Service trolley, complete with silver dome covering the scrambled egg, is wheeled into the sitting room. Two restaurant staff briskly lower the flaps and transform it into an elegant, white-clothed breakfast table – just like in the Marx Brothers film that gave this column its title.

We cannot help reflecting on the reactions of other (lesser) hoteliers when confronted with awkward guests who flout the rules. Clark Gable – alias Mr Chapman – has got the touch. The 'whatever you like' attitude, not to mention his hand-kissing abilities, say it all.

'My wife and I are happy that our twin sons (who have dual Swiss–British nationality) are now training with a view to joining the business in the future,' writes Tom Chapman, *'thus ensuring that Hassop Hall will continue to be run as a family hotel.'*

PS I take Mr Chapman's policy on dogs at face value.

Hassop Hall Hotel,

Hassop,
nr Bakewell,
Derbyshire DE45 1NS.
Tel: (01629) 640488.
Fax: (01629) 640577.
Tom Chapman and family.
Location: on the B6001 near Bakewell.
Open: all year, except Christmas and Boxing Day.
Rooms: 12. 2 single (£65–£85), 8 twin/double (£75–£95), 2 suites (£109–£119), all ensuite. Single in double (from £65–£109).
Restaurant: open for dinner from 7–9.30pm.
Chef: Michael Stones. Table d'hôte £16.50–£26.95. Continental breakfast £5.95. Cooked, £8.95.
Wine List: compact, carefully chosen, from £8.50.
Children: yes.
Dogs: bitches only, out of season.
Smoking: not in lounge.
And Also: Chatsworth, Haddon Hall, the Peak District.

*H*awes, *North Yorkshire*
COCKETT'S HOTEL

In Yorkshire I meet a hotelier who, when presenting the wine, asks: 'Who would like to taste it?' and glances in *my* direction. Good heavens. In my experience, women rarely get asked to taste the wine, even when they're paying the bill. This man is my friend for life.

The words carved above the stone doorway of Cockett's Hotel in the small town of Hawes seem pretty unique too, if a touch uncompromising: 'Anno Dom 1668. God being with us, Who can be against.' Trusting that He is, we enter hopefully through the paved forecourt set out with tables and chairs and open the front door. We find ourselves in a small, inviting bar. Out trips Mr Fred Bedford from behind the scenes.

'Mr and Mrs – ?' he beams, hand outstretched, offering in one breath to relieve us of our bags, show us our room and bring 'fresh milk if we want to make tea'.

Surely no one could be more obliging than Fred? Goodness, if I ask, he'll perform somersaults for sure. Now his wife Mary bustles in, as cheerful as he.

With pride he takes us up to a cottagey, simply furnished front bedroom. On the bedside cupboard is a clock – something that shouldn't merit special mention but does. Why don't more hoteliers realize that, if you wake in the night, you want to know the time at once, without fumbling for your watch or the light switch.

The room has not just one but two commodes, fortunately without hardware, as one serves as the bedside cupboard. Happily, in the bathroom, there are proper mod cons. There's also a squeezy bottle on the shelf of what I take, in the absence of any other likely looking bottle, to contain bath bubbles. Too late I discover it's window cleaner. No, it's not a good idea.

All polished up, we present ourselves downstairs. More guests are arriving, and Fred's doing a repeat welcome performance using a different script. Later he sits down for a chat. 'Those two came in off the street,' he confides. 'We bought this place five years ago. Used to run a pub in Coventry – nothing like this. But to the locals, I guess we'll always be foreigners.'

Fred and Mary's well patronized dining room has old lace curtains, cream-painted walls, polished kitchen chairs, candles and pink tablecloths. Across the room a bunch of academics is being refreshingly candid, not to mention catty, about an absent friend. At other tables, couples are gazing into each other's eyes.

The dinner that follows Fred's wine statement is very good: sautéed chicken livers with sage and garlic; half a Gressingham duck, perfectly cooked Wensleydale lamb cutlets. The French bread's delicious, so is the butter served in a little brown dish and scored on top. Afterwards Mary produces a plate of Yorkshire cheeses served with grapes and persuades me to try frangipane with Chantilly cheese.

Fred, meanwhile, is full of riveting information. '155 years ago the woman who owned this place had a big garden at the back she rented for 5/4d a year. I'll tell you what the dining room was used for *after* you've finished eating.'

Next morning, in striped apron, Fred is cooking breakfast. He reveals the dining room's secret – it was once an abbatoir. He also reveals another interesting side to his character – he is taking cooking lessons from his chef so that he can maintain restaurant standards on Sunday when the chef has his night off. A lesser man might have only been interested in the contents of the freezer.

While idly leafing through the brochure prior to leaving, I come across something that explains Fred and Mary Bedford's philosophy: 'When you arrive only you can decide if our accommodation entices you to stay. When you leave only you can decide whether our hospitality entices you to return. Our Hotel cannot live and grow unless you return and we therefore pledge to do everything possible to make your stay an enjoyable one.'

'We now offer a complete vegetarian menu as well,' say Fred and Mary.

Cockett's Hotel,

Market Place,
Hawes,
Wensleydale DL8 3RD,
North Yorkshire.
Tel: (01969) 667312.
Fred and Mary Bedford.
Location: in the centre of town.
Open: all year.
Rooms: 8. 6 twin/double (£54), 2 four-posters (£64), all ensuite. Single in double (£35). 1 ground-floor room.
Restaurant: open for dinner from 7–8.30pm.
Chef: Paul Noble. Table d'hôte £15.95.
Wine List: good value selection, from £6.50.
Children: yes, over 10.
Dogs: no.
Smoking: not in restaurant or bedrooms.
And Also: James Herriot country and Dales National Park. Pony trekking stables nearby. Special prices November - Easter.

In the crowded Saturday evening bar of The Old Black Lion in Hay on Wye (town of many bookshops), we are accosted by mine host, John Collins (man of many stories).

There's the one about how he is a surveyor by profession but bought 'this place for my retirement'. There's also the one about 'Mr Smith – ho ho – actually Ian Botham, that's between you and me, he comes here for the salmon fishing...' Then there's the other one about the two elderly ladies who phoned him from Argentina to book and 'Dammit they turned out to be perfectly serious, arrived on the appointed day...' Another time the 'entire staff of *Classic and Sports Car* magazine arrived: Couldn't believe my eyes. There they were, driving down the street, first this E type followed by this AC Ace, followed by...' Mr John Collins is in full flow.

The Old Black Lion is exactly what you'd expect an inn to be. Reputedly dating from 1370 and boasting a galleried room in which Cromwell reputedly stayed, it's noisy, friendly, convivial. Mrs Joan Collins, an ex-social worker, bustles about. 'Did you knit that jumper yourself?' she asks, giving me the once-over. No, I didn't. Oh, pity, she'd have borrowed the pattern.

To get to our room we climb a very short, very steep, staircase and mind our heads. The floors, covered in cosy red-patterned carpet, are creaky and sloping. Inside the room, looking down over the street, are some extraordinary pieces of painted furniture which, had they been left in their virgin state, would have been utterly unremarkable. As it is, they are – well – quite striking and certainly add to the general charm. There are also jugs, knick-knacks, chocolate biscuits. 'Things vanish,' says Mrs Collins, gazing sadly at an empty space.

Next to the bar is a restaurant that can only be described as inviting, though you've got to be into black beams, low ceilings, plates on walls, lots of dark-brown tables and chairs of the sort without which olde worlde pubs would not be olde worlde. There's what tastes like homemade bread and decent house wine. Candles flicker on the tables. Across the room is a group of Australians. A couple in the corner conduct a passionate whispered conversation. 'Lava cakes with bacon?' exclaims my husband. 'This is Wales,' I remind him. 'Huh, only just.' But he seems quite taken with his lava cakes, more so than with his salted Barbary duck with cider, which is large, menacing and exceedingly messy to eat. I choose chicken with Calvados sauce – very civilized.

After coffee and a drink in the bar, we park ourselves in the small sitting room with its television and piles of carefully chosen videos. Earlier Mr Collins had confided that he was a bit of a video freak. He had once gone down to the shop and got out *Brief Encounter* specially for two old ladies.

'They sat down and wept,' he said.

Instead of a video, we find things to read and, when John Collins pops his head round the door, the only sound is the rustle of paper. What, no television, no video. Who are these funny people? In he comes for a chat. Perhaps we need cheering up?

'Is this place really as old as it looks?' I ask. 'No. Older,' he quips, roaring with laughter. There's a pause as he slides into gear. 'I'm a surveyor by profession...bought this place for my retirement...Mr Smith – actually Ian Botham between you and me, he comes here for the salmon fishing... *Déja entendu* overtakes us and we bid him a polite good night.

Salmon fishermen are certainly well catered for at breakfast. For £6.75 extra they can indulge in a Fisherman's Special of smoked eel, horseradish sauce, and a large measure of Danish aquavit. For romantics, there's scrambled egg, caviar and a quarter bottle of Moët for £4.50 extra.

I think The Old Black Lion is just what an old inn should be: friendly, mercifully unmodernized, without all those pretentious little touches that would spoil it.

Oh good. I'm forgiven for sending up Mine Host: 'Nothing to forgive,' he assures me. 'Your description of The Old Black Lion and myself is absolutely correct. I'm still as jocular and cheeky as ever and try to ignore my age.'

The Old Black Lion,

Lion Street,
Hay on Wye,
Hereford and Worcester HR3 5AD.
Tel: (01497) 820841.
Joan and John Collins.
Location: in centre of town.
Open: all year.
Rooms: 10. 1 single with own bathroom (£18.95), 8 twin/double (£39.95–£41.90), 1 family room (£41.90–£64), all ensuite. Single in double (£25.90). 1 ground-floor room.
Restaurant: open for dinner 7–9.30pm.
Chef: John Morgan. A la carte only, average £18.
Wine List: global selection, from £6.95. Bar meals also served.
Children: yes, over 5.
Dogs: yes.
Smoking: not in restaurant.
And Also Hay on Wye is the secondhand book centre of the world. Fishing arranged for residents. Brecon Beacons, Black Mountains and Radnor Forest. Special 2-day Gourmet Breaks, please enquire.

*H*igh Offley, Staffordshire
THE OLD PARSONAGE

Through an excitable lady I meet at a party, I learn of The Old Parsonage in High Offley, Staffs. 'You must try it,' she gushes. '*Such* nice people. It's off the beaten track, mind.'

Exhilarated at the prospect of getting lost in dark country lanes, I telephone for a brochure. Instead, I get a dead-keen member of staff: 'English breakfast costs £5,' he volunteers, 'but you get a lot.'

Later, when I ring to book a room and dinner – 'We'll be there around seven-thirty' – the owner's wonderfully laid-back. He doesn't demand confir-mation, phone number, credit card or even deposit: 'Just your address, please, so I can send a map.' This arrives with a note that says: 'Look forward to seeing you.'

In fact, he has that pleasure later than we intend. Under-estimating the time it takes from Norwich to deepest Staffordshire and the country-lane factor, we arrive at nine. How rude. I haven't even phoned. 'If they're *such* nice people,' says my husband, 'they'll love us anyway.'

Beyond the reception desk, The Old Parsonage is buzzing. 'We thought you weren't coming,' says the owner's wife. 'Have you driven far? If you're tired, we can rustle up something light for dinner if you prefer.' She takes us up to a warm room in a professionally converted stable block done out in designer fabrics. 'There,' she says, 'come down when you're ready.'

Well. It's not hard to see why that large sitting room is bursting with punters sipping pre-dinner drinks. As a reflex action, we make a dive for the decanter of sherry thoughtfully provided. Looking around, this is a room with everything – even a clock.

Downstairs, we join the Saturday night crowd that includes a family party with baby, and a woman in a nail-biting strapless dress. Next door, in the pretty cream, green and pink dining room, a pearl-bedecked senior citizen at the opposite table is holding forth on a hotel she'd visited: 'There we were,' she sniffs, 'paying £90 for the privilege of sleeping in *their* bed.' Now her voice becomes conspiratorial. 'So while the barman was getting our drinks, we got him talking and he forgot to make a note of them. Oh, we did enjoy our free gins...' Well, *really*.

The wine list's inexpensive and they've won awards for their food: courgette and dill soup, garnished with smoked salmon; crab and lemongrass tart; local, partly boned roast duck with a garlic and red onion *confit* and sauterne butter sauce. 'This duck's very well organized,' says my husband, 'but I've *still* managed to splash myself.' My grilled fillet of red snapper, served with fresh tomato, Jalopeno pepper and basil sauce, has me sighing over a memo-rable dinner I once had in Sydney. And there are no extras: coffee and Belgian chocolates are included along with four courses at £18.50 per person. Service is laid-back to the point of lethargic – *not* a place for those who like to eat at seven-thirty and be tucked up by ten.

But what about that 'you get a lot' breakfast? In the morning, we find the owner roasting a pig on the terrace. 'Well, that's novel,' says my husband. 'Fool. That's for a charity lunch – look, there's freshly squeezed OJ and good strong coffee.' He settles for scrambled egg and bacon but somehow misses out on the cornflakes.

When settling up, the owner tells us their policy is to give good value: 'After all, better to take a minimal mark-up and be full...' A laudable aim that's reflected in the bill. Just as laudable is the easy-going atmosphere – *no* hotel guest likes being pushed around. As my acquaintance says: '*Such* nice people.'

Chortles Jeff Wilkinson: 'Overheard in the restaurant, one lady to another: 'Where did you find this place – it's wonderful!' Other lady: 'I read about it last week in The Telegraph *when I was in Borneo.''*

The Old Parsonage,

High Offley,
nr Woodseaves,
Staffordshire ST20 0NE.
Tel/Fax: (01785) 284446.
The Wilkinson family.
Location: where Derbyshire meets Shropshire.
Open: all year.
Rooms: 4. 4 double (£40), single in double (£40), all ensuite.
Restaurant: open for dinner from 7.30–9.30pm.
Chef: Ray Brown. Table d'hôte £18.50. Cooked breakfast £5.
Wine List: from £9.95.
Children: yes.
Dogs: no.
Smoking: not in bedrooms.
And Also: Alton Towers, Wedgwood Visitors' Centre, Gladstone Pottery Museum, the Peak District, Ironbridge Gorge.

*H*itchin, Hertfordshire
REDCOATS FARMHOUSE HOTEL

According to its brochure, the 15th-century Redcoats Farmhouse Hotel, set amidst the rolling Hertfordshire countryside, is 'only a few minutes from the A1'.

Apart from the fact that 'few minutes' is wildly over-optimistic for anyone unfamiliar with winding Hertfordshire lanes, the brochure neither reveals, nor even darkly hints at, the fact that Redcoats is one of the odder establishments 'Room Service' has ever discovered.

From the car park we are blown by strong winds through a door leading into a bar furnished with some handsome wooden antique furniture, where a group of locals, accompanied by blonde *décolletée* women, are engaged in TGIF conversation punctuated by much raucous laughter.

Now, owner Peter Butterfield mooches out from the nether regions, hunts amiably for our booking letter and offers to show us our room. He has a nice smile, but I fear the worst. 'Does it mean going out again?' I enquire, having spotted in the yard a row of unpromising-looking doors in what appears to be a converted stable block.

'Yes.' Off we go. Mr Butterfield opens one of those unpromising doors and turns on the light. 'Please call if you want anything.'

What I want is out. This room, a bit scabby round the edges, is surely aimed at the commercial traveller whose company is going down the drain. Just as we are resigning ourselves, Mr

Butterfield calls *us.* 'I thought you might prefer to be in the house and have a larger room,' he says suavely. 'I do hope you haven't unpacked.'

'Oh no, no.' Hastily we repack our bags. At this point the story takes on an Alice twist. Returning to the house, we are led by Mr Butterfield up an unexpectedly grand staircase lined with paintings and through the looking glass.

This is undoubtedly the best bedroom. Not only is it vast, it has a half tester bed, great swathes of heavy curtaining, a chaise longue, a desk, a round table covered with lace cloth, a massive mahogany wardrobe and matching dressing table, a brass-fitted bathroom complete with Alka Seltzer and that rare thing, a shower that works a treat.

What's more, there is Redcoats writing paper, Redcoats matches and Redcoats fine china mugs for tea. I collapse on the chaise in disbelief. Is Mr B one of these hotel proprietors who can spot a hotel reviewer a mile off?

On the desk is an enigma variation. 'Please let us know the night before in the bar,' says a note, 'if you require your bill phrased in a "special way". Bills cannot be altered in the morning.'

No time to work this one out. The enigmatic Mr Butterfield has promised us 'some good food'. Dashing through the sitting room we notice more choice antique furniture and paintings. We are booked into the Old Kitchen dining room which, though quaint, does not provide quite the sense of occasion offered by the formal dining room at front of house. I should feel conned if, as at the next table, I had taken the trouble to dress up in a satin jacket and put *diamanté* bows in my hair.

There are only two words to describe our meal for two at £55.30, excluding wine, and they are over-described and over-priced. Moreover, at this price level, I would expect it to be served by professional staff – the best one can say about these waitresses is that they have a wonderfully amateurish approach. Take the Wharfedale tart. 'Does it really come from Wharfedale?' I ask mischievously. I receive a blank look. 'I'll have to find out.' She returns, shaking her head. 'We don't know.'

Breakfast for two – only one cooked – costs an extra £14. The *real* enigma is that our lovely room is priced at only £35 even though, when booking, I was quoted £57 for the box across the yard. You see what I mean by odd?

'All rooms have been redecorated,' says the charming Peter Butterfield, 'and we now include breakfast in the room rates. We have also added a large Victorian-style conservatory restaurant for lunches and light suppers. And we're still only minutes from the A1, depending on your route and sense of direction!

PS: Our bar is not normally full of blondes you know.'

Redcoats Farmhouse Hotel,

Redcoats Green,
nr Hitchin,
Hertfordshire SG4 7JR.
Tel: (01438) 729500.
Fax: (01438) 723322.
Peter Butterfield and Jackie Gainsford.
Location: Hitchin/Stevenage.
Open: all year except 10 days over Christmas.
Rooms: 14. 1 single with shower (£52), 13 twin/double (from £70), 12 ensuite. Single in double (from £58).
Restaurant: open for dinner from 7–9.30pm.
Chef: John Ruffell/Jackie Gainsford. A la carte, average £25. Light suppers in the conservatory also available.
Wine List: extensive and carefully researched, from £7.50.
Children: yes.
Dogs: by arrangement.
Smoking: not in bedrooms and dining room.
And Also: Knebworth and Woburn Parks, Hatfield House and the Shuttleworth Aircraft Collection nearby.

REDCOATS
FARMHOUSE

$\mathcal{H}$oldenby, Northamptonshire
LYNTON HOUSE

Crunching up the sweeping gravel drive of Lynton House in smartest Northamptonshire, we think: oh dear. No, it's nothing to do with the pretty Georgian house and its bell tower – it's the dearth of other cars. It's going to be a 'just us' evening.

But as we pull our bags out of the boot and lock up, the front door's thrown open and a genial Italian man hurries out. 'How nice to see you,' he cries, hand outstretched.

Inside, the hall is full of paintings and the carpet is a rich deep red. Signing in, I enquire if we are indeed the only people staying. 'Friday is ze funny night,' he muses. 'The business people have moved out and ze weekend-a people come tomorrow. I hope you don't mind. Or would you like to move onto anozzer place?' he enquires affably.

'Absolutely not. I thought you might have been looking forward to a night off.'

'No, no. You have to be around in zis business...' He tells us his name is Carlo and that his wife, Carol, is the chef. 'I keep her chained to ze kitchen; she keeps me chained to ze bed,' he jokes. 'I've been in England for thirty years now, so I must like it a leetle.'

What an engaging man he is. Chatting us up the staircase, he takes us to a big room with comfortable pink velvet armchairs, pink blankets and curtains. When he's gone, we puzzle over the large but bare shower room. Where do we put our sponge bags? Ah,

the *floor*. (Note: don't forget to bring your shower cap.)

Making our way down to a plush little red bar, we find it full of water-colours. 'Who's the artist?'

'They're all mine – my hobby,' he says not-so-modestly.

Over drinks we discuss the classy menu and I'm tempted into choosing a dish called Bocconcini di Salmone (with dolcelatte and coriander): 'You won't find this anywhere else,' promises Carlo, 'maybe I should patent it.'

How swish, elegant and silent (ie no piped muzak) the restaurant is with its pink chairs and monogrammed carpet leading into a small conservatory. Ordering a bottle of Pinot Grigio, we settle back to enjoy ourselves. A mouthwatering Formaggio di Capra con Acciughe e Pesto is my husband's choice of starter while I – how boring, except it's not – have Melone e Prosciutto. This is Italian food at its best.

'While Carol gets ze fish ready, how about a little sorbet?' suggests Carlo later, mentioning almost in the same breath that Nigel Lawson was in the other night: 'A *very* entertaining man.'

It's easy to imagine how this restaurant must appeal to local people – though where are they tonight? Our main courses – the salmon, and a monkfish, squid and scallop casserole – are served with vegetables from the garden. We finish with a Crema al Forno, a sort of Italian crême brulée, and a Siciliano ricotta cheesecake made with fruit, chocolate and Strega. Beat all that.

In the morning Carol serves us breakfast in the conservatory overlooking pretty lawned gardens full of birds, squirrels and even, so our host had told us the night before, his friend the fox.

What *I* like about Lynton House is that, as usual, we book in anonymously (and, in this case, turn up just a few hours later) and are treated like special guests rather than strangers in the night. Although it's just us, dinner is served in a totally professional manner and, wow, do we get the works: the chat-up, the ceremony and, of course, the food. Strange: here's the classic Italian host, the classic Italian menu...cooked by the *very English* Carol. On getting the bill, we're further surprised: no one could accuse Carlo and Carol of over-charging.

PS. Recently I've been scolded for 'sending up' another charming Italian hotelier. I assure both these gentlemen that it's done with affection.

'Shower caps are now in all the rooms – of course zey should have been there anyway. After the article appeared, one man wanted to know the secret of the chains that kept my wife at the stove – he had been trying to do the same for years. Regards, Carlo.'

Lynton House,

Holdenby,
Northamptonshire NN6 8DJ.
Tel/Fax: (01604) 770777.
Carol and Carlo Bertozzi.
Location: on the East Haddon to Church Brampton Road.
Open: all year.
Rooms: 5. 1 single (£49), 4 twin/double (£55), all ensuite. Single in double (£55).
Restaurant: open for dinner from 7.30–9pm.
Chef: Carol Bertozzi. A la carte from £19.75.
Wine List: mostly Italian, including 'a good crop of classics from Piedmont and Tuscany', from £9.75.
Children: yes, over 5.
Dogs: no.
Smoking: no pipes or cigars in any food area.
And Also: Golf, tennis and riding nearby.

Ever left your car in an airport car park and forgotten, on return, which floor you left it on? I'll come clean. *I've* done it.

Now I discover a posh hotelier who'll not only clasp your BMW to his bosom while you're away but charge no extra for the convenience. Better still, he'll deliver you to the airport in his Daimler. The trick – and, incidentally, treat – is that you must first spend the night at Langshott Manor *circa* 1580 just eight minutes from Gatwick.

But as everyone knows, life hands out few real freebies, and Langshott Manor is not cheap. So is it value for money?

For those turned on by window-panel check trousers of the Duke of Windsor variety, owner Mr Geoffrey Noble is very good value indeed. Do I detect a hint of Kiwi accent here? I do.

It transpires that Mr Noble brought up his family in New Zealand before returning to this country in 1986 and rescuing poor dilapidated Langshott Manor. The only reason he could afford to buy this wonderful house, he explains, was because its land had been sold to builders – hence the surrounding cluster of red-brick executive homesteads.

Our room reveals books, magazines, a cricket bat (of all things), two beds pushed together with a hand-crafted wooden headboard and a guest book that confides: 'We bought this house at auction and have given her constant and ceaseless tender loving care ever since and have had the pleasure of watching the old lady respond and come back to life again...'

In 1991 Langshott became one of the RAC's 'highly acclaimed' small hotels. Clearly the Nobles are people of energy and resource. As we are the only overnight guests and there are two large private parties of diners to cater for, they have hit on the idea of putting us in a separate room for dinner. Mr 'Call me Geoff' Noble glints. There. Aren't you lucky. Haven't I thought of every-thing?

Yet we, his guests, are glum. There will be no other punters to eye up and down, no conversations to eavesdrop on. And what's the point of putting on one's glad rags when there's no one to admire them, hey?

With an imperious sleight of hand, Mr Noble – Geoff – whisks away such pleb reflections by whipping open crafty false panelling in the hall and leading us down a secret passage to a candlelit room with table laid for two and roaring log fire. Wow.

Dinner is served by French wait-resses, one of whose English is not of the best. When we comment mildly on the lack of kirsch in the Melon with Fruits and Kirsch, she replies, 'Mmm. Maybe someone forget.' You can't argue with that.

Yet when the excellent dinner – duck followed by summer pudding –is finished, the secret parlour loses its charms. There're voices and laughter from the diners across the hall. We feel left out. 'Let's go upstairs...'

On the ancient staircase, candles burn in metal holders attached to each newel post. All around is polished wood and antique furniture, lamps, pictures, pewter, flowers and a fat cat called Michael asleep outside a door.

Downstairs next morning the log fires are lit and one end of a large dining table is invitingly laid with a blue flowered cloth. Now we discover that Langshott Manor is indeed a true family concern. Mrs Noble and son Christopher do the cooking. Son Gregory, an architect, has set out the garden. Dogs Phoebe and Amy woof in the hall.

But the most formidable family member has got to be Grandma – the Esse stove. 'During our first months here, she was the only thing that kept us warm. When she needed repairing, we rang Esse who told us she had been installed in 1939. All the cooking is done on this stove, no microwaves for us,' says Patricia Noble, challenging me to disbelieve her. I wouldn't dare.

'We would be pleased to 'clasp your BMW to our bosom' and Daimler you to Gatwick any time,' wrote the Noble family after this piece appeared. Alas, I've never taken them up on it...

Langshott Manor,

Langshott,
Horley,
Surrey RH6 9LN.
Tel: (01293) 786680.
Fax: (01293) 783905.
The Noble family.
Location: off A23 at Horley.
Open: all year except 24–30 December.
Rooms: 7. 7 twin/double (£90–£128), all ensuite. Single in double (£78–£93).
Restaurant: open for dinner from 7-9.30pm.
Chef: Christopher Noble. Table d'hôte £25. Continental breakfast £5, cooked £8.
Wine List: created by Master of Wine to complement style of food, from £9.50.
Children: yes.
Dogs: no.
Smoking: not in bedrooms.
And Also: Winner Johansens Country House for Excellence 1993; AA Red Star & Rosette; Egon Ronay 1993; Michelin Award; County Hotel of the Year for Surrey, *Which Hotel Guide* 1993.

Friends who stayed at Esseborne Manor recently came back raving about its stylishness. 'Do go,' they purred.

In search, then, of this elusive thing called style, I find myself one snowy evening driving along the A343 between Newbury and Andover and turning left into a long driveway at the end of which stands a small Victorian manor house.

No manor house could fail to look utterly enchanting in this Christmas-card scenario: snow-covered roof; backdrop of trees garlanded in white; lighted windows that spell welcome. There's even a receptionist who comes tripping bravely out into the snow. 'May I help with your bags?' she smiles. Oh, it's a *very* stylish beginning.

The bedroom, however, has a style all of its own. Our noses twitch. 'What is that awful smell?'

'Drains,' says the housekeeper, appearing from nowhere. 'They've tried everything.'

'Oh, really, and do all the rooms smell like this?'

'No, just this one.' She is unnervingly matter of fact.

Very fairly, she offers us the room next door which, although sweeter smelling, is not, in my opinion, as prettily furnished. We decide to shut the smell in the bathroom, where we think it's coming from. After all, we *are* only staying for one night.

Apart from this obvious disadvantage, the room is pleasing on the eye. I approve of the thick wooden curtain rods and pretty patterned curtains, the matching antique wardrobe and dressing table with needlepoint-topped stool, the lace bedspread, the two pink velvety armchairs, the table with a bowl of truly appetising-looking fruit, the jar of peppermints, the thermos of iced water, the pile of glossy magazines.

Having arrived in good time, a soak before dinner seems a nice idea. Or is it? Level with the comfortable end of the bath is a window covered by a lace curtain. When we tentatively phone the manager to find out if there is supposed to be a proper curtain, we are told: 'There used to be a roller blind, but it got damaged.' So badly damaged, it seems, that neither it nor anything else is available as a cover-up, even on a temporary basis. 'You might think it looks public from the inside, but it is quite private from the outside,' reassures the manager. In the interests of fairness, my husband puts this theory to the test. Alas, it seems I am performing my ablutions in full view of the diners now beginning to park in the driveway.

Downstairs, though, nothing has been left to chance. The drawing room is elegant in blue and yellow. There are flowered ruffled blinds and curtains; comfortable armchairs and sofas; a window seat; a handsome mahogany Victorian round table; family photographs on small tables. The Pimms and orange juice arrive immaculately prepared, accompanied by stylish appetizers. A second room, done out in blue, has a log fire and a corner bar. The other guests are pretty stylish too.

And it is no exaggeration to say that dinner is brilliant. Pink candles, cloths and napkins. A five-course menu, perfectly cooked and served. The main course is set, unless you decide to make a selection from the opposite side of the menu and pay £3 extra for the privilege. There is a delicious choice of pudding and a large trolley of English cheeses. A basket of biscuits, including Bath Olivers, is left on the table, which seems more than generous, and coffee is served in the drawing room with a large – and I mean *large* – plate of chocolates.

I wish I could be as generous in my praise of the hotel as a whole. It is, of course, unfortunate for any hotelier when someone arrives incognito to review the place and she is put in the one room that smells and has a bath that comes under the heading of public. Nevertheless, £100 for a double room including breakfast is not cheap and most people would, I think, agree with me that for this price one is entitled to expect perfection or at any rate something approaching it.

Esseborne Manor,
Hurstbourne Tarrant,
Andover,
Hampshire SP11 0ER.
Tel: (01264) 736444.
Fax: (01264) 736473.
Michael and Freda Yeo.
Location: on the A343 between Newbury and Andover.
Open: all year.
Rooms: 12. 11 twin/double (£95–£112), 1 four-poster suite (£125), all ensuite. Single in double (£84). One room with wheelchair access.
Restaurant: open for dinner from 7.30–9.30pm.
Chef: Andy Norman. A la carte, average £25.
Wine List: catholic, with wide choice from New World, from £11.50.
Children: yes, over 12.
Dogs: no.
Smoking: if considerate.
And Also: Special racing weekends during season throughout year – please enquire.

Says owner Michael Yeo: 'At the time the piece appeared, we got a bit hot under the collar, but you were smack on the button. I said to everyone: just think, how many people who're not writers have stayed in that room and haven't said anything – they're the ones who never came back. Actually that smelly room brought business – it was amazing how many people turned up for Sunday lunch and said could they have a sniff please. We also had no fewer than five firms saying they were experts at getting rid of smells. It still persists, although less frequently. But we have repaired the blind!'

*I*psley, Worcestershire
THE OLD RECTORY

An Oxfordshire reader expresses astonishment that so many of the hotels featured in this column border on Fawlty Towers. Honestly I don't invent the singing waiters, acrobatic chefs, undiscovered Kenneth Branaghs and owners who tell the same joke twice. I just report on what I find. Everyone knows that England is full of eccentrics – if you want to meet one, book yourself into a small hotel.

Take Mr David Moore of The Old Rectory near Redditch. He's an actor *manqué* if ever there was one. In fact, he's a young acoustics engineer recently summoned from Paris to run the family hotel.

We are the only dinner guests at The Old Rectory this Friday evening, so the bespectacled Mr Moore has ample opportunity to demonstrate his wide-ranging talents. 'The whole evening will be a celebration of white,' he declares mysteriously just before seven-thirty dinner.

Alarm bells ring. 'Please tell us why.'

'A white first course. Definitely a lot of white in the second. A white pudding. But the candles are pink, I'm afraid. Now I'll get off my bottom and get it for you.'

The minute we arrived, we had received the full blast of his whimsicality. His ancient wood-frame rectory was modernized in 1812 (according to the brochure) by the great-grandson of Sir Christopher Wren. He literally bounces us up the stairs, throwing open the door of a small room painted buttermilk yellow in the converted stable. 'You can have a four-poster if you like. No problem,' he says.

But the four-poster has no bath, only a shower. Anyway, this room with its wormy beams, eaved ceiling and snug adjoining bathroom, is most attractive. 'There's the phone,' he says, pointing at it. 'The code for America is 0101 and it will make me very rich.'

We won't be dialling the States, thank you. Instead, we wander down to the conservatory where a lone table is laid, its pink candles flickering. And dinner's *very* white. First, there's a cauliflower and almond soup and we are issued with explicit instructions on how to eat it. 'The trick is to *cover* it with black pepper...and when that's gone, cover it again.'

It's good. The main course is a substantial dish of chicken with a creamy tarragon sauce accompanied by a baked potato and bowl of crispy veg. The pudding – a sort of syllabub – is also rich.

The only disconcerting thing about eating David Moore's food – 'never cooked before July 1991 in my life – you just need lots of cookbooks and a fertile imagination' – is that he can see you from his kitchen window. Try scribbling notes while your host is watching you with gimlet eyes.

Afterwards it's getting-over-it time in the drawing room. Will we ever want to eat again? Now he breaks the news that old schoolfriends are coming over. Suddenly they're here! We are surrounded by people who know each other very well indeed. There's even talk of a Chinese takeaway.

I groan. The smell will finish me off. We retire early to bed, wishing there was a TV set in the bedroom or, more particularly, a drawing room specifically for guests. This is supposed to be a *hotel* after all.

At breakfast his homemade marmalade is on the table and we nibble to the strains of Vivaldi or Big Viv, as he calls him. How did I discover The Old Rectory, he wants to know? When I tell him (truthfully) I can't remember, he asks me again.

His family home has tree-lined grounds – including an ancient mulberry – and the snowdrops are out. Once it must have been very much on its own, but now there are modern houses within spitting distance. As we get into the car, he nags because I haven't immediately put my seat belt on. 'You're extremely bossy,' I tell him.

'I am, rather, aren't I,' he says, pleased as Punch.

David Moore can't remember why he didn't take his friends into his own sitting room.

"Clearly you liked the look of us?" I suggest.

"Of course I did," he says. "You'll have to come again, won't you, and I'll organise more people. Incidentally, the room you had now has a bath and a shower. Apart from that, nothing changes...I'm still Mother Hen," he clucks.

The Old Rectory,

Ipsley Lane,
Ipsley,
Redditch,
Hereford and Worcester B98 0AP.
Tel: (01527) 523000.
Fax: (01527) 517003.
David Moore.
Location: on the fringes of Redditch.
Open: all year.
Rooms: 10. 2 single (£39.95–£49.95), 8 twin/double (£67.50–£77.50), 8 ensuite, 2 with private bathroom. Single in double (£49.95–£58.50).
Restaurant: Dinner at 7.30 pm.
Chef: David Moore. Table d'hôte £14.95.
Wine List: small, discreet, well chosen, from £6.50. Help yourself from fridge bar.
Children: yes.
Dogs: no.
Smoking: some rooms are non-smoking.
And Also: In the heart of the Midlands, 30-minute drive to Stratford, Broadway and Worcester.

'The Grange is proudly owned by Duncan and Jane Miller,' says the brochure. Hurrah. Some hotels I visit seem singularly lacking in that thing called pride – in which case, why do they bother?

Well. There's certainly more than a hint of pride when I ring to book and comment that their prices seem, well, reasonable. 'Someone said that to me this morning,' replies Mrs Miller delightedly, 'though I must tell you that these are our spring rates. I'm afraid it goes up on 11 May.' She's dreadfully apologetic.

The handsome Grange Country House Hotel, just outside Keswick, is built of grey Lakeland stone and over-looks a garden of rhododendrons just coming into bloom with majestic fells beyond. This Bank Holiday Saturday the car park's nearly full – can't wait to find out who all these other people are.

Jane Miller takes us up to a room with a half-tester bed, stripped pine wardrobe and dressing table, two Lloyd Loom chairs, clock phone and magnificent view. Mrs Miller tells us to be sure to call her if we want anything. 'We will. Thank you.'

First, we test the ensuite shower room – the shower's highly efficient. And six-thirty on the dot finds us scooting down to the bar – a large room full of sofas, a log fire and the chattering classes *en masse*.

Over drinks we get chatting too. Here's this pleasant middle-aged couple who've come to buy a Lakeland cottage and 'booked in here on impulse'. Then there's the substantial blonde woman and her attentive husband/lover; and a couple with elderly but marbles-intact mother in tow. I wonder what they think of us.

Because this hotel caters for hungry walkers (does Mother go too?), dinner is served early between seven-thirty and eight. Duncan, the thin and energetic other half of Jane, hops from sofa to sofa negotiating feet and legs with a flurry of jokes, though what I think he's really saying is: would we please all hurry up and order. Chef's waiting.

Chef? Somehow I had assumed that the diligent Jane was doing the slaving. 'No, no. Colin's our chef. Jane's number two, though tomorrow she's number one because it's Colin's night off.'

In the dining room, tall windows on two sides show off the view. Dinner is a five-course blow-out with choices. 'Who's doing the wine tasting around here?' asks Duncan, pointing the bottle of Rosemount Chardonnay in not quite the right direction. 'I can see whose side *you're* on,' I joke. 'I'm holding the bottle dead in the middle,' he says quick as Jumping Jack Flash.

The food is simple and appetizing: mushrooms *en cocotte* or egg and prawn mousse (mushrooms win on points), courgette soup with basil, salmon fillet or turkey with bilberries and orange. 'Brilliant,' says the bearded guy in navy blazer and striped tie, gazing intensely into the eyes of his *amoureuse*. Smacking his lips, he asks: 'Why can't you make crumble like that?'

After dinner we find lots of inviting places to park ourselves: the bar, the back end of the dining room furnished with armchairs, sofas and magazines, or a smaller room leading off. We listen in on Mother who's reading bits of *The Daily Telegraph* to her son and daughter-in-law. But goodness gracious. It seems they'd rather play chess.

Next morning, at breakfast, we find all these people, with the exception of Mother, dressed for action in red stockings, breeches and hill-walking boots. As we pay the bill, Jane tells us that she was brought up in the hotel business. 'Running a hotel's so much more than just being able to cook,' she says. 'It's about looking after people.' And she and her husband clearly take pride in doing exactly that – beautifully.

'Lots of reaction, lots of booking. Thank you,' says Jane Duncan.

The Grange Country House Hotel,

Manor Brow,
Keswick,
Cumbria CA12 4BA.
Tel: (017687) 72500.
Duncan and Jane Miller.
Location: just off the A591 outside Keswick.
Open mid March–mid November.
Rooms: 10. 8 twin/double, 2 half-tester (£86–£98), all ensuite. Price includes dinner. Single in double (£10 supplement).
Restaurant: dinner at 7.30 pm.
Chef: Colin Brown. Table d'hôte, £17.90 (included in room rate).
Wine List: changes with the seasons, from £7.90.
Children: yes, over 7.
Dogs: no.
Smoking: in bar only.
And Also: views, walks, lakes, the fells.

CONYGREE GATE COUNTRY HOUSE HOTEL

'Hold on while I swop my glasses,' says the proprietor of Conygree Gate Hotel, investigating what rooms he has available for Friday night. As I debate the merits of a twin room with shower or four-bedded family room with bath, he adds: 'If you want the room with bath, I won't charge extra.' I do – and he doesn't!

When we arrive in the small Cotswold village of Kingham, I decide that, if I were small again, I'd want a dolls' house just like this one. I do like leaded-light windows and flagged paths leading in straight lines to welcoming front doors.

As we push it open, the proprietor dashes into the hall. 'Brian Sykes,' he smiles, 'but Brian'll do nicely.' He whisks us up a short staircase and proudly shows us into the four-bed room. 'You can sub-let if you like,' he jokes. 'Must get back – I'm head waiter you see. When you come down, you'll find a bell pull with birds all down it – just give it a tug.'

Our room has cream-painted walls and bold turquoise stencils. A new dorm. I wonder what the other girls are like. Then I remember. It's just us two and all these beds. Fortunately we're too hungry to argue over them.

The pink drawing room is cottagey, with green velvet sofas and armchairs, patchwork cushions, books and pictures. Here's the string of birds and, when pulled, in dashes Brian from the kitchen. 'Have you come from *The Telegraph*?' he asks. Now he's rumbled me! 'We advertise there every week and get a good response,' says Brian. That's all right then.

He explains they serve a set main course – 'Tonight it's pork' – with choice of starter and pud. 'Let me read you our little list of starters – oh, must go and fetch my specs.' He comes back, bespectacled: 'My wife is deaf, she lip reads,' he says, 'which is why *I* do all the talking. She's a very good cook, you won't be disappointed.' He offers us a choice of house wine – dry, medium or red. We choose the dry. 'You'll like it. I've never had any complaints,' he beams.

The dining room is inviting: cosy, with knick-knacks everywhere and, better still, *people.* No wonder Brian is rushing around. And how sad, 'I used to love driving fast cars,' I hear a little old lady with a stick and carrying voice say.

Kathryn Sykes' food is simple and unpretentious. Coarse pâté and melon to start. And oh, it's ages since I had roast pork and all the trimmings – cooked slowly in an Aga too. To follow, a generous selection of cheese. There's a spirit of hospitality here that's warming. The homemade puddings, displayed on a table, are as splendiferous as they look. 'Please compliment your wife on the treacle pud,' I say afterwards. 'Oh, the butcher's wife made that one.'

In the drawing room over coffee, we meet the dog of the house: a large Bernese called Rupert. Now the cats,

Jimmy and Smokey, sidle in for a stroke. And then a merry party of six make their entry. They've had a good dinner. Now they want to play *games* for heaven's sake.

Our room grows on us. In the morning we discover it has a view over the front garden and quiet village street. 'My wife used to be a window dresser with Liberty's and she's a potter,' Brian tells us enthusiastically over breakfast. 'She's very artistic.' Well, I've had homemade marmalade for breakfast before, but never out of homemade pots...

'Ooh,' said Mr Sykes. 'The phone's never stopped ringing.'

Conygree Gate Country House Hotel,

Kingham,
Oxfordshire OX7 6YA.
Tel: (01608) 658389.
Brian and Kathryn Sykes.
Location: in the centre of Kingham.
Open: all year.
Rooms: 10. 1 single with private bathroom (£26), 9 twin/double (£48–£50), mostly ensuite. Single in double (£30). 4 ground-floor rooms.
Restaurant: open for dinner at 7pm.
Chef: Kathryn Sykes. Table d'hôte £12.
Wine List: French and German house wines, from £9.
Children: yes.
Dogs: yes.
Smoking: not in restaurant.
And Also: Cotswolds villages, Cotswold Wildlife Park, Batsford Arboretum and Falconry Centre.

$\mathcal{K}$intbury, Berkshire
THE DUNDAS ARMS

The Dundas Arms has it all: a canal, a river, a road and a railway. Swooshing into the car park and leaping out, we clatter through the bar door. Goodness, the place is swarming with Berkshire types. A chap in a jolly homeknit suddenly notices our bags and realizes we're queueing for attention not drinks. Throwing us an 'Allow me' smile, he bows out of the way. Thank you.

The barmaid looks flustered. 'You're booked in?'

'We certainly are.' She vanishes into the back and returns, smiling, with a key. 'Come with me.'

We are in our unremarkable ground-floor room in seconds. But there's a bonus: doors open onto a paved terrace and the River Kennet. A white table and chairs complete the idyll.

Alas, it's not the sort of warm evening conducive to lounging about outside peacefully knocking back a bottle. So after briefly savouring the riparian scene, we come back in and inspect our quarters instead, which have an oriental flavour with yellowy flowery wallpaper, matching curtains and Chinese lamps. There's the usual teapot – with unusually pretty cups – and also a couple of mugs with packets of chocolate tucked in. So inviting do these look, we promise ourselves we'll play Darby and Joan later.

For the moment, though, it's straight into the bar. No need to change. Taking our drinks to a cosy corner with a table made from a chopped-in-half barrel, it's easy to see why there's a crowd.

There's such a jolly atmosphere, what with polished wood pews, old photographs, caricatures, including one of the owner, and an amazing collection of blue-and-white china.

But what of the menu? 'All the main dishes have sauces,' I mutter. 'You must endure sauce then,' my husband mutters back. I choose a sauceless starter that's probably richer than anything *with*: grilled Italian bread with fresh pear and Gorgonzola. It's wonderful. My husband picks a simple tomato and mozzarella salad.

Roast duckling has a mint and lemon sauce; fillet of lamb, a port sauce; breast of pigeon, a bacon sauce; steak, a wild mushroom sauce; free range chicken, a sauce whose name I can't decipher. I decide on the grilled wild salmon with sorrel sauce. 'And I'll have the fried haddock with parsley crust, cockles and mussels. See?' says my husband triumphantly. 'No sauce with the haddock.'

From the wine list we note that this establishment won a Wine Award in 1990. It's not the cheapest list ever – even the house wine is £10. But we make an excellent choice: a New Zealand Cloudy Bay Chardonnay at £18.

The restaurant, decorated in shades of green, has a clubby feel and overlooks the garden and river. Olive green velvet banquette seats line the walls and some tables are in alcoves.

And there's a lot of what can only be described as dirty laughter coming from the party at the one other occupied table. 'Now, now, Harry,' says a woman's voice tartly. 'Well, when you get to *my* age...' grumbles Harry. We can just see the silvery tops of their heads.

When our fish dishes arrive, they are both covered with sauce. 'So yours *is* saucy after all,' I tease. It's all very rich stuff, so I can't imagine why I feel one of us ought to try a pudding. 'Apricot brûlé, please,' I say, naively thinking it'll be like a crème brûlée. Wrong. It consists of hard ice-cream that's actually rather unpleasant, topped with brulée and chopped hazelnuts. No, we don't fancy our bedtime cups of hot chocolate...

In the morning the bespectacled chef/patron potters about and amiably makes my husband some scrambled egg. 'First-class,' he says, tasting it. Why's it so good? We have to laugh. In our experience, the best scrambled egg *always* has cream in it.

David Dalzell-Piper sends me a reproving note: 'I have never and do not intend to use cream in my scrambled egg. It is just the way I do it that makes it so creamy in texture.' My husband stands corrected. What's Mr Dalzell-Piper's secret? He's not telling.

The Dundas Arms,

53 Station Road,
Kintbury,
Berkshire RG15 0UT.
Tel: (01488) 58263.
Fax: (01488) 58568.
David Dalzell-Piper.
Location: between Newbury and Hungerford.
Open: all year, except Christmas and New Year.
Rooms: 5. 5 twin/double (£65), all ensuite. Single in double (£55), all ground floor.
Restaurant: dinner served from 7.30–9.15pm. Also bar meals.
Chef: David Dalzell-Piper. A la carte, average £24.
Wine List: long, predominantly French, from £9.50.
Children: yes.
Dogs: ask first.
Smoking: no cigars or pipes.
And Also: watery pursuits.

$\mathcal{K}$nutsford, Cheshire
LA BELLE EPOQUE

La Belle Epoque calls itself 'Cheshire's Edwardian masterpiece' and one thing's for sure – it's not your usual building what with its towers, curly bits, steps, courtyards, windows of all shapes and bust of Mrs Gaskell.

Mrs Gaskell? What's *she* doing here? I consult a friend who's stayed. Hmm, it seems he's never heard of Mrs Gaskell, let alone Cranford. No, he's much more interested in the lady *he* took to La Belle Epoque. His face becomes soppy. 'Loads of atmosphere,' he promises. 'Cute little olde-worlde street. A very special place.'

Telephoning, I ask for a double room and dinner for the following Saturday. 'I'm sorry, the restaurant's closed on Saturday because of functions,' the receptionist explains. 'Well then, how about Friday?'

Parking just across the street, we waltz expectantly into this intriguing-looking establishment. '*Quelle epoque*?' you might ask as you look around the delightful pink-walled and decidedly characterful bar with wicker tables and mosaic tiled floor where a fire burns in the huge copper fireplace, Piaf warbles in the background and Edwardian portraits adorn the walls.

An inscrutable man called Dennis whisks us upstairs to a room that's warm, cosy and pleasing. By the door there's a Polite Notice: 'As we only have seven bedrooms we classify ourselves as a restaurant with rooms. In order to keep the room rates favourable, we would expect our guests to utilize the restaurant for dining. Thank you for your understanding.'

Some people might think they should have been warned in the brochure that rooms are cheap and dinner is not. But *we're* understanding the minute we discover the restaurant to be wildly over-the-top with emerald walls, ceiling fans, chandeliers, beams, a statue, yards of emerald and purple silk curtaining. A couple of American businessmen gawp: 'Whadda place,' says one.

But will dinner live up to the curtains? Doubts are drowned at the first sip of the NZ Montana Sauvignon Blanc that's sold as tasting 'like a mouthful of crushed gooseberries' – and it *does*. The next thing that impresses is the number of starters (eleven) and main courses (nine). I choose a flavoursome English cheese tart, with leeks and apple. 'Yummy.' My husband approves of his English skate and mash too. 'Quite delicious.'

Main courses of chicken breast in white wine and Gressingham duck with apricots produce similar platitudes, except I wish I'd had the duck because I'm covetous of the little sausage made from the legmeat and garden herbs. 'May I?' I enquire, helping myself. Somehow we avoid an argument, possibly because the sight of the cheese trolley with flags across the room has us agreeing that it looks just like a specialist cheese shop – or France.

Dennis is solicitous about our car and the Pay and Display regulations. 'Would you like me to take charge of it for you?' Next morning he assures us: 'Your car's fine, sir' as he serves the 'light breakfast' included in the tariff (orange juice, toast, croissants, no cereal).

Meanwhile, the owner, Keith Mooney, regales us with the story of La Belle Epoque. 'It was built in 1907 by an eccentric called Richard Harvey Watt. For some reason he named our left-hand tower the Elizabeth Gaskell Tower and had a list of all her novels inscribed on the side. Look hard, and you'll see the bust of her up there.' Good Lord, but why? 'He was an *admirer...*' says Mr Mooney vaguely.

Unlike my philistine friend, readers will of course know that Mrs Gaskell, born 1810, was long dead by the time her admirer built his commemorative tower. Never mind. I like to imagine that Mr Harvey Watt was thinking of those genteel Cranford ladies when he created all those different-shaped windows looking down on Knutsford's narrow King Street.

'We're now doing more brasserie-type food,' says chef David Mooney. 'Everything is still cooked to order, but we're slightly less formal with a wider price range.'
'What a pity,' writes a Knutsford reader, 'that no one at Belle Epoque told you that Mrs Gaskell once lived in Knutsford. It is because of the time she spent here living with her aunt during her early years that she based Cranford on 'our' town. That's why Richard Harvey Watt built a memorial tower to her!'

La Belle Epoque,

60 King Street,
Knutsford,
Cheshire WA16 6DT.
Tel: (01565) 633060.
Fax: (01565) 634150.
Nerys and Keith Mooney.
Location: mile and a half from M6, exit 19.
Open: all year except first week January.
Rooms: 7. 1 single (£35), 6 twin/double (£40–£50), all ensuite. Single in double (£40).
Restaurant: open for dinner from 7–10.30pm.
Chef: David Mooney/Graham Codd. A la carte, average £20. Cooked breakfast £5.
Wine List: ambitious, from £8.50.
Children: yes.
Dogs: no.
Smoking: if you must.
And Also: close to Tatton Park and Jodrell Bank. Conducted Mrs Gaskell tours available.

Lacock, Wiltshire
AT THE SIGN OF THE ANGEL

At this 15th-century, family-run inn, the welcome's decidedly frosty. True, when booking, I'd been told that dinner was between seven-thirty and eight: 'It'll be turkey and ham on Friday,' a charming female voice had confided – and, yes, we *are* late due to rain and motorway traffic. Except I've taken the trouble to telephone from a service station on the way, first to apologize and, second, to tell of our extreme hunger and to make sure of that turkey and ham dinner please. An equally charming female voice thanks me for calling, saying that of course dinner would be fine and adding a reassuring 'Don't you worry, dear.'

So I stop worrying – until we arrive to this welcome distinctly lacking in warmth and the news that we are not booked in for dinner at all.

What? Relenting slightly, the lady who is in charge of both reception and restaurant then offers to rustle up some soup. *Soup?* All around us in a wonderfully cosy dining room with stone fireplace, log fire, beams, old, polished furniture, a dresser stacked with china, people are munching away at platefuls of delicious-looking food and giving us curious looks. But we booked *dinner*. We rang to apologize for being late. The offer progresses to soup, bread and salad...but by now I'm too upset to care.

After much behind-the-scenes consultations, the ice eventually melts. We sit down at a corner table in what must surely be one of the most comforting rooms imaginable. Homemade bread and wine is brought, followed by a tureen of piping hot chicken and mushroom soup, and then that turkey and ham roast and piles of perfect vegetables. The spicy bread and butter pudding is the best I've ever tasted.

And so it becomes one of those memorable meals. The hotel has more than redeemed itself with the healing properties of its food. But would the 'welcome' have been different if they'd known I was from *The Telegraph*? So popular is this hotel, I almost suspect not.

Upstairs, via a crooked staircase, is an equally inviting drawing room complete with a ginger cat having a fuss made of him by the other guests who're relaxing over coffee. We relax too in the shabby but comfortable chairs and investigate all the old *Punch* annuals and *National Geographical* magazines, and have a game of Scrabble.

Our downstairs bedroom is equally cottagey though, studying the brochure later, I'm dismayed to discover it is intended for those 'not wishing to climb stairs'. Either my voice conveys the impression of wonky legs or it was the only room left. I do hope the latter.

A small table contains a tray with the usual tea and coffee and – a big plus – chocolate and homemade biscuits. There's a good selection of reading matter here too, including a book about the nearby Fox Talbot Photography Museum. Just as well because the telly growls and flashes at us, perhaps *it* has got beyond the age of climbing stairs.

In the hall outside, I admire the polished flagstone floor and am amused by the notice on the door leading out to the back garden where a notice exhorts: 'Please do not let the dog out. If he escapes, ring bell and tell me. Thank you.'

The garden is a dream: lawns, apple trees, wooden seats and tables, a bridge leading over a little stream to the 'annexe', with its extra bedrooms. A gnarled elderly man who's exactly my idea of what a gardener should look like emerges from a shed, followed by 'the dog'. We wish we could stay longer.

The 'Angel' has been run by the Levis family since 1953. 'As a direct result of your article,' writes Lorna Levis, 'more liberal hours of service have been introduced, with last orders at 9pm. 'One day,' she adds cryptically, 'we will tell you the real story of why you were originally only offered soup!'

At the Sign of the Angel,

Church Street,
Lacock,
Chippenham,
Wiltshire SN15 2LA.
Tel: (01249) 730230.
Fax: (01249) 730527.
The Levis family.
Location: in the heart of the National Trust village of Lacock.
Open: all year, except 1 week at Christmas.
Rooms: 9. 9 twin/double (£75–£93), all ensuite. Single in double (£55–£70). Wheelchair access to 1 ground-floor room (bathroom not specially adapted).
Restaurant: open from 7.30–9pm.
Chef: Lorna Levis. Table d'hôte £22.50–£30.
Wine List: ever changing, reflecting 'our own personal taste', from £10.
Children: yes.
Dogs: yes.
Smoking: grudgingly tolerated.
And Also: The Fox Talbot Museum of Photography; fishing and riding nearby.

*L*angar, Nottinghamshire
LANGAR HALL COUNTRY HOTEL
AND RESTAURANT

Here's a hotel that revives the spirits. Arriving at Langar Hall on a warm Friday evening, we find the car-park space full and punters in cheerful mood moseying through the door.

This party atmosphere is enhanced by a Bunter-ish man in a purple velvet waistcoat playing the piano and singing 'Who-o-o Stole My Heart Away' in a warbly voice at the far end of the impressive flagstoned hall.

'You must be the...?' says a charming receptionist, nipping out from behind a desk. 'Yes, we are.' After signing the book we are trotted upstairs to the Nursery Wing where we have been allotted a womblike room with gothic windows overlooking the herb garden and the church, known locally as 'the early English Cathedral of the Vale'.

The furnishings are a pleasing if unconventional mix – cane bedhead, flowery fabrics, a pair of modern green metal chairs, an elderly desk looking ill at ease, an attractive painting. There's also an adjoining single bedroom which, if used, costs an extra £25. If we'd known, we'd have brought my mum.

We hurry downstairs to join in what's going on. Pre-dinner drinks are being served in an elegant white-painted drawing room with views of parkland. On the opposite sofa, a flash Harry with slicked-back hair entertains his wife and daughter with champagne – or maybe they are *both* his wives?

Over dinner in the pillared dining room we discuss breasts. 'Do you like high and pointy ones?' I ask my husband. 'Not when they're made of stone,' he replies. If this seems an unusual topic of dinner conversation, it's because my chair is placed directly beneath a half-naked statue who effectively turns our dinner *à deux* into dinner *à trois*.

Candles burn in silver candelabras. All around is an animated babble of conversation. At the next table an attractive lovey-dovey couple are wearing evening dress. A celebration perhaps?

The food's good too. Well, some of us think so. Wisely choosing a goat's cheese salad to start, I laugh as my husband does battle with tiger prawns sautéed in garlic. My salmon fillet with lemon thyme and white wine sauce is also a wise choice. 'Very nice,' I comment smugly as he mutters that his fricassée of monkfish with americaine sauce is disappointingly bland. The pudding menu sounds suspiciously bought-in. I take that back. Our two ludicrously manic confections are delicious and taste freshly made.

Suddenly the tinkling music stops. The pianist, Crispin, announces that after dinner there will be an 'entertainment' entitled 'The Mad Hatter's Tea Party'. To his hushed audience he explains that this will involve guests following him and his fellow actors from the Scoundrel's Theatre into the herb garden and out onto the croquet lawn. He suggests that, like all good children, we visit the loo first.

The entertainment is sharp and clever – an unexpected bonus – especially when, with a cry like a banshee, Crispin minces down the fire escape dressed as The Red Queen.

Afterwards cafetières of coffee are brought into the dining room. Proprietor Imogen Skirving moves from table to table, cutting generous portions of Stilton and doling them out to guests, pausing to chat on the way round.

Our nursery bed is supremely comfortable, precluding the necessity for my husband to read in the bathroom. As for the bath itself, you can lie in it and watch the ivy curling round the windowsill.

Breakfast next morning is indifferent. Thin white toast served on a *plate?* There's the added entertainment of a cheerfully lugubrious waiter who complains he's run out of toast racks.

Later we talk to Imogen Skirving herself and it transpires that Langar Hall has been her family home since it was built in 1837.

'And *isn't* it nice,' she adds. 'That young man sitting next to you at dinner last night proposed to his girlfriend.'

'Oh, and did she accept?' we ask wide-eyed. She did.

'The Scoundrel Theatre evenings are still going strong, even though Crispin, our singing butler, has gone to join the Chichester Theatre Company,' reports Imogen Skirving. 'We have two new chefs, there's new better food and – you'll be pleased to know – toast racks at breakfast time.'

Langar Hall Country Hotel and Restaurant,

Langar,
Nottinghamshire NG13 9HG.
Tel: (01949) 60559.
Fax: (01949) 61045.
Imogen Skirving.
Location: between Grantham and Nottingham, off the A52.
Open: all year.
Rooms: 10. 1 single with bathroom (£60), 8 twin/double (from £80–£110), 1 four-poster (£110), mostly ensuite. Single in double (from £60).
Restaurant: open for dinner from 7.30–9.30pm.
Chefs: Stephen Douglas and Toby Garratt. A la carte, average £20.
Wine List: low mark-up, from £8.50.
Children: yes.
Dogs: yes.
Smoking: limited.
And Also: croquet lawn, medieval borders, carp fishing in newly restored moats – bring your own rod. After-dinner opera and theatre evenings – please enquire.

'Let's try The Lansdowne, a Regency townhouse. *You* book,' I say to my husband. The conversation with owner Mrs Allen goes like this: 'We've one double left, but it's only got a shower, sorry about that, sir.' Sir mutters something about an unreasonable wife who insists on having baths wherever she goes. 'In that case we have a twin with shower and bath, sir.'

'Yes please,' replies Sir, pretending it'd have been more than his life's worth etc. My heart *bleeds.*

Here's The Lansdowne, bang in the middle of town. Inserting the car in the small car park, we whisk in through a side door. Is that a picture of the *Queen* in the hall? Proprietors Mr and Mrs Allen seem delighted to see us. Would we like a morning paper? 'What about *The Telegraph,* that's always so good on Saturday,' purrs bespectacled Mrs A.

She takes us to an uninspiring ground-floor room – not one to linger in – and soon we're hot-footing it to the cluttered, velvety bar where Mr Allen is dispensing drinks, smiles and a dish of crudités. 'Dip in, old chap,' he says hospitably, aiming it at my husband with one hand and producing menus with the other.

In the corner a prodigal son(?) is regaling his family with his travels. 'They eat iguana in Mexico,' he remarks. '*I'd* rather have spinach soup and rack of lamb,' I mutter. My husband chooses crab salad followed by lemon sole. The iguana-eater wants sole too. 'I'm sorry, there isn't any

more,' says the cheery Mr Allen, 'but you can have brill instead.'

Oh, their wine list's reasonably priced – my favourite Burgundy Aligoté is £11.95 as opposed to £17.50 in some hotels. 'Mmm, reckon we've a bit of that,' murmurs Mr Allen, clearly a wine buff, and, in the dining room, he says 'Cheers now,' as he pours it.

This room boasts a red carpet, dark-red shades on both the chandelier and wall lights and small square dark wood tables. What looks like a treasured collection of highly varnished wooden wine-case plaques crowds one wall. And if Mr Allen wonders why I haven't finished my soup (he doesn't) it's because it's watery rather than spinachy.

'Feel free to pick up the bones, won't you,' he urges next, as he brings plates of lamb and sole, accompanied by roast potatoes, plus an extra plate: 'For the bones. Enjoy yourselves now.'

While appreciating the thought, I find myself glancing enviously at my husband's grilled-to-a-golden-tan sole. Wish I'd chosen that – the lamb's fatty. 'Very nice,' he declares smugly, helping himself to sweet corn and scallop-cut carrots.

After an earnest pudding discussion with Mrs Allen, we decide on café Liegeois and crisp tarte with apricots and almonds – both excellent. Suddenly I realize my husband's finished off my wine (absent-mindedly, he claims). 'Never mind, have a glass of Muscat,' says Mr A, arriving at this fraught moment. After pouring one, he leaves the bottle on the table. 'There's a drop left, do finish it.' How nice of him – it's a generous 'drop' too. Grinning, he bumbles off, still talking – to himself I think.

Our room's so well equipped, there's even that rarity – a clock radio alarm. Just to prove it works, it wakes us with a blast of sound at 5.45am and, again, ten minutes later. The Allens are mortified: 'We *should* have checked.'

By the small reception desk a pokerwork wall plaque bears the inscription: 'One nice person and one old grouch live here.' So who's the grouch then? 'Oh ho, ho, ho,' says Mr Allen, coming over all shifty-eyed. '*Most* people,' says Mrs Allen, popping up from nowhere, 'don't even bother to ask.'

'We've been teased rotten ever since,' say the Allens.

The Lansdowne,

Clarendon Street,
Leamington Spa,
Warwickshire CV32 4PF.
Tel: (01926) 450505.
Fax: (01926) 421313.
David and Gillian Allen.
Location: in the centre of town.
Open: all year.
Rooms: 15. 5 single (£29–£49), 10 twin/double (£39–£59), most ensuite. Single in double (£52). 2 ground-floor rooms.
Restaurant: open for dinner from 6.30–9pm but 'we're flexible.'
Chef: Lucinda Button. Table d'hôte £16.
Wine List: emphasis on value for money, from £7.95.
Children: yes, over 5.
Dogs: no.
Smoking: not in restaurant.
And Also: Warwick University, Warwick Castle (5 mins), National Agricultural Centre, Stoneleigh (10 mins), NEC Birmingham (30 mins).

*L*eeds, *Yorkshire*
42, THE CALLS

Driving round (and round) a Leeds one-way system in search of our smart city-centre hotel, we encounter a chap with a stride as long as Jack and the Beanstalk's giant's. *'He'll* know.' Winding down the window, I yell: 'Can you direct us to 42 The Calls?'

'Sure...' He grins. 'Are you staying there?'

'We're trying to.'

After giving copious directions, he ends up in a *verbal* one-way system. 'I'll take you,' he offers, folding his long legs into the car. 'I used to work there.'

42 The Calls is in a dark, empty street in the middle of a re-development area. 'You'd never believe this was a swish hotel,' I murmur as we carefully lock the car.

'Designed by individuals for individuals, a deluxe hotel in miniature,' trills the brochure. Step inside...and you begin to see what they mean. The interior's knock-you-back modern and gleams with newness. It's warmed by a sweet little flame-haired receptionist who hurries forward with glasses of mulled cider. 'Welcome,' she cries. After downing the cider and signing the book, we hand over keys and she promises faithfully our car will be put in the lock-up. 'Enjoy your stay,' she urges.

The genial Billy swooshes us up in the lift to the fourth floor, where our very large room gives us black looks. Why? Walls, curtains, bedhead, lamp-shades, desk, three telephones and two TV sets are all a sophisticated *noir.*

Exposed wooden beams and white-painted brick arches make sure we don't forget we're in a converted-warehouse environment.

Someone's keen on animals round here. We have a Cheshire cat key ring and there's frog soap in the bathroom. Peeping out onto the landing we encounter wooden ducks.

The luxurious bathroom's all you'd expect from such a slick city hotel. But wait. Here's a notice explaining why the water's discoloured, something to do with peat from the moors, though when I run a bath the water's not peat brown but a disconcerting golden yellow.

As I step out of it, someone knocks on the door. It's an anxious little lady trying to turn down the beds and leave two wee boxes of Smarties. We end up striking a deal in which I get the Smarties and she doesn't get to turn down the bed.

Later, we swish downstairs to supper at the next door Brasserie 44, part-owned by the owner of 42. Here's another world, in which the beautiful people of Leeds are out in force, dressed to kill and *how.* An automatic piano plays, complete with large-as-life animatronic pianist. There are bare brick walls, a wide expanse of polished floor and not quite enough places to sit.

Of course you can sit at the bar, though don't expect anything as prosaic as bar stools. Good heavens no. It has swings. This presents a problem for a person with little legs. Clutching the ropes, executing a huge jump, I promptly slide off again. 'Has anyone – er – ever done themselves an injury?' I ask the pretty bar girl. 'There've been near misses,' she replies jauntily. 'A chap fell backwards only the other night.'

'Oh, and what happened?'

She giggles. 'He was lucky. Someone caught him.'

Dinner in the large restaurant, overlooking the river, is a delight. In among the parties, families and the aforesaid smart set, we enjoy efficient brasserie food, the view and all those fascinating conversations.

I cannot fault this hotel, although it could equally be 141 not 41 rooms. The service is impeccable, ditto breakfast sitting at a sunny table overlooking the river where I dive into a bowl of freshly prepared hot porridge and yummy marmite toast – nursery food at its best.

As we leave, the manager puts on a fierce expression. Oh dear, have we upset him? 'You can only have your car back if you tell me the *exact* mileage...' he quips. I can't even think of the registration number.

'The area surrounding the hotel has been vastly improved, with virtually all building and road works completed – at last,' writes the jolly manager. 'Do come back and see us soon!'

42 The Calls,

Leeds,
West Yorkshire LS2 7EW.
Tel: (0113) 2440099. Fax: (0113) 2344100.
Jonathan Wix.
Location: in the city centre on the canal, directions sent on booking.
Open: all year, except Christmas.
Rooms: 41. 7 studies (£95), 25 standard (£120), 6 directors' rooms (£125), 2 junior suites, (£150), 1 penthouse (£195). Single in double (as above). One room equipped for disabled.
Restaurant: Brasserie 44. Dinner served from 6.30-10.30pm.
Chef: Geoff Baker. A la carte menu, average £20. Continental breakfast £6.95, cooked £10.
Wine List: comprehensive, including 24 house wines from £8.95. Cocktails served.
Children: yes.
Dogs: by arrangement.
Smoking: no pipes or cigars in restaurant, some non-smoking rooms available.
And Also: secure lock-up garage. Classical music concerts.

Growls a Somerset 'fan': 'It's fair enough for you to slag off food and wine and furniture, but when you turn your attention to the personal qualities of host or hostess you overstep the boundaries of good behaviour...'

Alas. If there's one thing reviewers *aren't* employed for, it's good behaviour. How disappointing it would be if there were no comments on the funny little ways of hosts and hostesses. It's those 'personal qualities', after all, that help determine whether a hotel's going to be a pleasant experience or not. Owners *matter*.

Take Upper Buckton Farmhouse in very rural Shropshire where we're welcomed not by owners but by three waggy-tailed farm dogs who lead us round to the open front door. On the verandah we pause and gaze down at the beautifully laid-out sloping gardens with millstream and bridge at the bottom – a perfect setting for *Madam Butterfly*.

A nice country lady takes us up to our room. 'Duck or Grouse' says the notice on the perilously low beam above the ski slope staircase. 'Your bathroom's across the landing and round the corner,' she says, 'or, if you prefer, there's a shower room on the next floor...'

Much tender loving care has been expended on this Georgian farmhouse. Everywhere we look there's stripped and polished woodwork. Covetable pieces of family furniture abound. It's very much a home.

In the drawing room, couples are sitting about not saying a lot. In comes a young man: 'I'm Richard, Yvonne and Hayden's son, I'm home from college for the weekend and I'm in charge of the dining room tonight.' I think he's saying dinner's ready.

We sit down. No fancy stuff like menus. This is a working farm. Two wine glasses sit on the table but – er – no sign of anything to put in them. 'Do you suppose this is a temperance establishment?' asks my one-track husband.

Richard brings first courses. 'Do you serve wine?' I ask. 'Oh yes. Some people bring their own. What would you like, red or white?'

'White, please.'

'Oh Lord, it's just us,' I murmur, feeling positively decadent. But no – we have started a trend. Another couple want a bottle too. Meanwhile, we plough into our prawn and cucumber salads, accompanied by a yoghurt dressing. Then Richard brings the wine, tied up jauntily with a red napkin: 'To catch the drips,' he explains.

Our second course is a homely chicken and mushroom pie with a breadcrumb topping, boiled potatoes and a salad of peppers, two kinds of lettuce and a ready-mixed dressing that's a mite too sweet. Puddings consist of a geometrically perfect crème caramel and spiced apple slice – too sweet even for me.

As we chat and drink coffee on the verandah with a Cambridge professor and his wife, Richard appears. 'Just to let you know breakfast's at eight-thirty.'

'On the dot?'

'Yes. I mustn't get on the wrong side of Mum.'

Whew! In the morning the Upper Buckton dining room bursts into life. 'I'm Hayden,' declares the grey-haired farmer striding in. 'I hope we didn't wake you when we came in last night?' Beaming, he introduces his daughters, explaining they'd all gone to hear Kiri te Kanawa in Birmingham. 'I normally see more of our guests,' he adds.

Now his wife, a cheery, white-haired lady in green gardening apron, bounces forward. 'Hallo, everyone, I'm Yvonne...I'm *so* sorry we weren't with you last night...' And although Hayden knows one set of guests well enough to give the wife a kiss, he doesn't for one moment make us one-nighters feel excluded.

'What lovely people,' we agree. We can also vouch for Yvonne's scrambled egg and homemade marmalade. When it's time to settle up, she invites us into the kitchen where we cannot resist buying a couple of pots of that marmalade at £1 each. Wish the entire family *had* been here...except that would be a different story.

'After reading about your visit, we went to stay at Upper Buckton Farm,' writes a reader. 'We were treated in every way as rather more than guests – nothing was too much trouble to Yvonne and her family. We shall be going back.'

Upper Buckton Farm,
Leintwardine,
Craven Arms,
Shropshire SY7 0JU.
Tel: (0154) 73634.
Yvonne and Hayden Lloyd.
Location: off the A4113 Knighton road.
Open: all year.
Rooms: 4. 4 twin/double (£40). 3 public bathrooms (luxury wrap-around bath towels provided). Single in double (£20).
Restaurant: open for dinner at 7pm.
Chef: Yvonne Lloyd. Table d'hôte £14–£16.
Wine List: red or white, or guests may bring their own.
Children: yes.
Dogs: no.
Smoking: this is a no-smoking house.
And Also: walking, nearby golf and pony trekking centres. No credit cards.

THE BOW WINDOW INN & RESTAURANT

'The-Bow-Window-Inn-Hotel-and-Restaurant-how-may-I-help-you?' a woman's voice announces in one breath. *phew.* In answer to my enquiry, she shoots out the information that they charge £35 dinner, bed and breakfast per person. Done. We'll have two, please.

Driving into the car park, we spot a notice that says 'Under New Management'. Maybe this is why the 300-year-old Bow Window Inn Hotel and Restaurant is in darkness, except for a few flickering candles – well, how romantic. But, as we open the door, *pow,* all the lights come on. We blink. What a welcome. Alas, the truth is more prosaic. 'We've just had a power cut, it lasted for two whole hours,' says the blonde and breathless lady owner.

As we sign in at the bar, she's still fretting. 'You may find your room a little cold or your water not as hot as you'd like. Bear with us,' she says.

We sympathize. The power cut has mucked up things in the kitchen too. 'My husband's the chef, he's doing his best, but supper will be a little late,' she apologizes. 'Bear with us, won't you.' We will, we will.

To get to our beamed room, we climb a glum back staircase – no doubt, being keen new owners, they plan to refurbish. Inside, all is pink: walls, velvet headboards, candlewick spreads, armchairs, a mottled carpet that defies description. It's also comfortable and well-equipped and, despite the owner's apologies, much warmer than many hotel rooms that haven't had two-hour power cuts.

Hmmm, in the bathroom, decor's less than conventional. Turquoise fittings are teamed with sort-of-tan tiled walls and a large rounded bath that I have to climb into before I can reach the taps. Oh, some joker's left the tap turned to shower. Remind me to take my clothes off next time.

Over drinks in the brightly lit lounge, we chat to a mother, son and daughter-in-law trio – regular diners, it seems, under the old regime. Bustling over with menus, our hostess is soon acquainting us with the way *they* do things. Someone mentions frozen food and she's horrified: 'Everything's freshly made here, down to the puddings,' she assures us. 'In fact, we don't even have a freezer in the place. Which is why supper may take a little longer than we'd like. Bear with us.' Her name, we discover, is Carol and her concern for her guests' welfare is touching.

The attractive beamed restaurant is full of couples and the odd European. Two waiters whizz about dispensing plates and *bonhomie*. It transpires the hunkier of the two is a junior Rugby International, still at school. 'I work here evenings and weekends.'

Now we discover The Bow Window's secret. It's a family affair. And, yes, they've *always* been hoteliers – all over the world, you name it. 'Dad's the chef. My brother, the other waiter, is a chef too. My uncle, he's doing the washing up.

My mum and me, though, we're not so good...'

We eat flavoursome homemade Stilton and celery soup, followed by *coq au vin* for my husband – 'very nice indeed' – while I choose 'oven-roasted rack of lamb served with a classic redcurrant and rosemary sauce'. There's lots of it and it's slightly pink, just as it should be. 'Everything all right for you?' enquires our Centre Threequarter, bringing two freshly-made Tartes aux Pommes.

Very much so. And next morning we've just one small request. Another time would it be possible to have our own pot of coffee on the breakfast table, so we could pour it when *we* want instead of when *you* remember?

'When the children went back to university,' writes one reader, 'a mini break was called for. The Bow Window Inn Hotel and Restaurant seemed just the ticket. Yes, we also had the one-breath reply on the telephone, but, no, we didn't have a power cut and the staircase is much brighter. We loved it...'

And oh. It seems the one-breath reply won't be quite so breathtaking in future. They've shortened the name to The Bow Window Inn and Restaurant. Was it something I said?

The Bow Window Inn and Restaurant,

50 High Street,
Littlebourne,
Canterbury,
Kent CT3 1ST.
Tel: (01227) 721264.
Fax: (01227) 721250.
The Steinmetz family.
Location: in middle of village.
Open: all year.
Rooms: 8. 1 single (from £35), 5 twin/double (from £50), 2 four-poster (from £60), all ensuite. Single in double (£40).
Restaurant: open for dinner from 7–9.30pm.
Chef: Rolf Steinmetz. A la carte only, average £16.50.
Wine List: international, from £7.75.
Children: yes.
Dogs: guide dogs only.
Smoking: smoking and non-smoking tables.
And Also: Canterbury, Channel ports and the Tunnel are close by.

ℒittlebury, Saffron Walden, Essex
THE QUEEN'S HEAD INN

The chap on the phone is most obliging. 'Yes, we can do you a room next Friday. Oh, you might want to come *Saturday*? We can do that too...'

Arriving in Littlebury (on Saturday), we find the Queen's Head on the corner. What an inviting-looking pub. Swanning through the bar, we ping the reception bell. A brisk chap in shorts hurries in – owner Jeremy O'Gorman we presume. 'Ah, yes,' he grins, pushing a form across the counter top. 'Please sign that and then I'll need to know what you want for breakfast.'

But breakfast's the last thing on our minds! 'We do Continental in your room, and if you want English we make a charge.'

Oh? We hum and ha. 'If I make up a tray for you, I can do it in my dressing gown,' he cheerfully explains. 'If I've got to serve it in the restaurant I reckon I'm entitled to a gratuity because I have to *get dressed*.' We burst out laughing. How can we possibly force someone so honest to *get dressed*. 'Continental in our room, please.'

This important point sorted, he marches us up the stairs. A large tabby cat precedes us. 'It'll do anything to get in one of the bedrooms,' he grumbles mildly. Unlocking a door, he breezily points out the amenities. 'If you want the heating on, just twiddle the knob,' he instructs.

We do. And it works. What's not so hot is the one bedside light. Heads I win. Tails it is. Just as well I've forgotten my book.

The unpretentious beamed room, decorated in pale pink, has furniture that's reputedly come from The Waldorf Astoria Hotel in New York. We examine it carefully. Hmmm.

Downstairs, the bar is furnished with antique chairs and tables and has a traditional black and terracotta quarry floor. At the back is a children's garden with swings between the shrubs and, in the paddock, a lugubrious hound hangs its head mournfully over the gate pretending to be a horse.

Later, wandering into the restaurant, we suddenly remember what the man said: 'If you come down before eight, you'll get served at once. After that you'll have to wait.' He's right. The restaurant is buzzing. Pink candles flicker. Two large parties arrive as we sit down.

We've already ordered from the blackboard menu in the bar: melon and parma ham, salad with beef tomatoes, onions and herbs, followed by grilled tuna steak with limes and swordfish with pink pepper sauce. Except we *don't* have to wait. Service is efficient and unobtrusive. Unpretentious too: the head waiter's still in his shorts and trainers.

'This sauce is extremely good,' exclaims my husband, remembering the last time he'd had pink pepper sauce and how it had made him queasy. In fact the food's so simple and tasty we have this little fantasy we're eating in France.

Next morning we know breakfast's on the way when we smell toast in the bathroom. In the *bathroom?* Sniffing around, we trace the toasty aroma to the heating duct. Apart from toast, the tray left outside our door consists of two pots of coffee, packets of this and that, and tins of juice.

When we come downstairs, the bar is spotless and there's our host – dressed – sitting at a table, reading. Leaping up, he apologizes for breakfast being late. 'The dog decided to go for a walk and I had to go and find her.'

As for the furniture, it seems Mr O'Gorman didn't personally remove it from The Waldorf: 'But that's where the shop down the road said it had come from.'

'Tell us about your chef. We had such a good dinner.' 'Actually, he used to work with Marco Pierre White...' says Jeremy O'Gorman.

'I only appear in my dressing gown now on Monday mornings,' says Jeremy O'Gorman. (Shame. They've got themselves a breakfast waitress.) 'And our-then chef didn't actually work with Marco Pierre White...he prefers to be remembered as the man who cuckolded him!'

The Queen's Head Inn,

Littlebury,
Saffron Walden,
Essex CB11 4TD.
Tel: (01799) 522251.
Fax: (01799) 513522.
Debby and Jeremy O'Gorman.
Location: in Littlebury village.
Open: all year, reduced service over Christmas.
Rooms: 6. 2 single (£29.95), 3 twin/double (£44.95), 1 family room (£49.95), all ensuite. Single in double (negotiable), including continental breakfast in room.
Restaurant: open for dinner from 7–9pm.
Chefs: Jeremy O'Gorman/Tim Barr. A la carte £10.50–£18.50. Continental breakfast in restaurant £4.50, cooked £6.
Wine List: small, international, from £7.50.
Children: yes.
Dogs: yes, but not in bedrooms.
Smoking: 1 non-smoking bedroom, also area in bar.
And Also: special bridal package: champagne on arrival, breakfast, flowers and chocolates – please enquire.

ℒlandrillo, Clwyd
TYDDYN LLAN

Peter Kindred's letter inviting *The Daily Telegraph* to visit his hotel in deepest Wales is entitled 'A Fawlty Experience'. Not only was he once set designer for *Fawlty Towers*, he tells us, but he and his wife – both in television – used to travel all over. Those were not the days. 'We were rejected, made uncomfortable and financially abused by hoteliers. We were well qualified to write the *Worst Hotel Guide to Britain*,' he claims.

Twelve years ago they found a dilapidated Georgian country house called Tyddyn Llan – meaning 'smallholding attached to the church'. Throwing caution to the winds: 'We decided to redress the balance and turn it into the perfect small hotel...'

One's heard these fairy stories before. But Mr Kindred does sound – well – characterful. Could he and his hotel really be fawlt-less? Off we go in search of Tyddyn Llan. This involves driving through some of Wales' most spectacular scenery, finding the lake at Bala and turning right.

Mr K promises perfect peace for stressed townies – it's one of those no-TV's-in-the-bedrooms kind of places. Turning into the drive, we discover a tranquil grey stone house with clipped lawns on which a game of croquet is in progress. There's a shady verandah, too, where people are lounging about reading newspapers.

A friendly girl takes us to our attic room – 'It's the *one* room left,' Bridget Kindred had told me on the phone the day before. 'I'm glad you've confirmed, someone else wanted it...'

Our room is light, airy and pale pink. There's a brass-trimmed, white-painted bed and nice old furniture. Nothing too grand. Coming downstairs, we have to make the onerous choice of which sitting room to disport ourselves in. There are three, all equally elegant and relaxing.

Swanning over, Mr Kindred asks what we'd like to drink. 'Pimms, please.' There's a pause. 'I used to be too mean to buy it,' he says. 'Then so many people asked for it I thought I'd better get some. Now I want *everyone* to order it.' His Pimms is strong, accompanied by tasty appetizers.

The restaurant – reached through a snug bar area – is exceptionally attractive: large, high-ceilinged and painted in discreet tones of blue-grey. All tables are full. Dinner is silver-service and formal, the view stupendous. Mr Kindred helps serve. He's perfectly nice to us, though clearly on more intimate terms with other guests – after all we've only just arrived and are staying only one night. I amuse myself by wondering what his reaction would be if he knew I was writing notes beneath his crisp white cloth.

At the next table is a loud party who've come to fish on the hotel's private stretch of the River Dee. The food's good: lamb's liver salad in balsamic vinegar; carrot soup with cardamon and coriander; turbot in a white wine sauce; grapes in puff pastry with a Grand Marnier sabayon. Afterwards we take our coffee into one of the sitting rooms and chat to an American couple who're 'doing' Britain. And then we go for a peaceful walk into the nearby village of Llandrillo.

This place could be addictive. After a day or two of such a relaxing atmosphere, we'd be zombies for sure. To assist the zombie process, Mr Kindred has even laid on Deep Muscular Massage plus the added benefit of the 'ancient Japanese art of Reiki'. Mmm, wouldn't mind a bit of that.

'Of course,' admits Mr Kindred, 'we do have our Fawlty moments...' He cites guests with bathtaps in their hands, power cuts and bats in the hall. 'Are we really to believe all this?'

'These stories pass into legend and we laugh about them in the bar on a winter's night,' says Mr Kindred, the perfect urbane country gentleman.

I have to smile. He's got the touch. Two stressed townies are now so relaxed they can hardly summon the energy to climb into their car. Or perhaps we just don't want to leave?

The Kindreds describe one of their worst experiences when staying in a hotel: 'Halfway through the bacon and eggs, we noticed a large puddle forming round our feet and then observed the host's elderly labrador relieving itself at the next table. To date, no such incidents at Tyddyn Llan!'

Tyddyn Llan,

Llandrillo,
nr Corwen,
Clwyd LL21 0ST.
Tel: (01490) 440264.
Fax: (01490) 440414.
Peter and Bridget Kindred.
Location: just outside Llandrillo village.
Open: all year, except February.
Rooms: 10. 10 twin/double (£88–£96), all ensuite. Single in double (£56–£61, sometimes less).
Restaurant: open for dinner from 7–9.30pm.
Chef: Dominic Gilbert. Table d'hôte £21.50–£23.50.
Wine List: both Old and New World, from £9.
Children: yes.
Dogs: by arrangement.
Smoking: feel free.
And Also: croquet, walking, private fishing on 4-mile stretch of River Dee, ghillie available. Jazz, musical weekends and wine tastings – please enquire.

'At weekends we get werry booked up,' the receptionist at London's Academy Hotel explains. 'Zers just one room left.'

'I'll take it...'

Dashing through the hotel's smart front door, we're amazed to find ourselves in a smart hall with polished wood floor and modern paintings lining its pale cream walls. Turning into reception, the scene changes to smart drawing room. Can this *really* be a terraced house hotel a stone's throw from Euston?

From behind the tall reception counter, a blonde head pops up. Greeting us in Dietrich tones, its owner gives us key, room number and a ticket for a free drink each. The scenario's unreal.

We return to earth when climbing heavenwards. A word of advice for those with fragile legs: *don't* book The Academy's 'one room left', it'll be the small one at the top for sure. Being impatient, we rush up three flights before realizing we've taken the wrong stairs – The Academy is not just *one* terraced Georgian house but three knocked into one. 'We're next door, pity you didn't look where we're going,' comments my husband acidly, but, then, he *would* insist on carrying the bags.

Our room is small, freshly painted, with folded towels laid neatly on the end of the bed. 'Oh, not another duvet,' I groan, visualizing a complaining man and sleepless night. 'I'll ask for a sheet,' says my husband, picking up the phone. The receptionist promises to see what she can do.

Making our way downstairs, our sense of unreality increases with the 'ocean liner' mural that covers the entire wall at the top of the basement stairs. The theme is continued in the basement bar and restaurant with bright yellowy-orange wood fitments and lights with a porthole effect. 'They've really set the scene and created an atmosphere, haven't they,' I marvel.

There's a convivial buzz of conversation too. Someone mentions the hotel manager is German. Now we realize that not only are the bar staff German, but most of the punters too. We order drinks and choose from the menu. The young, trendily dressed waiter/barman returns looking worried: 'I need to ask a leetle question: do you want wegetables or salad with your meal?' Good heavens, it's not life or death then. 'Vegetables, please.'

What fun dinner is: the asparagus salad with Gorgonzola sauce and fish soup full of mussels served with a creamy yoghurt dip are delicious. Oh, how *conscientious* is our lovely waiter. When I mildly comment that the 'Chinese greens' accompanying my salmon aren't green – 'Perhaps there's been a mistake?' – he immediately says he'll ask the chef. He comes hurrying back. 'The chef says those are Chinese greens.' Oh? Pardon my ignorance then. For pudding my husband orders Chocolate Marquis. 'Werry, werry wich,' warns the waiter.

At this point I notice that a discretionary 12.5 percent will be added to our restaurant bill. Well, at least they tell you in advance here. As it's a fine evening, we ask if we can have coffee outside. Wandering back upstairs, through a library with French doors, we go down an iron staircase to a delightful walled patio. Coffee is brought and we sit and listen to the police sirens and helicopters. What *is* going on out there?

Back in our room, two sheets have been laid on our bed. Actually, I don't mind the duvet at all. What I *would* mind, if I hadn't brought my own, is the lack of shower cap in the shower room.

But oh: come breakfast time those tall pasta jars of dried fruit that, the night before had decorated the bar, are now arranged on the buffet table, together with sacks of cereal and bright blue pots of help-yourself preserves. Very stylish, very still-life. 'We will always accomodate your needs,' says The Academy blurb and, from our brief experience, this could well be true.

'We try to teach our staff that, if they give, they will get back – I don't mean money – but nice conversations with people and so on,' says manager Mette Doessing, who also wishes to point out she's Danish not German. 'Guests are extremely pleased that we take an interest in them – "how was it last night, mind the step." It's the small, silly things... but we think they make a difference.'

Of course they do. This caring attitude has now earned The Academy three AA stars.

The Academy Hotel,

17–21 Gower Street,
London WC1E 6HG.
Tel: (0171) 631 4115.
Fax: (0171) 636 3442.
Manager Mette Doessing.
Location: in the University quarter.
Open: all year.
Rooms: 33. 5 single (£42), 3 twin/double (£63), all with shared facilities. 4 single (£74), 19 twin/double (£88), 2 studio suites (£115–£143), all ensuite. Single in double (£42). Prices exclude VAT and breakfast.
Restaurant: open from 7pm till late (5.30 pm on Saturdays).
Chef: Mads Begtorp. A la carte, average £15.
Wine List: mainly European, from £9.95.
Children: yes.
Dogs: no.
Smoking: feel free.
And Also: British Museum, Covent Garden, theatreland.

London SW1
THE GORING HOTEL

Just behind Buckingham Palace is what's described as 'one of London's best-kept secrets'. So proud is The Goring Hotel of being so secret that it likes to call itself the *discreet* Goring Hotel.

I am not certain whether this is intended to suggest The Goring is the sort of place for liaisons of a romantic not to mention *dangereuse* nature, or simply that it exudes suave, unostentatious comfort. At a wicked guess the couple throwing discretion to the winds over pre-dinner drinks in the Garden Lounge are probably long-time marrieds – if not to each other – and as for comfort, The Goring has loads.

At breakfast, however, liaisons are not on the menu. On this brisk Friday morning, the elegant dining room is full of men in grey suits holding earnest discussions and the only females are a power-dressed foursome at the next table conducting a high-level conference on the travel industry.

The Goring scores highly in its residential proprietor, the indefatigable George Goring, who dashes hither and thither and is apt to greet strangers with the information that he 'was born in Room 114 in 1938'.

He'll go on to say that the hotel was built by his grandfather in 1910 and has been in the family ever since. The dynasty flourishes. 'There will always be a Mr Goring at The Goring to welcome you,' he declares.

A family-run hotel, with all the dedication that implies, is a scarce commodity in London and, in 1990, George Goring was named Hotelier of the Year. 'When your name is above the door, you try that much harder,' he tells me modestly. Trying harder includes making sure that noisy kitchen fans are switched off at ten o'clock each night and, when on duty, sleeping in each room in turn.

I thought of writing him a letter:

Dear George,
Your hotel is delightful, the food delicious, the courtesy of the staff most warming and I love that soft yellow colour scheme but, when next sleeping in Room 118, may I suggest you take a companion who has left her book behind. You will then discover that the lights above the bed cannot be switched off separately, a source of aggravation to any would-be sleeping partner.

Then there's the wardrobes. No one could complain they are not generously large, nor stocked with the best class of hanger, but for those of small stature one vital piece of equipment is missing. A step ladder. As a result, this five-foot-nothing person's clothes spent the night draped across the back of the chair.

Sincerely etc

As for loos, Harrods had better watch out. To think I might never have discovered them if my husband had not checked out the Gents and reported it was full of naked women. 'Pictures,' he adds. This compels me to find out whether the Ladies is crammed with naked men. Sadly not: naked women predominate, elaborately framed. Walls and ceiling are smartly covered with delicious flowery wallpaper and pelmets trimmed with frills and green bows. Basins have brass taps – elegant brass, as you might expect in a place like The Goring, is a speciality – yet such luxury has me wondering why there's no bidet in our ensuite bathroom.

Our room looks out over a lovely garden courtyard surrounded by the backs of houses. Alas, under the term of an ancient covenant, this garden may not be used commercially. Gorings can sit in it, but not their guests. It would be a churlish guest, though, who did not appreciate what The Goring *does* have to offer.

'The most important thing is enthusiasm,' says George Goring. 'It's easy for me to be enthusiastic about The Goring because it belongs to me, but when the guy at the top is enthusiastic, then everyone underneath him is too. The doorman, when he opens the taxi door to someone arriving, will say: "Welcome to my hotel." He takes a pride in his job. I want all our staff to know the importance of their contribution to the hotel's success.'

The Goring Hotel,

Beeston Place,
Grosvenor Gardens,
London SW1W 0JW.
Tel: (0171) 396 9000.
Fax: (0171) 834 4393.
The Goring family.
Location: close to Victoria Station.
Open: all year.
Rooms: 78. 25 single (£125), 48 twin/double (£155–£175), 5 suites (£195), all ensuite. Single in double (£135).
Restaurant: open for dinner from 6–10pm.
Chef: John Elliott. Table d'hôte-menu, £25. Continental breakfast, from £8. Cooked breakfast, from £11.
Wine List: international, from £15.
Children: yes.
Dogs: no.
Smoking: feel free.
And Also: ramp for wheelchairs. Buck House and St James's Park just around the corner.

London WC2
MANZI'S RESTAURANT AND HOTEL

I always thought this jolly Italian restaurant off Leicester Square was just for eating fish in. But a colleague suggests there's more to Manzi's than greets the eye: 'They've got rooms upstairs, didn't you know?' she asks, surprised. No, I didn't. I'm so surprised that I book dinner and a room for the following Friday. When I arrive, it's the same as I remember – chaotically efficient – and I haven't been here for three years.

The woman who welcomes us doesn't understand a word we say and tries to direct us into the restaurant. No, no. We persevere up the narrow staircase. Here, on the first floor, we find rows of Rexine-covered chairs, complete with resting elderly ladies, hotel reception desk and mournful-looking Italian man, whose fish and chip supper we interrupt. Inexplicably he has reserved *two* rooms for us.

We accept one on the fourth floor. It's just like other seedy rooms I've stayed in, in various cheap European hotels. There's a faint musty smell, ceiling tiles on the ceiling and the fluorescent tube over the mirror is missing. The bedspread boasts a couple of cigarette burns. Dismal, but adequate, is our verdict.

Coming down again, we're referred to a waiter who appears utterly amazed that we've booked dinner. 'But there's no reservation!' he points out.

'Well, I did book.'

'No problem, you can have dinner whenever you want,' he says expansively.

'8.30 then?'

'Why not,' he says. That settled, we saunter outside for a quick whizz round Chinatown to work up an appetite.

Later, at the restaurant door, there's a gleam of recognition in the maître'd's eye. 'How are *you*?' he enquires warmly, as if it were but yesterday, tossing a mere good evening to my husband. 'Huh, are you sure it was your *friend* who told you they let rooms by the afternoon?' my husband asks. 'Why shouldn't he remember me?' I respond haughtily.

The restaurant's full, tables squashed together, paper napkins, workmanlike glasses, red check cloths, mermaids on the wall, can-can girls on the ceiling and hundreds (yes, I exaggerate) of Italian waiters dashing about.

On our left, we have a trio of cheerful theatrical types with moustaches, while the couple on our right have definitely come here to enjoy themselves.

'You were an hour and a half late,' he accuses. 'What were you playing at?' His companion, aware that discretion's better than valour, remains silent.

'The only reason I waited for you was because it's our wedding anniversary. I suppose you want *champagne* now,' he grumbles. *My* husband collapses into his eels.

'Are they good?' I ask. 'Very,' he says, still choking on mirth or eel bones.

'So's my fried calamari.'

Bello, our waiter, keeps a sharp eye on proceedings, whisking away plates, bringing main courses *con brio*: grilled turbot, grilled Dover sole and lots of chips. Now, a single red rose wrapped in plastic has appeared on the next-door table. 'You've got *butter* on it,' he complains.

For puddings there's fresh fruit salad – how much nicer if the grapes had been de-seeded – and ice-cream, made to a Swiss recipe. 'We hope you have enjoyed the personal experience', it says on the bill. Of course we have. I wonder if our neighbours could say the same.

Upstairs, in spite of a missing control panel, we coerce the air-conditioning system into life – only to find it makes a noise like an old-fashioned aeroplane.

Over breakfast next morning in the dark Cabin Restaurant – decorated with portholes, *SS Manzi* lifebelt and ships' wheel light fittings – we speculate on the other guests, mostly Europeans. We're agreed. Anyone wanting some-where central, cheap (?) and cheerful to stay – whether Dutch, Norwegian, Belgian, German or even British – could do worse than Manzi's.

Manzi's is a family run outfit. Says Daniel Manzi: 'We've got new air-conditioning units in all the rooms now and they don't make any noise at all. We've also replaced most of our bedspreads. We are very conscientous here – you can see we take everything on board.' Indeed I can.

Manzi's Restaurant and Hotel,

1/2 Leicester Street,
London WC2H 7BL.
Tel: (0171) 734 0224.
Fax: (0171) 437 4864.
Daniel Manzi.
Location: off Leicester Square.
Open: all year, except 24 and 25 December.
Rooms: 14. Single (£40), double (£63), all ensuite. Single in double (£47).
Restaurant: open for dinner from 5.30–11.30pm.
Chef: Leonardo Grisales. A la carte fish menu, average £30.
Wine List: mainly French, from £9.30.
Children: yes, over 5.
Dogs: no.
Smoking: feel free, no pipes.
And Also: Chinatown, theatreland.

London W2
PEMBRIDGE COURT HOTEL

'Welcome to the hotel, you are in Portobello, my *favourite* room,' purrs the receptionist at the Pembridge Court Hotel, London W2, giving us a key and a ginger cat.

The cat is most obliging. It guides us to the lift, accompanies us to the third floor, takes us to our room. Should we offer it a tip? Or will a stroke suffice?

But – good heavens – when we unlock the door, the cat's through it before we are, pointing out the room's many amenities, although it is unable to explain how to work the video or find the clock (that's because there isn't one!)

Pembridge Court is a 19th-century townhouse in a leafy street close to Portobello market. It has pot plants, window boxes and steps that positively lure you inside. We feel at home at once. And I suppose that if I lived in the next street to Portobello, *I'd* collect things too. How intriguing are all these framed fans, lace collars, the baby's Victorian nightdress, granny specs, caps, glittery evening bags and, on the stairs, a 1940s cigarette case. At least no one's framed the cat.

And the cat's right. Our room is lovely: comfortable, smart without being pretentious (difficult to achieve) while a wide staircase leading up to the bathroom creates a very luxurious effect indeed.

Deciding it's time to eat, we leave cat and key at reception and ask where the restaurant is. 'Just down that staircase,' instructs the receptionist,

handing us a card that says: 'We'd like to offer you a complimentary drink in the bar of Caps Restaurant this evening.'

Caps Restaurant and Cellar Bar is named after the owner Paul Capra and now it seems there's another special offer: our three-course dinner will cost us £9.95 each. 'Could we have the special offer menu?' we ask. 'This is it,' says the waitress. 'Choose any three courses you like.'

'That's a real bargain,' I exclaim. 'I think it's stupid,' she grins. And I do see what she means – the menu isn't an expensive one anyway.

It's such a good atmosphere in here this Friday evening that we forget to claim our free drinks and order a bottle of wine instead. There are lots of people, lots of noise, lots to look at: the walls are crammed with memorabilia, rugby caps, cricket caps, knives, bottle openers, you name it. Behind us a reunion of what my husband uncharitably christens the Addams family is getting under way. Over there a girl waits – in vain – for her friends to turn up...

What to eat? I choose Tom Yum Goong HOT Thai king prawn soup, which the waitress promises will be very hot indeed. It *is*. My husband has chicken satay, and we follow with mustard-glazed chicken and halibut with a herby crust from the blackboard menu. It's all good bistro stuff.

Afterwards, we have coffee in the drawing room and I'm able to read all the glossy magazines that I never buy for myself. Much later, when we collect our key, the cat – an opportunist, if ever there was one – comes too and insists on staying the night, stretching itself out luxuriously on the nice green sofa specially provided. While we are happy to have it as our guest, we're not *quite* so happy when it decides at 3am that it's time to get up.

There are plenty of people around at breakfast time – no danger of being bored. Afterwards, we decide to walk back up the stairs and are amused to see two litter trays discreetly placed behind a couple of large pot plants. 'We have two cats,' explains the receptionist. 'Their names are Spencer and Churchill. Spencer's the one who likes sleeping with the guests.'

'Spencer and Churchill, our two ginger cats, are the best PR people in the business,' says Valerie Gilliat. 'Now we hope to acquire a Winston to help cope with the demand.'

Pembridge Court Hotel,

34 Pembridge Gardens,
London W2 4DX.
Tel: (0171) 229 9977.
Fax: (0171) 727 4982.
Paul Capra (Manager: Valerie Gilliat).
Location: close to Notting Hill tube.
Open: all year.
Rooms: 20. Single (£90–£120), twin/double (£110–£150), all ensuite. Single in double (£110–£120).
Restaurant: bistro with bar, dinner served from 6.00–11.15 pm.
Chef: Philip Writworth. A la carte, average £16.
Wine List: small, international, from £8.95.
Children: yes.
Dogs: yes (and cats!)
Smoking: feel free.
And Also: Portobello, Earls Court, Olympia. Regular restaurant 'specials' – please enquire.

*L*ower Swell, Gloucestershire
OLD FARMHOUSE HOTEL

'Good evening, welcome to Old Farmhouse Hotel,' says Mr Erik Burger in that extra-perfect English we do not expect to hear in the Cotswold village of Lower Swell.

This amiable Dutchman has three rooms available, all very comfortable. Two are in converted outbuildings, one in the main house. Would we like to see them all before making our choice? We would.

I choose number six because it reminds me of a Wendy house and is only a short sprint to the hotel entrance. Later I discover that both this room and number seven once housed the pigs. See if I care. This is a *farmhouse* hotel. It would be a pity not to enter into the spirit of the thing.

Entering into the spirit means *not* having to dress up for dinner – even the staff are in shirtsleeves, admittedly worn with ties – so we make it to the bar in double-quick time. What an appealing place this is, dimly lit, log fire flickering, the Liverpudlian barman in the corner making jokes as well as drinks and handing out dinner menus. 'Have whatever you don't have at home,' he advises one couple. 'You can only make one choice, so you'll never know which was best...'

The 16th-century Old Farmhouse Hotel has a warming lack of pretentiousness. For instance, the wine list is set out according to taste rather than region. Better still, there are half bottles. We get the feeling the place is run for the guests' pleasure rather than the management's convenience.

The two adjoining dining rooms are small with beams and low ceilings. Tables are casually laid, cutlery being brought as and when required. We sit between a lovely hot radiator and a loving couple who emit almost as much heat. The first course is brought by the cheerfully lugubrious Jordan, the second by our Liverpudlian barman-turned-waiter: grilled plaice stuffed with spinach leaves and salmon accompanied by a lemon cream sauce. Vegetables – served separately – include a big wodge of dauphinoise potatoes. My husband's grilled liver – 'perfect,' he says – is part of the good value table d'hôte menu.

In the middle of this repast, the punctilious manager dashes in with a note confirming our booking together with two postcards with line drawings of Old Farmhouse Hotel on one side and, on the other, a first-class stamp and a PS: 'We are staying in this hotel which is in the heart of the Cotswolds.' A nice touch. Good PR too.

At the mention of puddings, we declare ourselves full. 'I'm sure you can manage something,' coaxes our Liverpudlian friend. 'You obviously know a bit about human nature,' comments my husband. 'We *cater* for it...' Now I add my own PS: the treacle pudding is delicious.

This place is a haven for cheese addicts as well as the treacle pudding ones. We are invited to help ourselves from a generous trayful of local cheeses and exhorted to come back for more. The competitive spirit is alive and well too. When we opt to take coffee in the residents' lounge in the adjacent stable block, Jordan does a nifty sprint with the tray and arrives before us, panting slightly, a triumphant grin spreading across his face.

It's time for bed. The room may be small, but it has everything: velvet-buttoned headboard, bedside tables and lamps, an electric clock, tea-and coffee-making equipment, a full-length mirror – even a mini safe. In the bathroom, water is boiling hot, though the shower isn't brilliant – showers rarely are. There are even two drying racks, so I wash my cotton socks to see if they will be dry by morning. They are.

At breakfast, the same help-yourself attitude prevails. 'Brown or white toast?' asks the waitress. On the table are bowls of both brown and white sugar. Other smarter hotels please note. Is it really eccentric to want to sprinkle brown sugar on your cereal? Not here it isn't.

'Alas,' says Erik Burger, 'I regret to say the shower in Room 6 is still a little inefficient! Nothing else has changed here since your visit, except our restaurant has just been awarded an AA Rosette...'

I'm happy to say Mr Burger doesn't seem to have changed much either!

Old Farmhouse Hotel,

Lower Swell,
Stow on the Wold,
Gloucestershire GL54 1LF.
Tel: (01451) 830232.
Fax: (01451) 870962.
Erik Burger.
Location: in the centre of Lower Swell.
Open: all year.
Rooms: 14. 2 twin/double with shared bathroom (£41), 10 twin/double (£64–£84), 2 four-poster (£73), all ensuite or with private bathroom. Single in double (on request).
Restaurant: open for dinner from 7pm.
Chef: Graham Simmons. Table d'hôte £14.50.
Wine List: good value, from £7.50.
Children: yes.
Dogs: yes.
Smoking: not in restaurant please.
And Also: mountain bikes for hire, air-pistol target shooting, golf, trout fishing. Riding and clay-pigeon shooting nearby. Walled rose garden with apple tree.

'Do let me carry your bags,' insists Guy Crawley, opening the smart burgundy door of Number Eleven in Ludlow.

'No, really. They're not heavy.'

Behind his specs, Guy's eyes flash warning *tsk tsk* signals. 'It's what you're paying us for...' *He* carries the bags.

Trotting us briskly up the staircase of his elegant house overlooking Ludlow Castle and furnished and decorated to exact Georgian Society specifications, we arrive at the Master Bedroom. Why this honour? There's no honeymoon involved, nor even proposed.

Our admiration of his best room he takes entirely for granted. Handing us a key, he remarks po-faced: 'Don't bother to lock your door, unless of course you have thousands of pounds' worth of travellers cheques...in which case do, because I'm *very eager.*'

He turns to leave. 'Come down to the drawing room when you've changed and have a cup of tea or coffee. On *us,* of course.' (How nice. Your average hotel offering tea or coffee on arrival sticks an extra £1.50 or more on the bill.)

The Master Bedroom is awe-inspiringly perfect. A high iron and brass four-poster bed is hung with lace and, as Guy helpfully points out, a stool awaits to help the littlies climb up. I think he means me. A couple of red-and-black striped bows add a finishing touch, as does a dear little velvet draw-string bag containing shoe-cleaning materials that hangs on the door.

In the even more elegant drawing room, we meet co-owner Michael Martin (he's the chubby one), who brings a tray of tea and settles himself down for a good chat.

'We call ourselves a private house hotel. I deal in antiques and Guy was a teacher. Never having done anything like this before, we weren't sure at first whether it would work. To our amazement, we were busy from the word go. Never had to advertise. It's all been word of mouth.'

He had been saving the cream of his furniture and paintings for exactly the right house, he reveals. 'We were sick of London. We tried the Cotswolds, but the Cotswolds are so crowded. So we fled to Ludlow. As soon as I saw Number Eleven, I knew this was the one. Mind you, what a state it was in...' He rolls his eyes heavenwards.

Much later we discover that, although there are other guests, they are not eating in. So it's just us two facing each other across the highly polished dining table, our loneliness relieved by strains of opera from the kitchen and the impact of Michael's beaming face as he bears food prepared by Guy. 'What happens when you have more diners?' we ask.

'Oh, we get out the Pembroke tables over there.'

Bowls of carrot, orange and coriander soup are followed by plates of delicious ragôut of lamb accompanied by rice and veg cooked to exactly the right degree of crispness. Puddings match the soup: slices of orange in an alcoholic sauce. Compliments to the cook.

Earlier Guy had emphasized there were no house rules. The exception *could* be breakfast. 'He won't do bacon and sausages unless he knows the night before,' Michael announces, glancing nervously in the direction of the kitchen.

'How about poached eggs?' He looks relieved. 'Oh, he won't mind those.'

Peering through swathes of bathroom lace curtains the following morning, we spot two little white designer dogs dashing to and fro in the neatly paved yard leading to a garden that slopes down towards the river. Over breakfast Michael asks if we slept well. 'You didn't fall out of that bed then? Someone did once. It was a honeymoon couple...'

Now he launches into a story about the English Tourist Board and how Number Eleven had first got into one of the guides. Suddenly he claps his hand in front of his mouth. 'Oooh. Why am I telling you all this? For all I know, *you* could be an inspector.' The very idea.

Says Guy Crawley (he's the thin one): 'Since your visit, I trust my cooking has become more varied and imaginative. It remains our aim to provide the best service and care we can at the fairest price. It's a tough life but we enjoy it!'

V. good effort, Guy.

Number Eleven,
Dinham,
Ludlow,
Shropshire SY8 1EJ.
Tel: (01584) 878584.
Guy Crawley and Michael Martin.
Location: overlooking Ludlow Castle.
Open: all year.
Rooms: 4. 2 twin (£56), 1 four-poster (£60), 1 double with private sitting room (£60), single in double (as above), all ensuite.
Restaurant: dinner served at 7.30 pm.
Cook: Guy Crawley. Table d'hôte £12.50.
Wine List: varied, from £7.50.
Children: yes, over 12.
Dogs: no.
Smoking: no.
And Also: Christmas and New Year breaks with 'no organized fun and games' – please enquire.

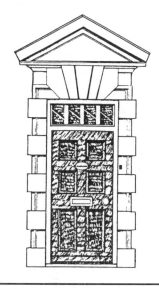

THE RISING SUN HOTEL

Mr Hugo Jeune, owner of The Rising Sun, a cute smugglers' inn, proves the perfect host when I telephone to grovel for not sending a deposit and to confirm his errant guests will shortly be on their way. 'Ah, if only all guests were as thoughtful as you,' he cries.

'Ahem, I just wanted to make sure you didn't give our room to anyone else...you *did* say you were full.'

'Tch tch,' he says, muttering something I cannot catch about being an award-winning hotel. 'Besides, we do have your phone number,' he reminds me sweetly.

So he does. Now he's giving me intricate instructions on how to proceed to The Rising Sun in torrential rain: M4, M3, A39 to Lynmouth, turn right. What a letdown then, upon arrival, to discover that this maestro of the charm-school style of hotelkeeping is conspicuous by his absence.

His staff, with the strong Antipodean element now mandatory in the more desirable parts of holiday Britain, are well trained in the art, but, alas, cannot make up for the lack of the charismatic Mr Hugo Jeune.

'Last orders for dinner are eight-thirty,' the receptionist tells us. We look at our watches. It *is* eight-thirty. No time for a relaxing drink.

So it's up the narrowest staircase in the world, a quick peek at our small, pretty room with authentic creaky floor, and, swooosh, down again to the dining room where we are about to discover a new meaning to the term 'intimate dining'.

One punter is performing an elaborate routine, winding a long leg above the pink tablecloth, in an attempt to shoe-horn himself in. We watch, fascinated. Will he do himself an injury? Our bosom neighbours have whispered Northern accents and their best clothes on. Psst... *honeymooners.* What was it Mr Jeune had said? 'We appeal to the romantics...'

I may now be accused of crass *unro-manticism* when I murmur that, lovely though it is to be in such an attractive panelled dining room decorated with plates, the chef is having an off night. A bland tagliatelli starter reminiscent of school milk pudding, followed by rack of lamb complete with fat, is not my idea of the food of love.

The puddings, however, are definitely Barbara Cartland and are all accompanied by clotted cream. 'Two pineapple *beignets*, please.

'You mean the fritters?' asks the Australian waitress.

Afterwards the ration is one cup of coffee per person. Shall I do an Oliver Twist? No. Instead I amuse myself by talking to Gypsy, the bar dog with a talent for soliciting, and wonder why the pub bar is almost empty – surprising after the crush in the restaurant. We wander to the sitting room upstairs, where a solitary couple decides to leave as soon as we appear.

In our room we turn on the nice new television set and relax. All has been carefully thought out in here: attractive pink and cream cotton curtains, a chair upholstered in the same material, pink wall lights and, a rare luxury, a clock. In the morning we open French doors onto a small terrace and hillside garden from which, if you climb to the top, you can see the sea. Heaven.

At breakfast, the space race is on. Oh Lord, here comes the fat couple. Too close for comfort behind me sits a group of professional guests: 'And have you got a shower attached to your bath?'

'No.'

'We have.'

'When I was at The Palace in Torquay...'

Once again coffee is rationed, though I notice the tea drinkers get a pot to themselves. The OJ isn't freshly squeezed, but the scrambled egg is exemplary, as is the note on the menu: 'If you're leaving us this morning, we wish you a safe journey and hope to see you again in the future...'

Hugo Jeune was not happy when this piece was published. I am sorry he felt I had criticized him for his absence when, in fact, I had genuinely hoped to meet him. Of course it is not necessary for the proprietor of a small hotel to be present day and night: what is important is that his influence should be felt when he's not around.

'The main change,' writes Mr Jeune, 'is a great improvement in the restaurant with the result we received the RAC Restaurant award, the AA rosette and Les Routiers Casserole award.'

The Rising Sun Hotel,

Harbourside,
Lynmouth,
Devon EX35 6EQ.
Tel: (01598) 53223.
Fax: (01598) 53480.
Hugo Jeune.

Location: harbourside.
Open: all year.
Rooms: 16. 2 single (£44.50), 13 twin/double (from £79.00), 1 suite (£110), all ensuite. Single in double (£59.50).
Restaurant: open for dinner from 7–9.30pm.
Chef: David Lamprell. Table d'hôte £21.50.
Wine List: emphasis on fine New World, from £8.75.
Children: yes, over 5.
Dogs: by arrangement.
Smoking: not in dining room.
And Also: seaside, Exmoor.

Matlock Bath, Derbyshire
HODGKINSON'S HOTEL

A London reader writes: "I would value your opinion on Hodgkinson's Hotel. It's run by two young gentlemen and is quite an experience." She adds darkly: "Very enjoyable – so long as you like museums."

Who can resist a museum posing as a hotel? I get on the phone. 'You want a room? Hang on. I'll just get Nigel,' says a girl's voice. Nigel's fearfully obliging. Double rooms cost from £40 to £60, he announces smoothly, giving away no clues as to their museum-like tendencies. Rashly, I book a £60 front.

Belting up the M1, I dream of a long hot bath before dinner. Too late I consult the guide book. Oh. Hodgkinson's don't have baths, only showers. So it can't be *that* museum-like then, I mutter to my husband. A long hot shower's not the same at all...

From the outside, Hodgkinson's is positively uninteresting. But wait. As we push open the Victorian coloured-glass front door, a shop bell tinkles. Walking into the restaurant/bar, we're bowled over by gleaming mahogany panelling, old glass lights and a carved stage-set of a bar filled with as many *objets* as bottles. A young chap whistles forward. 'I'll just get Nigel...'

Beautiful blond Nigel is dragged, smiling, from the kitchen in his chef's apron. Picking up our bags, he hurtles us up three flights of stairs. On each landing our astonished gaze takes in a series of still lifes: a dressmaker's dummy attired in silk dress and leopard- skin coat; a hat stand smoth-

ered in hippy hats; an ancient birdcage sprinkled with rose petals; an arrangement of the sort of shoes you might find at Portobello.

Nigel throws open a door. 'This – ahem – is our best room,' he murmurs. Oh, very nice: William Morris paper, king-size brass bed, lace bedcover, pink velvet sofa and the most outrageous chandelier I've ever seen. Museum-ish? Oh yes. Happy and gloriously so. We discuss dinner arrangements. 'We've a party arriving at eight. Would 8.30 suit you?' Perfect!

On our way downstairs we stick our heads into the high camp Victorian drawing room on the first floor. Party members are congregating, so we whisk on down. 'What would you like to drink?' asks a chap with ponytail and soulful eyes. 'Campari and orange please.' 'What sort of orange: Britvic, fresh, or freshly squeezed?' Well, you could have knocked me down with a feather boa...

We plonk ourselves on a sofa in the equally Victorian downstairs drawing room. Mr Ponytail brings us drinks. His name is Malcolm and he's one of the 'young gentlemen'. 'I'm the collector,' he enthuses, gesturing in all directions. 'Actually – ' he confides – 'I'm a hairdresser, I have a salon on the first floor.'

Oh, really? 'When we arrived seven years ago, the place was semi-derelict. Nigel's the interior designer, you know. He trained at the Royal College of Art...' Oh, *really*? It's so boring when Malcolm's gone that we're forced to tune into the conversation of the trio opposite. '*Undertakers,*' whispers my husband confidently.

In the restaurant we're ushered to a table half hidden behind an ornate wooden screen. How thoughtful – perfect for note taking. The multi-talented Nigel's five-course dinner at £22.50 (with coffee) is quite mouth-watering: spicy soup; stuffed grilled mussels with garlic and fresh fruit salad with passion fruit sorbet; two differently flavoured fillets of beef. Now comes the pudding trolley: 'All freshly made, Nigel *just loves* making puddings,' says the waiter. I recommend his classic lemon tart from a recipe by Mrs Beeton.

Next morning, in between getting our breakfast, Nigel's making more puddings. 'It'll be busy tonight,' he smiles. Gazing around, we comment on the room. 'It's beautifully done – such attention to detail.' 'Well, it's our *home,* you see,' explains Nigel.

In answer to my reader's question, yes, I do like museums. Not at home perhaps – but certainly in hotels. And certainly when they're as cosy and immaculate as this one.

'We cannot stop buying bric-a-brac all the time,' writes Nigel. 'I've just found myself a piano, which is now standing at the hotel entrance. I'm also working hard to get the garden together – it's still a bit like a builder's yard...but it's coming on.'

Hodgkinson's Hotel,

150 South Parade,
Matlock Bath,
Derbyshire DE4 3NR.
Tel: (01629) 582170.
Malcolm Archer and Nigel Shelley.
Location: in the middle of town.
Open: all year, except Christmas.
Rooms: 7. 1 single (£30), 6 double (£50–£80), all ensuite. Single in double (from £40).
Restaurant: dinner served from 7.30–8.30pm.
Chefs: Nigel Shelley and Malcolm Archer. Table d'hôte £22.50.
Wine List: mostly French, but a few Australian, from £9.95.
Children: yes.
Dogs: yes.
Smoking: yes.
And Also: local stately houses, golf, boating and fishing on the River Derwent.

*M*awnan Smith, Cornwall
NANSIDWELL COUNTRY HOUSE

Not for this host the ubiquitous grey suit or country-tweed jacket. Mr Jamie Robertson of the wisteria-clad Nansidwell Country House is a sight for sore eyes.

Popping his head out like Punch from a booth in the hall cunningly disguised as a bar, he first booms a welcome, then springs forth to shake hands. He is wearing dress trousers with velvet cummerbund topped with flowing fine cotton shirt and delectable red brocade waistcoat and his black velvet slippers are monogrammed. Beside him, his blonde wife Felicity, in black jacket and short flirty skirt, is positively mouselike.

'We've a lot of doctors here today,' he announces. 'They've just had their conference...and now they're going to have their wives.' We *think* he means over dinner.

Felicity ushers us up a staircase lined with paintings to a pink and green room furnished in pleasing if eclectic fashion: bold pink striped wallpaper, pink-trimmed green and white flowered curtains, a couple of carved inlaid chairs, candlestick lamps with pink shades either side of the large, lace-covered bed. Generous piles of up-to-date glossy magazines are strewn on window sills and tables – even in the bathroom.

In the double sitting room downstairs, there are more piles of magazines and a plethora of books. We are lured by roaring log fires and the onerous decision of which squashy sofa to sink into. Other guests seem an amiable bunch, mostly of the twin-set and sensible-shoe kind, and we gravitate towards a rather more jauntily attired couple arguing over a game of Scrabble. 'We've been here a week. We are *utterly* wound down. We were even allowed to bring our dog...' Oh, and where is your dog? 'Upstairs sleeping off the long walks she's had.'

Now the Robertson's own canine – Barney, a black labrador – comes bounding joyfully in, though he promptly exits when confronted by the stern sound of his master's voice. The nice thing about this place, I decide, is that there's no hint of the joyless good taste one so often encounters and, to coin that well-used phrase, it looks lived-in.

Fastening my gaze on Mr Robertson's fancy waistcoat, I enquire if he is the architect of all this lived-in loveliness? He looks terrified. 'No, my wife does all that. She's now taken to designing *me*.'

His pretty paintings are, he claims, car-boot sale finds . 'All bought locally,' he boasts. Follow that man.

Dinner is eaten in a dining room that, by comparison, is plain: white cloths, white candles, white napkins laid flat rather than being contorted into elaborate shapes. Tables are big enough to seat four. In one corner the doctors are making merry – loudly.

The wine list is as plain as the napkins. Let's try the Spanish house white at £9. 'Is it good?'

'We are *privileged* to have this wine,' Mr Robertson assures us po-faced.

In fact it's all right. The food, though, is impressive. We eat home-smoked salmon accompanied by walnut bread; warm crab and avocado pancake on a piquant coriander butter sauce; followed by a plainly grilled fillet of beef and breast of chicken with wild mushrooms and thyme. Puds are wonderfully over the top. It's a memorable dinner, we decide, heightened by the views from large, uncurtained windows of a wet and windy sub-tropical garden landscape leading down to the sea.

By morning, our host has shed his peacock plumage and looks like any other chap in a perfectly ordinary pullover and cords. He has lost none of his panache, however, as he tells us over the freshly squeezed OJ and home made (runny) marmalade that his restaurant is in *The Good Food Guide* and that he is offering 'substantially reduced rates for dinner, bed and breakfast'. He smiles mournfully. 'No one seems to want to come to Cornwall in winter...'

After this piece appeared, Felicity Robertson left a message on my ansaphone: 'You got him to a T,' she giggled. Her husband, who describes himself as a Punch and Judy operator, writes: 'Thought you'd like to know that more doctors and their wives are coming here!!'

Nansidwell Country House,

Mawnan Smith,
nr Falmouth,
Cornwall TR11 5HU.
Tel: (01326) 250340.
Fax: (01326) 250440.
Jamie and Felicity Robertson.
Location: just by the Red Lion pub.
Open: all year, except January.
Rooms: 12. 12 double (£90–£146), all ensuite. Single in double (£80).
Restaurant: open for dinner from 7–9pm (can be later).
Chef: Anthony Allcott. Table d'hôte £23.
Wine List: reasonably priced, from £10.
Children: yes.
Dogs: yes.
Smoking: feel free.
And Also: 5-acre sub-tropical gardens, tennis, croquet; close to sea, with bathing, fishing, windsurfing and riding nearby. Surrounded by National Trust coastland.

*M*iddleham, *North Yorkshire*
MILLERS HOUSE HOTEL

At first it seems there's only one small room available for Saturday night at Millers House Hotel – though when I ring back there's been a cancellation. 'You can have a nice twin-bedded ensuite room, dinner, bed and breakfast at £48 per person,' says a brisk female voice. 'Right... we'll take it.'

Opening the front door of what the brochure calls 'our peaceful Georgian country house', we follow the hall down to a reception desk at the back where, after pressing a bell, a tall, angular man with a beard leaps into view. Presuming this to be the owner, Crossley Sunderland, I repeat the details of my telephone conversation. 'Ah,' he cries, raising his arm in a sort of Heil Hitler salute, 'You must be in Swaledale...'

Are we? Noticing our bemused glances, he adds that all rooms are named after various Yorkshire Dales. Of *course.* Is he pleased we have come? Impossible to tell. Taking us up to our room, he first, somewhat myste-riously, opens the bathroom window, then recites a set of house rules. We must order dinner a good half hour before we want it, he explains in busi-ness-like fashion, because 'all food is specially prepared'. Only a brave couple would argue.

The house has been the subject of enthusiastic refurbishment. Doors, cornices and picture rails are painted ginger to complement the flowery wall-paper. White-painted wooden shutters are decorated with flowery motifs. A ruffled kidney-shaped dressing table is a perfect partner to white candlewick bedspreads. Curtains and pelmet are made from not one but two different flowery fabrics. Cream-painted wood-chip paper and brown sculptured pile carpet complete the effect. In the adjoining bathroom the fittings are mahogany and brass. All is immaculate.

Down in the bar other guests are congregating. Once we have ordered our dinner from grandiose leather-bound menus, Mr Sunderland mixes us drinks and tells the story about his friend with a gas-operated bottle opener that 'hangs from his belt like a Kalashnikov ha ha'. His wife, attired in bright flowered dress, swishes in. 'Have you told them about our friend with the...?' We are saved from a repeat performance by a sudden excitement. 'Lord W...is coming down,' hisses Mr Sunderland, practically standing to attention. Disappointingly, all His Lordship wants to do is sip his sherry and read his book.

In the formal dining room Mr Sunderland enquires about my glass of house white. 'Very dry,' he warns. I take a sip: 'Perfect.'

'Sure it's not *too* dry?'

'I *like* it dry.' My husband treats himself to a half bottle of claret and keeps quiet.

After the big build-up, the 'freshly prepared' four-course dinner is a bit of a let-down. Apart from unexciting starters and a dish of unappetizing-looking boiled potatoes, my noisettes of lamb have lost their pinkish hue and arrive with fat round the edges. Puddings are decked out with piped cream, in much the same way the ceiling rose above is picked out in gold and the glass-topped candleholders have little flower wreaths arranged around their bases.

Conversely, breakfast next morning is beautifully done: a vast array of cereals, grapefruit, prunes, exotic marmalades and bowls of tomato and brown sauce are invitingly set out on a white-clothed centre table.

If I sound lukewarm about Millers House, it's because I wish the house had been decorated more in sympathy with its natural elegance and its restaurant had lived up to its claim of 'a deserved reputation for excellence'. But what Millers House may lack in sparkle, it makes up for in comfort, cleanliness – and a very reasonably priced wine list.

The Sunderlands write: 'The room you stayed in now has a soft pastel green and rust-flecked carpet, new beds, new drapes, new bathroom and the wood-chip paper has been replaced with a delicately patterned cream wallpaper. Furniture is now more in keeping with the period and style of the property. We have just completed a large conservatory restaurant and engaged a professional chef...with the result our food has won the AA Red Rosette award. We have also just been awarded the Yorkshire and Humberside Tourist Board Hotel of the Year runner-up for 1994.'

Millers House Hotel,

Middleham,
Wensleydale,
North Yorkshire DL8 4NR.
Tel: (01969) 22630.
Fax: (01969) 23570.
Judith and Crossley Sunderland.
Location: off Middleham's cobbled market square.
Open: all year, except January.
Rooms: 7. 1 single with private bathroom (£33.50). 5 twin/double (£67), 1 four-poster (£82), all ensuite. Single in double (price on application).
Restaurant: open for dinner from 7.15–8.30 pm.
Chef: Mark Gatty. Table d'hôte £19.50.
Wine List: reasonable, from £5.15.
Children: yes, over 10.
Dogs: no.
Smoking: not in dining room or conservatory.
And Also: special Dales Weekend Breaks: gourmet wine tasting weekends; also racing weekends. House parties of 10–14 people can be arranged.

*M*iddleham, North Yorkshire
WATERFORD HOUSE

Driving through Middleham a year or so ago, we'd peered through the windows of a small hotel on the hill. Waterford House it's called and it looked so inviting that my husband promptly nipped in for a brochure and was taken on a guided tour by an amiable pink-and-white man.

When booking, I'm told there's just one room left at £55. 'If you're having dinner,' adds the friendly female voice, 'it'll be £50.' What a business-like arrangement. 'Dinner for two, please.'

Parking the car in the market square, we knock on the smart brass-trimmed front door. Our blonde, be-aproned hostess takes us to the top of the house. 'I'm waiting for a family,' she says, glancing at her watch. 'They probably won't turn up now. Pity, I could have given you the better room.'

This one looks fine to us, especially as it's cold and she's turned the radiators on full. My husband suddenly spots the duvet. 'You wouldn't have a blanket, by any chance?'

'I'm *sorry*!' She throws up her hands. 'There isn't one in the place.' I hasten to add it's a very nice duvet (as duvets go), it's simply that he and they aren't compatible.

'One of the warmest hotel rooms we've been in for ages,' he declares when she's gone. 'I rather like the fact the television doesn't work too well, it's like home.' This is a lovingly decorated, creaky-floored attic room with a view over the market square, an assorted collection of furniture and half a bottle of sherry and generous-sized cartons of nuts on the dressing table.

Having sampled the sherry, we swan downstairs. The crammed drawing room's a delight. Where to look? At the grand piano and all that sheet music? Into cupboards crammed with china? The lacy antimacassars? Or the log fire, brass fire irons and the cat who knows she's beautiful? Soon we're gossiping with the couple on the sofa. 'Great atmosphere,' I comment. 'It's like home,' says the woman, who's been here several days.

Our ebullient host, Brian, comes charging in, waving arms, menus and wine list. 'Let me tell 'ee what I've got,' he offers. 'The chicken's already taken; I've just *one* calves' liver...'

'Looks like everything's cooked to order?' I interrupt. 'Certainly is,' says Brian, adding he has over 700 wines to choose from. Good heavens. And good heavens again with the arrival on the family scene of a three-legged cat called Tripod, along with a couple who describe how they like their steak cooked: 'Just walk it through a warm kitchen.' A knock on the door heralds the arrival of the missing family and their two small children. It's full house.

In the Regency dining room, we find more ephemera, chiming clocks a speciality, and candles, flowers and technicoloured peppercorns on our table. Mmmm. All this *and* Mozart too.

Now the family's sitting down at the big table. The mother tells the assembled company that they've driven from

Hampshire that morning for the rugby in Edinburgh. 'The boys went to the match, us girls went shopping. Now we're on our way back.'

'Take your time to enjoy it, that's what it's all about,' says Gloria, the large and cheerful waitress, serving us with plates of delicious calves' liver and pheasant. 'My, you're too generous,' comments my husband. 'No one goes hungry here,' states Gloria. We also recommend Everyl's 'wonderful' summer-fruit crème brulée and the 'best sherry trifle ever'.

When paying our bill, we're invited into the chaotic Aga kitchen to meet our hosts' one-year-old son. 'When you're in the area again, do pop in and see us,' they say hospitably. As for us, we need pinching to remind ourselves we've been here *only one night.*

'We've just had showers put in all bathrooms,' announces Brian Madell, 'and blankets are now available for those who don't like duvets. PS: I'm now known as 'that amiable pink - and - white man'. Kindest regards.'

Waterford House,

19 Kirkgate,
Middleham,
North Yorkshire DL8 4PG.
Tel: (01969) 22090.
Fax: (01969) 24020.
Everyl and Brian Madell.
Location: on hill overlooking Market Square.
Open: all year.
Rooms: 5. 4 twin/double (£55–£90), 1 four-poster (£70–£80), mostly ensuite. Single in double (£40–£45).
Restaurant: open for dinner from 7-9.30 pm.
Chef: Everyl Madell. Table d'hôte £17.50–£25.
Wine List: over 700, many unusual, from £8.50, 50 by the glass.
Children: yes.
Dogs: yes.
Smoking: not in dining room.
And Also: horse racing, hiking, caving, fishing, golfing, shooting all nearby. Wine and Food weekends – please enquire.

Mousehole, Penzance, Cornwall
THE LOBSTER POT

What a dear little place Mousehole is. So is The Lobster Pot hotel, originally five fishermen's cottages, which leans out magically over the harbour.

My friend, Lenore, now back in New Zealand, once worked in the bar at The Lobster Pot. '*I* reckon it was the best job I ever had in England,' she reflects. I reckon it was because she had a twinkle in her eye...but that's another story.

On booking I'm offered a room that 'has a harbour view, though it's on the side.' This description mystifies me. I imagine painfully craning my neck. What the hell. It's different. 'OK,' I say, and promptly send off the requested £40 deposit.

We cannot believe our luck upon arriving at The Lobster Pot and being taken by the receptionist to 'the room on the side'. What we, in fact, get is a tiny room with a stable door that leads onto a small almost-private walled terrace furnished with table and chairs. As soon as she's gone, we peer over the wall. It's an idyllic scene. The harbour's directly below. The gulls are squawking. Little boats bob up and down.

Inside, the room is pink, beamed and, well, cosy's the best I can manage. Although it's not furnished with amazing flair, a patchwork quilt I've just purchased in a Penzance antique shop livens it up considerably.

We dress up for dinner – not that The Lobster Pot is a dressy-up sort of place but because Mother-in-Law's joining us and she *is*. We've booked a table for seven-thirty, too early really,

but we've been persuaded that if we leave it later we might not get a 'harbour-view' table.

At seven then, throwing open our stable door, we saunter along the short outdoor passage that leads to the restaurant and bar, and swan inside. Mother-in-law awaits. Ordering drinks, we begin the serious business of studying the menu.

No, we refuse to be bullied into ordering at seven-fifteen. If we did, we'd probably be finished at eight-thirty, and what then? So we dally. 'There are a lot of people coming in shortly,' urges the receptionist-cum-waitress. 'I'm just trying to make life easy for myself.'

There are certainly some unusual-sounding dishes here. What about Scallops Elizabeth, 'succulent queen scallops in a garlic and granary mustard sauce'?

'Yes, please,' says Ma-in-Law. My husband rashly chooses Patrick's Orchard, described as 'deep-fried smoked cheese in a Guinness batter served with apple and clove sauce'. 'Well, someone's got to try it.' I choose melon.

At some stage, the restaurant has been added onto the original structure and appears almost to hang out over the water. Most of the tables are on the window side and the room is lit by soft orange lights that shine through trails of plumbago hanging from the ceiling.

Ma-in-Law declares her scallop starter to be 'Very nice, dear,' though

Patrick's Orchard isn't as successful. 'It tastes mostly of apple purée,' comments my husband, making a face. 'But it's supposed to have Guinness in it,' I exclaim. 'Oh?' he says.

The main courses are monkfish Kashmir, accompanied by a 'light curry sauce', something called turf and surf, in other words 'steak with a prawn and nut stuffing', and brill Penberth, 'whole Newlyn brill pan-fried in butter sprinkled with grated cheese and flaked almonds and finished under the grill' – all typical pub grub. Coffee is served in a horribly bright room upstairs – a shock to the system after the subdued ambience of the restaurant.

In the morning it's a perfect autumn day. At breakfast we note that sugar (brown), butter (in curls) and marmalade are in pleasing little dishes. There's a pleasantly relaxed atmosphere and the cheery Scots waitress informs us she cycles to work each day. We envy her. We've got to leave at ten and belt back to a London that suddenly seems rather unattractive.

'Nothing changes here,' says Patricia Deakin, 'but we have done something about those bright lights in our lounge...'

The Lobster Pot,

South Cliff,
Mousehole,
Cornwall TR19 6QX.
Tel: (01736) 731251.
Fax: (01736) 731140.
Manager: Patricia Deakin.
Location: right on Mousehole harbour.
Open: all year, except January.
Rooms: 24. 1 single, 2 twin/double with shared bathroom (£39.50), 21 twin/double (from £67.20), all ensuite. Single in double (when available, half double rate).
Restaurant: open for dinner 7.30–9.45pm.
Chef: David Tregear. Table d'hôte £14.95.
Wine List: classical choices, from £8.95.
Children: yes.
Dogs: no.
Smoking: not in restaurant.
And Also: the fairytale setting.

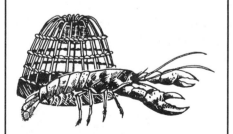

'I thought you said this was a hotel!' A pair of pristine, lace-trimmed Victorian pantaloons swings from the handle of an ancient pram at the gate. At the end of the drive is a stone-built dolls' farmhouse. I take a deep breath. I see what my husband means.

In the guide book I'd consulted the previous day, I'd been seduced by a photograph of the Fosse dining room with its red-and-white checked cloths, bread sculptures and blue-and-white china piled onto a pine dresser of comforting proportions. I am further intrigued by the unusual rise and fall lamp, *circa* 1900, hanging over one of the tables. How strange. Over *my* dining table is its twin, purchased from a West London antique shop I'd haunted until its owner inconsiderately upped sticks and retreated to the country.

All of which seems a good reason for belting down the M4 one hot Saturday afternoon and the fact we find it only with difficulty says more about our stupidity than the owner's precise instructions over the phone.

Fosse Farm Hotel stands by itself in the middle of fields on the Roman Fosse Way. Around it is a rambly orchard and garden set out with tables from which to indulge in cream teas or quaff the homemade cider.

'I bought this place in 1984 when it was an absolute wreck,' owner Caron Cooper tells us. Later on, her mother June arrived to help her transform it into the delectably pretty hotel it is today. And when Mother and I meet,

yes, she *is* my antique shop lady and she even manages to recall some of the treasures I'd bought in the dim and distant – like the pine clock with the painted face that my husband hated then and still does.

Adjacent are the converted stables with three bedrooms, one of which is ours. It has white lace bedspreads, a tiny shower room and brass taps. Downstairs is the breakfast room, with a flagged floor, a huge black polished range with tiled surround and old French furniture. With its beamed ceiling, metal candelabra and bunches of herbs, it's just like being in the sort of French gîte you always hope to find and never do...

Caron beckons conspiratorially. 'Come and have a look at the honeymoon suite,' she says, leading us across to the main house and up the stairs to a room elegantly furnished with pine furniture. Wow. There are ribbons everywhere and a bottle of celebration champagne awaits on a tray. 'They don't arrive till midnight, we're leaving the key under the mat,' she confides.

Dinner by candlelight in the farmhouse kitchen is a pleasant affair. There's even something hypnotically pleasing about the muzak tinkling just beneath conversation level. To begin, I choose melon liberally doused with port, while my husband has the Provençal fish soup. 'No one could complain it lacks fish,' he says.

The set main course of grilled trout cooked with dill, accompanied by garden vegetables, is plainly cooked, just the way I like it and, with it, we knock back the perfectly adequate house wine. Now the cabaret begins. The couple behind us are in a wicked mood. They torment the young French waitress, whose English isn't quite up to it, by pretending they are Egon Ronay inspectors. Poor girl, I wonder if she ever did suss their little game.

In the morning, the newlyweds appear. 'I do hope they liked their room,' we say and then overhear June Cooper ask the same question. 'Very nice,' says the bridegroom abruptly. Gosh, that *was* an anticlimax. If *I* had gone to so much trouble I'd have been mortified by such a reaction. June Cooper merely shrugs. He's probably shy, she says. But when mother and daughter pay such infinite attention to detail, how sad when it's so summarily brushed aside.

As for me, I cannot leave empty-handed. From the many antiques for sale, I find a teddy bear to add to my collection and he costs a lot less than he would have done in London.

This was my first 'Room Service' hotel. 'Why didn't you tell me why you were here?' June Cooper asked when the piece appeared in The Telegraph. *'I couldn't. You'd have been on your best behaviour.'*

Says Caron: 'Nothing's changed. My mum is still out searching for antiques, between baking scones and making jam. The Japanese have discovered Fosse Farmhouse, but this makes no difference as I only take independent travellers – there's no room for coaches thank goodness. It's the Alice in Wonderland feel they find so attractive. Did you know it's the most popular English-language book in Japan?'

Fosse Farmhouse Country Hotel,

Nettleton Shrub,
Nettleton, Chippenham,
Wiltshire SN14 7NJ.
Tel: (01249) 782286.
Fax: (01249) 783066.
Miss Caron Cooper.
Location: off the B4039, approx 1 mile from the Salutation Inn.
Open: all year.
Rooms: 6. I single (£40–£48), 4 twin/double (£98), 1 family room (up to 4 people) (£110–£130), all ensuite. Single in double (£50–£70).
Restaurant: dinner served at 7.30pm.
Chef: Caron Cooper. Table d'hôte £21.50.
Wine List: French, from £9.50.
Children: yes.
Dogs: by arrangement.
Smoking: not in dining room.
And Also: tea room and garden. Antiques shop. Watercolour painting weekends in summer; Christmas Decorations weekend November – please enquire.

It's an unlikely setting for a romantically named country hotel: on an industrial estate, off a roundabout, beneath a giant pylon. But, sure enough, here's Hotel des Clos, complete with Roller parked outside.

At this point I recall my conversation with proprietor, John Abbey. The subject is Gourmet Evenings. 'We have them once a month. This Friday most diners are staying. So I have only one room left – the four-poster,' he says.

In my experience, four-posters are either antique – wonderful to behold, not always wonderful to sleep on – or they have that factory fresh look. 'I don't want a four-poster and, anyway, you'll charge me extra,' I say, being difficult. 'No, I won't,' replies Mr Abbey briskly, quoting his weekend rate of £48 per person dinner, bed and breakfast.

Hotel des Clos chooses a cliché to describe itself: 'a tasteful conversion of Victorian farm buildings.' We're greeted by Mrs Abbey, in leggings, who takes us, quick march and smiling, across a paved terrace to our colour-matched room.

This boasts an unusual arrangement: two bathrooms and a single bedside light. One bathroom has everything you'd expect; the other a fiercely efficient shower in a proper cubicle with nowhere to put the soap. 'All very nice,' grumbles my husband, still clutching it, 'but where am I supposed to shave? They forgot to put a mirror in this bathroom.'

Across the terrace, in the bar, it's impossible to miss the fact they're keen on Chablis here – four pages of it, for heaven's sake, on the wine list. I catch Mrs Abbey in mid dash: 'You, er, specialise in Chablis?' She discloses that her husband is a Francophile: 'It's an obsession,' she adds darkly. 'He's off to France every six weeks to buy the stuff.' We choose a white Burgundy – it's cheaper.

Soon we encounter the Gourmet Diners *en masse*. Boy, are they enjoying themselves – the atmosphere's terrific. Stuff the set menu, I'd thought earlier, ordering from the à la carte a 'small salad with quails' eggs and walnut vinaigrette' followed by 'sea bass with basil, tomato and beurre blanc'. My husband, sticking to the party line, had chosen a 'warm salad with guinea fowl and bacon' starter. Now – lo! – he's being offered a perk: a surplus portion of Gourmet roast pheasant accompanied by duck pâté. 'No extra charge,' coos Mrs Abbey. 'Yes, please,' he says.

Dinner's wonderful. Can't get enough of that beurre blanc. As I curse the inadequacy of forks, a spoon is silently slid onto the table. I look up to find Mrs Abbey slyly grinning. 'You've got eyes at the back of your head,' I declare, hoping she hasn't spotted my notebook.

Later, her husband (the chef) makes his entrance. Should we applaud? He's just as interested in us one-nighters as in the local Gourmet lot. 'Where did you learn to cook so brilliantly?' I ask. 'Oh, I just picked it up.'

After all that cordon bleu, the factory fresh four-poster's very comfortable, thank you. Alas, my insomniac husband prefers the comfort of the carpeted bathroom floor, reading Auberon Waugh and clad in one of the towelling bathrobes provided.

For breakfast we're offered freshly squeezed OJ and the muesli comes with blueberries and slices of orange. Delicious. But, well, life just isn't fair, is it? In reply to my question, Mrs Abbey confirms her husband really did 'just pick up cooking', his apprenticeship consisting of a mere few days in a French kitchen: 'As a skivvy. But, you know, that man can do anything. I'm still looking for my talent.' 'You have a special talent,' I tell her, 'for making your guests feel very welcome indeed...'

'Can you imagine how we felt when we saw our name at the bottom of your column this morning,' writes John Abbey. 'We have never before had a review published and, while it is easy to imagine how we would feel if we'd received bad publicity, it has come as a shock to both of us to realize how exciting it is to receive a nice review. The first call I received was from an unknown gentleman who merely rang to offer his congratulations!'

Hotel des Clos,

Old Lenton Lane,
Nottingham NG7 2SA.
Tel: (0115) 9866566.
Fax: (0115) 9860343.
John and Rosemary Abbey.
Location: 5 minutes from Nottingham city centre, on the banks of the Trent.
Open: all year.
Rooms: 11. 3 single (£70), 8 twin/double (£70–£90), all ensuite. Single in double (£70–£90).
Restaurant: open for dinner from 7–9pm.
Chef: John Abbey. Table d'hôte £19.50. Continental breakfast £4.50, cooked £7.50.
Wine List: All French, majoring on Chablis, from £8.50.
Children: no.
Dogs: yes.
Smoking: feel free.
And Also: Gourmet evenings on Fridays – please enquire.

*O*ckham, Surrey
THE HAUTBOY

At the The Hautboy hotel – 'one of Surrey's finest' – we are welcomed by a dishy waiter. Sweeping us up the staircase, he shows us to a large, extravagantly decorated room. I ask if all the Hautboy rooms are as grand as this. 'No, zis is ze best room.'

'And what time are we booked for dinner?'

'Any time to zoot you. If you want zumthing meanwhile, you just go toot, toot, too...' he urges.

Ignoring my husband, who's now practising *toot, too* in a light falsetto, I knock back the sherry thoughtfully provided by the management. Dialling 222 on the internal phone seems easier somehow.

The Hautboy (we are reminded) has a history. Built in neo-gothic style in 1864 by the flamboyant Earl of Lovelace, its name comes from *haut-bois,* alluding to 'the high-pitched note produced by an oboe' and, no, I still don't know what that's got to do with it. Our room's called Lovelace. Another is Byron – the Earl married Byron's daughter Ada.

'Men,' my husband is now intoning solemnly, 'grow up accepting that certain things are best done standing up.' *What?* I hurtle from the bathroom. 'Why are you on your knees?'

'Trying to tie my tie, there's no full-length mirror.' Oh, for heaven's sake.

Skimming downstairs at last all dressed up, we are directed to a large basement bar full of sofas, cane chairs, mirrors, muzak and – oh-my-God – a fountain. Our dishy waiter – presto! – presents us with His' n' Hers menus, but I spoil the ritual and grab the His – I do like to know how much everything costs.

We reject the à la carte – 'Yes, Madam, I think perhaps you would find our fish soup (£9.50) a little too much,' coos Maître'd – in favour of the £17.50 and £22.50 menus and decide on a 'cheap' wine at £13.95. Apart from drinks, crisps and eavesdropping, there are also magazines with intriguing titles like *Monacle* and *Surrey Occasions* to amuse us.

Oh, how posh the restaurant is with pink cloths, candles and waiter-ish waiters, one of whose specialities is flame-throwing – sorry, flambé-ing. Somehow my gaze zooms straight across the tables to the chap with tattoos so dense I don't realize he's rolled his sleeves up. He's ordering champagne. The best. '*I* don't get picked on,' he confides to his blonde companion. 'I'm shrewd...I'm *slippery*...

He's more fun than the food. My melon and Parma ham is fine, ditto my husband's avocado, buffalo mozzarella and tomato platter, but we both agree that the main courses could do better. 'Mmmm, they have that "sales convention" touch,' comments my husband. From the sweet trolley I choose cheesecake. Cheesecake? It's got to be strawberry mousse – or *hair* mousse.

The ceremony of dinner is further enlivened by the Oriental waiter who clearly learned the art of wine pouring in a military academy: '*Pre*-sent bottle...hup, two, three...pour...two, three...' If only he'd just leave it on the table.

Back in our pretty pink room, we remark on the decorative hip bath, now a repository for dried hydrangea, and the rows of little framed portraits hanging on tasselled ribbons decorated with bows. As for that four-poster, it's wonderfully comfortable.

We are the only guests, so a breakfast table has been specially laid for us in reception, overlooking the terrace. 'Brought the sun with you,' remarks David, a wide-awake Yorkshire lad, who's been up all night doing the tables for a wedding breakfast that day. But he still finds time to show us the Minstrels' Gallery, where we could have eaten last night, and recommends a stroll round the gardens...Yes, The Hautboy's all very pristine, very Home Counties. Not quite us, perhaps, but an enjoyable experience .

Owner Ian Shier wasn't delirious with this account of our stay in his hotel but recovered sufficiently to want to be included in this book. The good news from The Hautboy is: full-length mirrors have been installed in all bedrooms and a new chef and pastry chef have arrived. 'I am working with them to try and improve our standards,' says Mr Shier. 'All bread and petit fours are now made in The Hautboy kitchens.'

The Hautboy,

Ockham Lane,
Ockham,
Woking,
Surrey GU23 6NP.
Tel: (01483) 225355.
Fax: (01483) 211176.
Ian and Piera Shier.
Location: in the Surrey Hills.
Open: all year.
Rooms: 5. 5 twin/double (£98), all ensuite. Single in double (£78).
Restaurant: open for dinner from 7–10pm.
Chef: Phil Richards. Table d'hôte £17.50 and £22.50. Cooked breakfast £5.95.
Wine List: mainly French, from £9.95.
Children: yes, over 8.
Dogs: no.
Smoking: feel free.
And Also: Hampton Court, Windsor, Ascot, the gardens of Wisley. Special evenings hosted by sports celebrities, also cookery demonstrations by well-known cooks – please enquire.

*O*ldbury, West Midlands
JONATHANS' HOTEL AND RESTAURANT

At first sight, Jonathans' Hotel – on a busy roundabout near Birmingham – isn't promising. It doesn't look like a proper hotel at all, more like a row of little shops, though, on closer inspection, the 'shops' are all restaurants: Jonathans' Original, The Fishmarket and Littlejohn's Bistro.

No grand entrances either. Finding an unassuming door at the end of the parade, we erupt into a potted-palm reception area where a girl in black dress and white pinny hands us 'passports' to the Amazing World of Jonathans'.

Duly amazed, we are whisked up steep stairs, round corners, across landings, catching glimpses of secret passageways, archways, Grannie's Kitchen, a roof garden and corners stuffed with bric-a-brac. 'No good for Aunt Jane and her poor leg,' I whisper.

Our passports tell us our room is Upper Gornal. In the manner of a conjuror producing a rabbit, the receptionist throws open the door of a dark-papered Victorian sitting room. We blink. 'Is there a bedroom too?' I ask, half expecting her to magick a bed from the wall. 'Round the corner,' she smiles.

Round I trot. The bathroom's a masterpiece of Victoriana and there are teddy bears on the beds. I'm *more* amazed. 'What an unusual place, when did Jonathans' open?'

'Four years ago,' she says. 'They started with three or four rooms and gradually bought up the row of shops.

They've extended and extended...' She raises her hands wide. *They* are Jonathan and Jonathan, proprietors, entrepreneurs.

'I like this funny place,' announces my husband when she's gone. 'It's been very carefully thought out.'

'Sure has,' I reply, fishing a newspaper dated 12 August 1870 from a drawer, 'though this may be carrying authenticity *too* far.'

On our way down to Jonathans' Original Restaurant for dinner, we explore Grannie's Truly Amazing Kitchen and discover a warren of sitting rooms where you can browse through shelves of books or play 78s on a wind-up gramophone.

To our astonishment the upwardly mobile view from our restaurant table is of a galleried room heaving with people. A private party? Looks like fun. We devote ourselves instead to white linen napkins clasped by silver rings and the Mrs Beeton menu where courses are described as 'First Remove' and 'Main Remove'. For his 'Main', my husband chooses Newcastle Fillet 'dusted with our patent Newcastle spice mix, pan fried with slivers of bacon and mushrooms with good English gravy enlivened with a dash of Mrs Beeton's Carrack Sauce'. For me, it's The Birmingham Market, in other words 'fish delivered daily from Birmingham wholesale market'. Puddings are disgustingly rich and wonderful. All this scoffing is accompanied by frequent solicitous enquiries as to whether 'Everything's all right?' Yes, chaps, it is.

'We'll have coffee in an upstairs sitting room, please.'

'Would you like me to take you up?' asks the waiter. 'No thanks, it's more of a challenge to us to find it.'

And we do. Suddenly we tune in to distant sounds of music: 'The Lambeth Walk', 'Roll A Ball A Ball A Penny A Pitch', 'Any Old Iron?'. Yes, it *is* a party – an Edwardian music hall one at that. Can we join in? Yes, we can!

From the crowded gallery we look down upon the champagne scene: the staff in their Edwardian dresses; the Master of Ceremonies; the merry punters; and the cabaret who're cracking unsophisticated and amazingly vulgar jokes. 'Do they *pay* you for working here?' we ask a passing Edwardian waiter. 'Only just,' he quips back. Joke. Which sums up Jonathans'. Life here appears laugh-a-minute but hotel keeping, I suspect, is taken very seriously indeed. Which reminds me. I hope the Jonathans will take seriously my one quibble: the amazing all-or-nothing lighting arrangement in Upper Gornal.

We're still very much occupied with the day-to-day running of Jonathans' and find it gives us as much pleasure and satisfaction today as when we started,' say Jonathan and Jonathan.

Jonathans' Hotel and Restaurant,

16–24 Wolverhampton Road,
Oldbury,
Warley,
West Midlands B68 0LH.
Tel: (0121) 429 3757.
Fax: (0121) 434 3107.
Jonathan Baker and Jonathan Bedford.
Location: 4 miles from Birmingham city centre.
Open: all year.
Rooms: 29. 5 single (£69–£89), 24 double suites (£80–£118), all ensuite. Single as double (£69–£89). Luxury penthouse apartment (£150).
Restaurant: open for dinner from 7–10.30pm.
Chef: Graham Bradley. Table d'hôte £16.
Wine List: mainly French, from £11.50.
Children: yes, over 10.
Dogs: no.
Smoking: not in restaurant.
And Also: special theatre, murder mystery and old-time music hall weekends – please enquire. Substantial reductions at weekends.

$\mathcal{P}$ainswick, Gloucestershire
THE PAINSWICK HOTEL

Among the 'Room Service' letters forwarded to me from *The Telegraph* some months back is one from Somerset Moore of The Painswick Hotel. Oh dear. Mr Moore's got his envelopes in a twist. He's sent me the letter intended for a Famous Restaurant Critic – maybe *he* got mine? Simpers Mr Moore: 'Dear Wayne Black, I've been reading your amusing and some-times frightening column...we should be delighted for you to pay a visit.'

Shooting into The Painswick, we're delighted with the stereophonic welcome: 'Good evening,' trills a girl entering from right. 'Good evening,' warbles a girl from the back. 'Good *evening*,' enthuses another sidling down the stairs. It's good to see there's no shortage of ministering staff at The Painswick. Quite right too...it isn't cheap.

Painswick is a pretty, architecturally correct little Cotswold town and the hotel, built in Palladian style, was once the rectory. Our first-floor front room is suitably reverent with good pieces of heavy antique furniture, serious curtain-ing, a four-poster – oh, didn't ask for *that* – and much Oriental accessorizing. A few niggles though: in a room costing £95, we don't expect to find the full-length mirror lolling against the wall, a naff gilt triple mirror on the dignified chest, a lopsided casket in the bath-room (two legs missing) and a compli-mentary basket of wizened apples...

And in the luxurious bathroom I get wetter than I mean to. 'You've been behaving like a duck again,' I accuse my husband. 'Nothing to do with me,' he shouts back. I remain unconvinced – there's a mini flood in here. Crossly I wring out my spongebag.

Sort of reconciled, we go down a few stairs to the drawing room where a glowering fire smokes in the huge grate and couples sit on sofas looking self-conscious. It ought to be nice in here, and we puzzle over why it's so cheer-less. The noisy extractor fan? The light-ing? No time to reflect. Our host is sashaying in bearing titbits, menus and *bonhomie*. 'Had a good journey?' he asks us. 'I'm afraid the lobster's off, *just* sold the last one from our tank.' When our table's ready, he urges: 'Enjoy your supper, won't you?' Supper? We're expecting a feast, Mr Moore.

The elegant dining room has chan-deliers and much stripped panelling. 'We're only twenty-two for dinner tonight,' laments Somerset Moore, looming up behind us. 'Oh, who'd be a hotelier!' we sigh. 'Tomorrow, though, we're full,' he beams.

Our bottle of wine arrives with its cork attached by an elastic band. The chap at the next table is intrigued: 'Perhaps we're supposed to fire them across the room with the elastic band?' he speculates. What a tempting idea but not half as tempting as the food. I love my salad of smoked salmon, Ogen melon and lightly poached quail eggs even more than the breast of chicken filled with herb mousse served with grain mustard sauce. 'What's yours like?' I ask my husband, but he's too busy mopping up his ragôut of hare with lardons of bacon, red wine and shallots to give a coherent reply.

Declining the Arabica coffee with homemade fudges, we return to the smoky drawing room full of whispering, well fed couples – oh look – there's some *serious* hanky panky going on over there. Back to reality and our bathroom: 'See, there's water running across the ceiling and down the wall and it's not *new* either,' says my husband smugly, pointing to tell-tale brown marks on the ceiling.

Over an excellent breakfast, Mr Moore engages us in a flurry of conversation about how long it'll take us to drive to Cumbria – 'Three hours,' he confidently asserts – with the result we entirely forget to mention his water leak. Later, when we're paying the bill, he's nowhere. We tell the girl instead. 'Oh...' she says.

After this review was published, I met Somerset Moore at a London reception and got a somewhat po-faced look. Now we're the best of friends. I do like cherubic hoteliers who get huffy, calm down and send me notes saying Kind Regards.

And I had a letter from the grandparents of the Painswick chef, saying that, as we'd liked the food so much, how they wished he'd been given a mention. Here goes: thank you Robert Maughan for memories of an excellent dinner.

The Painswick Hotel,

Kemps Lane,
Painswick,
Gloucestershire GL6 6YB.
Tel: (01452) 812160.
Fax: (01452) 814059.
Somerset and Helene Moore.
Location: in one of the most desirable parts of the Cotswolds.
Open: all year.
Rooms: 20. 2 single (£65), 18 twin/double (£90–£120), all ensuite. Single in double (£72–£92).
Restaurant: open for dinner from 7.30–9.30pm.
Chef: Robert Maughan. Table d'hôte £23.50.
Wine List: 'Chosen to be drunk now,' asserts Somerset Moore. From £10–50.
Children: yes.
Dogs: yes.
Smoking: feel free.
And Also: croquet lawn at hotel, antique hunting, pretty Cotswold villages.

HEDDON'S GATE HOTEL

And is there honey still for tea? Well, no – it's cucumber sandwiches actually, followed by fruit cake, scones, jam and clotted cream. 'We *always* make sure we're back in time for tea,' confide the couple we meet over the silver teapot in the hall.

Tea's the thing at Heddon's Gate Hotel. So's the view – a wild landscape of forest, hills, valleys and mist. There's also the womblike thing. We speculate on the reason: is it (a) because this former hunting lodge was built in the golden age of country estates (1890) by Mr Hartley, maker of jam or (b) because owner Robert de Ville's been here 25 years. 'A bit of both,' suggests my husband unhelpfully.

In a letter to guests, Mr de Ville says: 'The enthusiasm I still feel for Heddon's Gate rubs off on the staff, some of whom have been here for years. This is my home and it is my wish that, for the time you stay, you will feel it is yours too.'

Such old-fashioned sentiments are echoed in the ambience: pictures hang from brass hooks on picture rails; a treadle sewing machine lurks in a corridor complete with *Book of Hobbies*; and, goodness gracious me, if pelmets are your thing, Heddon's Gate has turned them into a whole new art form.

We're soon running off the clotted cream down the steep hill at the end of the drive and along a footpath leading to Heddon's Mouth and the sea. What we totally forget is having to stagger back *up* that long, leg-aching hill –

though give us a week in this lovely place and we'd be as fit as Linford Christie for sure.

After a bath – no shortage of hot water here – we explore the downstairs: here's the lace antimacassared room where we'd had tea on the window seat; here's the library; and here's a 'bridge, anyone?' room; not to mention a large drawing room with piano. There's a little bar too. I ask for mineral water. 'Bottled or tap?' enquires the nice girl who'd greeted us earlier.

'Tap, please.'

'It's spring water from our own spring,' she explains. 'You've bathed in it, now you can drink it...'

Dinner's at eight and, in the dining room, we meet the ex-department store dummy called Rose dressed in black and gold with a feather in her hair – one of Mr de Ville's little eccentricities.

We have French onion soup; roast leg of new-season English lamb; breast of guinea fowl in mushroom sauce served with devilled 'bones', followed by old-fashioned baked rice pudding and – oh no – more clotted cream. 'Real food', the brochure calls it...and it is.

We drink our coffee on the silent terrace and, when cold, retreat to the drawing room and the merry party of eight whose jokes we couldn't miss over dinner. One plays the piano: 'I'm Devon's answer to Andrew Lloyd Webber...'

'Huh,' says his friend, 'Devon's answer to Les Dawson more like...'

What's specially nice about Heddon's Gate – apart from the comfort and attention from staff – is its breakfast menu. Its tempting offers include: fresh orange juice; fresh pink grapefruit; grapefruit segments; figs and yoghurt; porridge and cream; the best sort of muesli; kipper with butter; boiled eggs with soldiers; perfect poached egg accompanying two crisp rashers of bacon.

There's strong coffee, butter in a dish, brown and white sugar in bowls and myriad jars of different kinds of marmalade and jam. Surely more hotels could produce breakfasts like this if they wanted to. So why don't they?

There's just one thing that's puzzling us. What's all that whistling behind the scenes? Managing to drag modest Mr de Ville from his kitchen, we compliment him on his whistling while he works... only to be told it's his parrot.

'We've redecorated the reception area,' says Robert de Ville. 'We've over decorated it! Now we have the French look, blue and pink floral wallpaper, bevelled mirrors, French glass globes while our new reception desk is an old pulpit...'

Heddon's Gate Hotel,

Heddon's Mouth,
Parracombe,
North Devon EX31 4PZ.
(015983) 313.
Robert de Ville.
Location: on hillside above Parracombe.
Open: 1 April–1 November.
Rooms: 14. 1 single (£57.20), 10 twin/double (£110–£126.20), 3 cottage rooms (£120–£132.60), mostly ensuite. Single in double (subject to negotiation). All room prices include afternoon tea, dinner and breakfast.
Restaurant: open for dinner at 8pm.
Chef: Robert de Ville. Table d'hôte £20 (included in room rates).
Wine List: mostly from small producers, from £7.80.
Children: yes, over 10.
Dogs: yes, but not in dining room.
Smoking: yes, but not in dining room.
And Also: walking, horse riding and trekking, fishing, bird watching.

$\mathcal{P}$enzance, Cornwall
THE ABBEY

The romantic Abbey hotel sits on a narrow hilly street overlooking the harbour front in Penzance and its walls are painted a bright cobalt blue. Gulls swoop and wail. The large solid front door is crammed with brass fittings lovingly polished.

For me, a junk and antique shop habitué, the main reason for staying at the 17th-century Abbey is to sigh over its collection of antiques, curios, paintings and, most particularly, its style – though '60s people may also want to sigh over its owner Jean Shrimpton, who runs it with husband Michael Cox.

We're let in by the chef, who fetches our bags from the car park at the back and brings them – and us – the short-cut way through the kitchen. And even had we come here to meet the '60s legend, we wouldn't have had the chance because, according to the girl in charge, the owner's 'at the sale room acquiring more stuff for her hotel. Mrs Cox just loves buying things.' She points to a glass-fronted cabinet in the red-painted hall crammed with rings, brooches and trinkets, all for sale. 'This cabinet – well – it gives her the excuse, you know.'

And there's 'stuff' everywhere we look. On the front of the postcard confirming my booking (£50 deposit please) is a photograph of the drawing room, from which it's easy to spot the compulsive collector – though when we walk into the real thing, nothing's quite the same. Furniture's been moved around, pieces added. Regular visitors, I suspect, find The Abbey looks different each time they visit.

It's the chef who escorts us to our harbour-view bedroom on the first floor – he doesn't seem to mind at all being dragged from his kitchen. This room is huge with two comfortable pink armchairs, antique rugs and a canopied bed covered with a quilt. While it's stunning to look at, as are the other rooms I peep into, anybody who's forgotten their hair dryer or likes bath bubbles in their bath might feel irritated by their absence.

Yet – for me – how hard to complain seriously of such trifles (even the lack of a proper shower), when the bathroom is large, elegantly wallpapered, pine-panelled and has a cheval mirror and an ancient weighing machine that, surprisingly, works.

Going down to the drawing room for drinks before dinner, we chop and change among the tall armchairs and squashy sofas in order to get better views of the books, the lacquered chest, the decorative boxes and pictures. And we're faintly surprised by another lack – not even a couple of crisps are offered along with the drinks.

Similarly with dinner. The chef is chatty and charming, but is he, we wonder, understaffed? There are only three tables taken in the dining room, yet we wait ages between starter and main course. While no one wants to eat in a tearing hurry, there should perhaps be some sort of flow.

And the food is disappointing: king prawns flambéed in Pernod are drowned by the Pernod; grilled lemon sole is *devastated* by the capers beurre noisette. And so on. Dinner is strictly three-course and we are not offered cheese. It's a lacklustre meal. Coffee is taken in the drawing room and, a nice touch, is accompanied by a pot of hot milk.

It's mid April – the holiday season hasn't begun. And how do we know that the nice girl who makes our breakfast is the only one on duty? Easy. When asked for one poached and one scrambled egg for breakfast, she hesitates. 'It might take a little while...' she says. To help breakfast along, we decide on two poached, which arrive – dreadfully lonely, minus toast – in the middle of large plates. Oh well. At least the orange juice is freshly squeezed.

The Abbey is beautiful to look at, but I wonder whether the proprietors are more interested in buying antiques than in the everyday, nitty gritty of running the hotel. The laid-back attitude will suit some, not others.

Later, on another visit to Penzance, I do meet Jean Shrimpton. Wearing specs, she was deep in a book at the back of her antique shop just up the road from The Abbey. I liked her very much and we chatted about 'stuff' generally. No, I didn't tell her I'd stayed in her hotel and written about it in The Telegraph, *but I did buy one of her patchwork quilts...*

The Abbey

Abbey Street,
Penzance,
Cornwall TR18 4AR.
Tel: (01736) 66906.
Fax: (01736) 51163.
Jean and Michael Cox.
Location: off Capel Street down towards the sea front.
Open: all year, except Christmas period.
Rooms: 7. 1 single (£60–£65), 6 twin/double (£80–£130), mostly ensuite. Single in double (£75–£100).
Restaurant: open for dinner from 7.30–8.30pm.
Chef: Glyn Green. Table d'hôte £22.50.
Wine List: not extensive, starting from £8.
Children: yes.
Dogs: yes (not in public rooms).
Smoking: not too excessive.
And Also: close to Minack clifftop theatre, Lands End and the Cornish Coastal footpath.

*P*ortmeirion, Gwynedd
HOTEL PORTMEIRION

In one of the grand, Indian-inspired public rooms of this hotel a gurgling baby kicks its heels on the carpet while its parents, as elegant as the decor, sip Bloody Marys and converse in an unfamiliar language.

On arrival, we check in at the reception office at the top of the hill – where the staff converse in the same language – before driving down through the holiday village to the hotel which sits in white and turquoise splendour on the edges of a sandy estuary.

The village itself, vaguely Mediterranean in style, is a magical place. A cluster of pink, blue and yellow-painted houses (available serviced or on a self-catering basis) look out onto an unreal world of trees, exotic foliage, Italian arches, a high-spired church, pillars, statues and tiered gardens sloping down towards the water.

Here is a hotel like no other. Portmeirion was the dream of architect Sir Clough Williams-Ellis, who intended his romantic 'folly' to prove wrong all those who muttered that development of such a spectacular site would spoil it.

When Hotel Portmeirion opened in 1926, celebrities were quick off the mark. George Bernard Shaw, H.G. Wells and Bertrand Russell soon became regulars. Noel Coward wrote *Blythe Spirit* during a two-week stay. And during the '60s Patrick McGoohan filmed his TV series 'The Prisoner' here.

In 1981 the hotel mysteriously burned down. 'How?' I ask the friendly Welsh receptionist. 'It was *supposed* to be a cigar butt falling down the inside of a chair.' She shrugs. 'But who knows.'

Hotel Portmeirion Mark Two, *circa* 1988, is still very much a family concern. Robin Llywelyn, the founder's grandson, is MD. His wife Sioned, a fashion designer, has created a highly inventive new interior with fabrics from Kashmir, paintings from Rajasthan, wallpaper from New York and radiators from Harrow School.

Dashing through its portals, we stop short in the dramatic black-and-white marble tiled hall with stone lions guarding the entrance. On top of an enormous fireplace carved from French limestone is a collection of menacing black china cats. A sofa and chairs are covered in red-and-cream striped Oriental fabric.

The staircase leading off is carpeted with an eastern runner held in place with brass rods. The Jaipur bar has fretwork screens and chairs designed to resemble elephants.

There's also a formal library with ornate carved woodwork; an exotic, green-and-gold mirrored sitting room; and a window-seated garden room that overlooks the terrace and the estuary. Vases of fresh flowers stand everywhere.

'You're in room nine,'announces the receptionist. She throws open the door and we blink. Polished antique walnut beds covered in bright Indian blue-patterned material; blue-striped wallpaper; blue-striped curtains; blue-and-white tiled bathroom. A view that encompasses sand, sea and a fig tree. Heaven.

I ask what time we are booked for dinner. Oh. It seems I forgot to book. 'Not to worry,' says the restaurant manager when I phone. 'Come at eight-thirty – it won't be so busy then.'

What next? A swim in the outdoor heated pool perhaps? But we haven't brought our swimming things. We settle instead for a walk along the sandy beach and rocky headland, followed by drinks on the terrace where a stone boat, copied from a wrecked ketch, is moored alongside. Is there anything Sioned hasn't thought of?

At dinner, the guests are dressed up. Outside, the tide fills the darkening estuary. We don't even mind when the food turns out to be OK rather than brilliant and when coffee is distinctly on the weak side – something we remedy at breakfast next morning by asking for a pot of double strength which is brought at once with apologies.

The Hotel Portmeirion has to be one of the most enchanted hotels I've visited and one of the few places I am sorry to leave.

'We have a new head chef who has improved the cooking,' says Robin Llywelyn.

Hotel Portmeirion,

Portmeirion,
Gwynedd LL48 6ET.
Tel: (01766) 770228.
Fax: (01766) 771331.
General Manager: Mrs Menai Williams.
Location: midway between Penrhyndeudraeth and Porthmadog.
Open: all year.
Rooms: 34. 34 twin/double from (£58–£150), all ensuite. Single in double (£48–£140).
Restaurant: open for dinner from 7–9.30pm.
Chef: Craig Hindley. Table d'hôte £25.
Wine List: international, from £9.50.
Children: yes.
Dogs: no.
Smoking: not in dining room.
And Also: heated outdoor pool, tennis, croquet.

THE PEAR TREE AT PURTON

My main impression of The Pear Tree at Purton is that it's very pink. The simple answer could be that the owners like pink, but I think it's more subliminal than that because other P-words keep springing to mind such as pretty, polished, professional, perfect.

I mustn't give the wrong impression. The outside isn't pink at all, it's that nice honeyish colour that's so Cotswoldy. Not that The Pear Tree (once a vicarage) is deep into Cotswold-land – in fact, it's only five miles from industrial Swindon where undoubtedly many of the weekday guests have business to conduct, resplendent in their trouser-pressed suits.

At weekends, though, The Pear Tree drops its prices to attract people like me (well, perhaps not quite like me) in search of a brief respite from town life.

Back to the P-factor. I had an unusual experience when booking into The Pear Tree, which illustrates how much of a seeker-after-perfection this hotel is. I had been asked to fax confirmation; what I did not expect was a Thank-You fax by return and the proprietor's wife looking forward to welcoming me to The Pear Tree at Purton, and assuring me of their best and personal attention at all times. Isn't that nice?

We're greeted by the polite Australian receptionist, who takes us to a room called James Kibblewhite. All The Pear Tree's eighteen rooms are named after characters from the village of Purton. Ours is a runner, though don't ask me where he ran to.

It is a pleasing room – pale pink – with flouncy blinds, pink fringed lamps and personal attention to detail evident everywhere you look: clock, TV guide, in-house movies, twenty-four-hour reception, generous decanter of sherry, sugared almonds, biscuits, bowl of fruit and – yippee! – pink starched napkins for messy fruit-eaters.

Sinking into pink armchairs, we get acquainted with the sherry and contemplate a long, slow bath before dinner in the immaculate bathroom, where you know without trying it that the shower works.

Pristine, pink and panting with anticipation, we wander downstairs. The drawing room is prettily lit with pink lamps and filled with the babble of conversation from punters sitting on pink-ish settees. Now's the chance to meet our suave and unobtrusive host, Francis Young, as he glides to and fro with menus.

In the conservatory restaurant, we find pink cloths and candles. Next to us is a party of what appears to be TV types, while the rest of us are couples having (we hope) romantic dinners. We start with the light celery and duck soup. 'Very ducky,' comments my husband. 'Mmmm,' I agree.

He's not quite so enamoured of his poached breast of chicken in an Irish whiskey, tomato and cream sauce served with a tart of chicken livers: 'Bit too creamy and buttery for my taste.'

'Then you should have asked for it without the sauce, as it suggests on the menu,' is my stern reply, though I rather wish I'd done just that with the baked fillet of Looe halibut served with glazed shallots in a Burgundy sauce. Can we manage pudding? Perhaps not.

After a brilliant night's sleep – comfy everything – we trip down to the perfect breakfast: porridge, with cream and Purton honey, freshly squeezed orange juice and strong coffee. In the hall, we encounter a couple just leaving. 'Lovely hotel,' says the man. 'Really enjoyed it.' Us too, us too.

Paying the bill, I prod Mr Young into conversation. He mentions it's the nanny's weekend off. 'Otherwise you'd have met my wife...' Oh, wish we had. Sssh...guess what? He's wearing a pink shirt.

'Our pinkness was a conscious decision. My wife, Anne, did all the design – although perhaps not the shirt. The room you had is probably the pinkest of them all.'

The Pear Tree at Purton,
Church End,
Purton,
Swindon,
Wiltshire SN5 9ED.
Tel: (01793) 772100.
Fax: (01793) 772369.
Francis and Anne Young.
Location: on the outskirts of the village.
Open: all year.
Rooms: 18. 3 single (£92), 10 double (£92), 3 four-poster (£105), 2 suites (£130), all ensuite. Single in double (£92).
Restaurant: dinner served from 7–9.15 pm.
Chef: Janet Pichel-Juan. Table d'hôte £27.50.
Wine List: subjective – Francis Young likes them all – from £11.
Children: yes.
Dogs: yes, if well behaved.
Smoking: no pipes or cigars in restaurant.
And Also: 6 ground-floor rooms, ramps, disabled WC. Learn to drive a steam locomotive: special weekends throughout the year, please enquire.

*R*edmile, Leicestershire
PEACOCK FARM COUNTRY RESTAURANT AND GUEST HOUSE

Just to confuse things, when searching for Peacock Farm Country Restaurant and Guesthouse, there's another Peacock en route. 'Ah, the one you want is down the road,' explains the Peacock Inn obligingly. Why this proliferation of peacocks? Ask the Dukes of Rutland. Pre-1936, it seems, they were the owners of Peacock Farm and the peacock is part of the Rutland family crest. Nearby is the Rutland family pad, Belvoir Castle.

Peacock Farm itself is in what I call real country, surrounded by fields. In the yard, behind the house, a cat with three legs and baleful stare hops about. We push open the door into a small beamed bar and a fat labrador called Cassy plonks herself at our feet, bestowing pleading glances.

Actually it's food – not labradors – that is really on our minds. Will we get fed? When booking I'd mentioned the possibility of arriving late and had been reassured that food would still be available. Even so, we shouldn't expect miracles at nine o'clock on a wet Friday evening when other, more sensible – and replete – guests have left the dining room.

What a relief, then, to be greeted with a smile and the offer of a steak and to be shown into a room reminiscent of a log cabin, just across the yard, and to be commanded to 'Come back when you're ready.'

In the dining room in the old part of the house, beams criss-cross a low, white-painted ceiling. An impressive collection of long-past-their-sell-by-date farm implements decorates the walls, as do paintings, water colours and framed *bon mots*. Perhaps antique tins are your thing? If so, you'll want to open each one.

Tables in an adjoining room are laid for a celebration dinner the following evening. 'A sixtieth,' confides blonde owner, Nicky Need, bustling about bringing wine, bread and herb butter to accompany our homemade soup followed by steak and salad.

Later, taking a closer look in the next room, we discover a brick wall – too precious to be covered with panelling – together with the fascinating information that in times gone by Peacock Farm was a brick factory where children were employed. 'While demolishing part of this wall to make the restaurant extension, Peter found this brick with a child's imprint,' says a notice. The handprint is very little indeed.

Peter Need, his wife and daughter run Peacock Farm together. Not so long ago, he tells us, it used to be a proper working farm but one day it seemed just too much like hard work. So they began to develop the guest side of the business. 'Even businessmen feel at home here,' they say.

Our log cabin is full of behests: 'Please request any facility you would expect to find in your own home' – and Yves St Laurent and Chanel goodies in the bathroom. Furnishing is idiosyncratic – some would describe the curtains and lampshade as garish – with a tin wind-up alarm clock, but somehow it adds up to a nice atmosphere. A bookcase spills over with a weird collection of books: an English dictionary; the *Book of Worries; Car Spraying Made Easy* and *Child Care Made Simple.*

In the morning we discover there's more to Peacock Farm than we'd thought. The old stables at the back have been turned into a games room, and sunbed and exercise equipment are available. Bicycles are there for borrowing: 'no charge, but contributions to the on-going repair fund welcome'. In the large garden are swings, see-saws and slides – even a swimming pool. The family pony, now getting on, is called Gig, and the pet goat Tuppence.

After breakfast we set out for a walk along the canal bank. Perhaps we'd like to take Cassy, suggests Nicky Need. 'But don't let her go in the canal, will you.'

The dog I'd thought so soppy the night before turns into one of fiendish cunning. Waiting until the very end of the walk, when she thinks no one's looking, she leaps into the sluggish water and flops energetically about. Nicky Need is not surprised. 'But she needn't think she's coming into the house.'

'We are now installing phones in the ensuite rooms,' writes Marjorie Need. 'As for the restaurant, it's going strong, thanks to Nicky's eagle eye.'

My eye, it seems, wasn't so eagle. I got lectured by one reader for getting the address wrong. Peacock Farm is in Leicestershire, he grumbled, suggesting I buy myself a proper county map. Thank you E.E. Snow.

Peacock Farm Country Restaurant and Guest House,

Postal address: Redmile, Nottinghamshire NG13 0GQ.
Tel: (01949) 842475.
Marjorie, Peter and Nicky Need.
Location: follow signs for Belvoir Castle. The farm is half a mile out of Redmile village.
Open: all year.
Rooms: 10. 6 twin/double (£42) ensuite. 4 double with shared facilities (£34). Single in double (£19.50–£30). 2 rooms with wheelchair access.
Restaurant: open for dinner 7.30–8pm.
Chef: Nicky Need. Table d'hôte £12.50–£16.50.
Wine List: comprehensive and affordable, from £6.90.
Children: yes.
Dogs: yes.
Smoking: not in restaurant.
And Also: small bar leading into conservatory, games room, unheated swimming pool. Bicycles available, also dog for walking.

*R*olleston-on-Dove, Staffs
THE BROOKHOUSE HOTEL

Here's a William and Mary Grade II listed hotel furnished with real antiques on the banks of a brook in a village close to Burton on Trent. What do people come to Burton on Trent for, I wonder? Let's go to the Brookhouse Hotel and find out.

In our guidebook, the owner of the Brookhouse is described as 'the welcoming John Westwood'. I don't think I'd be too keen on that if I were Mr Westwood. It raises too many expectations along the lines of, if he's so welcoming, why isn't he here to greet us, pumping our hands and saying Welcome? (Before he gets huffy, this *is* a joke.)

There are compensations, though, in the form of a nice young man in waiter's gear who smiles, fusses, chats, seizes our bags. Taking us upstairs, he conversationally points out a couple lurking in the bar: 'They've been with us for two weeks now. Don't know what they do exactly, but they eat and drink a lot...'

Riveting. Now he whips open the door of a bedroom with a whirlpool bath. Oh. *Very* nice. He explains how to work it: 'Wait till it's nearly full before you turn it on,' he warns. Then he checks out the room in businesslike fashion, leaving us with the impression of a most efficiently run establishment.

Downstairs in the dark-furnished bar, a man brings us menus. There's – er – something – about him. Could this be – ? 'Are you the owner?' I tentatively ask. He is! 'Yes, of course you can have your Dover sole lightly oiled instead of buttered,' says John Westwood welcomingly. 'It'll look a little anaemic though.'

Lighting a cigarette, he settles down for a chat. How does he *know* we don't smoke, I wonder? He tells us that he and his wife have been here for eight years – the chef and most of the staff for much longer. 'During the week we're full of business people,' he says. 'Friday night's our quiet night and, then, on Saturday the honeymooners arrive.' 'Most of them stay one night,' adds Elaine, the cheerful receptionist-cum-barmaid-cum righthand woman.

'Just the one night?'

'Maybe that's all they can afford,' she muses.

At dinner there are crystal glasses, heavy silver cutlery and mahogany antique tables. The whirlpool bath expert is also our waiter. He's pretty good at silver service too.

The asparagus starter is impeccably served. A large fork is first carefully placed on the mat with the plate on top at an angle so the butter runs down – I wish I were a businessman trying to impress an important client. As for the Dover sole, it's perfect – not at all anaemic.

Drinking coffee in the bar area, we listen in to a conversation at the next table. The daughter-in-law seems to be trying to impress her in-laws. Her husband says not a word.

On first inspection, our room is gorgeous; on second, not quite so. It's the little things: the bathroom mirror's so high I need a stool to see in it, except there's no stool; the plastic wash-basin has been damaged by what might have been nail polish remover (and, boy, it shows); and in spite of a generous supply of towels, there's no towel rail to hang any of them on. As for that antique wardrobe, it contains a motley selection of old wire hangers. All of which contrasts oddly with the grandeur of the antique dressing table, the draped bed, the magnificent wood frame sofa.

What *really* disappoints, though, is my brief parting encounter with the woman who settles our bill. 'When I booked, I was told the price included VAT and complimentary newspaper,' I begin. 'Did you order one?' she asks.

'No.'

'I'll have to find you one then – *Telegraph* or *Express*?'

'*Telegraph*, please.' She brings an *Express*. 'But I asked for...' Grimly, she shoots off in another direction and, although I get my *Telegraph* in the end, a goodbye and a 'I hope you enjoyed your stay' would have been more welcome.

'I think you were unkind to Brookhouse Hotel for not having any towel rails,' writes a reader. 'In hotels we have stayed in, towels are changed practically every time we use them – so a rail isn't necessary, is it?'

I must confess to being baffled by this one.

The Brookhouse Hotel,

Brookside,
Rolleston-on-Dove,
Burton on Trent,
Staffordshire DE13 9AA.
Tel: (01283) 814188.
Fax: (01283) 813644.
John Westwood.

Location: between M1 and M6 – ask for directions when booking.
Open: all year.
Rooms: 18. 7 single (£65), 11 twin/double (£85), all ensuite. Single in double (£69). 4 ground-floor rooms.
Restaurant: open for dinner from 7.30–10pm.
Chef: David Bould. A la carte only, average £23.
Wine List: extensive, including some rare wines, from £8.50.
Children: yes, over 12.
Dogs: yes, not in public areas.
Smoking: of course.
And Also: the Derbyshire Dales, the Potteries and Alton Towers. Golf, shooting, trout or coarse fishing can be arranged – please enquire.

DANEHURST HOUSE HOTEL

Through the uncurtained window a table's laid for two. 'We've come to the wrong place!' exclaims my husband. 'This is someone's *house*.'

Oh no. Dashing to the gate, panic subsides as I check that the Danehurst Hotel sign is actually outside *this* house. 'You found us all right then?' asks Angela Godbold, opening her front door.

'We have six rooms,' she tells us, pointing out the guest drawing room on the way upstairs. 'Come down for a drink when you're ready' Then she shows us into a spotless, small ensuite room with a half-tester bed and pink velvet curtains. 'Here's the breakfast menu. May I ask you to fill out your order before you retire?' Breakfast? I haven't had dinner yet.

Looking around, I'm impressed. This room has absolutely everything: shower gel, bubble bath, mending kit, shoe polisher, you name it. Pink bows adorn the lace bedside tablecloths and – how sweet – there's even a lace-trimmed satin nightdress case on the bed. 'Why didn't I bring a lacy nightie to put in it?' 'Because you don't possess one,' says my husband. Clearly the country house hotel has had its day. This is the era of the suburban house hotel.

At least we don't have to dress up here. After all, Mrs G's wearing her casuals. But by the time we've dressed *down*, she's dressed up and now looks the part of the perfect Maîtresse d'.

Downstairs, the drawing room door's propped open with a stuffed frog. Two antimacassared armchairs draped with fringed silk shawls are arranged in front of the gas coal fire and its collection of real and faux copper. Spirit bottles with optics decorate the wall behind the small bar. Are we the only guests? It seems so.

The Maîtresse d' explains her dinner arrangements: set main course with choice of starter and pudding. We discover she's hairdresser turned hotelier and has three boys aged twelve, ten and five. 'You must be extremely busy.' 'I never stop,' she says.

We choose tomato and avocado salad and smoked venison, plus a bottle of Muscadet from the informative and inexpensive wine list. Soon she's back: 'When you're ready, we're ready for you...' she trills.

She certainly knows how to set the scene. The curtains are now cosily drawn; the lighting is soft and, on the table, a gleam of silver coasters and candle holders. She hands us hot rolls in a silver basket. 'I hope the music's not too loud?' she enquires anxiously. 'No,' we say, though actually we're not mad about Sing Something Simple and the Cliff Adams singers. 'A lot of our guests like the heavy classics,' she confides. When we say we quite like them too, she immediately puts on a 'Four Seasons' CD.

Our main course of salmon steaks in a creamy sauce is very good, the vegetables nice and crisp. But remind me to ask for a *half* portion of pudding next time: the meringue nest with raspberries is just too generous. Afterwards we flop in the drawing room with coffee and read all those *Country Living*s and *Hello*s.

In the sunny, added-on conservatory, we breakfast with Beethoven (his Fifth), *The Times* and, guess what, *The Telegraph*. Beside the DIY toaster is a pile of wonderful thick granary bread. The milk jug is covered with an old-fashioned square of muslin trimmed with coloured beads. She's provided butter *and* low-fat spread as well as a choice of marmalade, jam or honey. Suburban house hotel? Yes, but run as meticulously as any top country house hotel.

So I'm not surprised when my husband reports favourably on his scrambled egg. 'I slipped up on one thing, though,' he confesses. 'I used my *fingers* to get the toast out...' Grinning, he holds up a pair of silver tongs.

'I am a regular reader of your weekly hotel reports,' writes Angela Godbold. 'I have always taken notice of your comments and made various amendments to improve our quality and service – always praying you would never come to our house!'

Danehurst House Hotel,

41 Lower Green Road,
Rusthall,
Tunbridge Wells,
Kent TN4 8TW.
Tel/Fax: (01892) 527739.
Angela and Michael Godbold.
Location: village outside Tunbridge Wells.
Open: all year, except last 2 weeks August.
Rooms: 6. 1 twin with shared bathroom (£39.50), 5 twin/double (£49.50–£55), all ensuite. Single in double (£29.50–£45).
Restaurant: open for dinner at 7.30pm.
Chef: Angela Godbold. Table d'hôte £18.95–£22.95.
Wine List: sensibly priced, including local wines, from £5.95.
Children: yes.
Dogs: no.
Smoking: no.
And Also: Tunbridge Wells, the Kent countryside.

$\mathcal{R}$ye, East Sussex
THE OLD VICARAGE HOTEL

The Old Vicarage Hotel in Rye, *circa* 1706, sounds just right. It's small (four rooms), has a history (Henry James once lived here) and all the reverend gentlemen have long since departed.

On the phone Mr Foster, the owner, announces he has a double room costing £70 a night. 'It happens to be a four-poster,' he adds. Oh. Am I supposed to be impressed? Well, I would be – honest – if I could count on this ubiquitous piece of hotel furniture being antique rather than new and shiny.

The Old Vicarage four-poster, though, is neither. It's a four-*curtainer* – four sets of curtains hanging from a rail in all the right places; of posts there's no sign.

But I quibble. The room has a delightfully tranquil ambience with a low window, chairs either side, and a view of steeply sloping gardens over-looking the River Rother and the Romney Marshes.

Ensuite arrangements, however, are unusual. In one corner is the bath with shower curtain, while, opposite, the miniscule loo and wash basin compart-ment is divided off by see-through louvre doors. Squeeze yourself inside and you are confronted with a net-curtained window. This arrangement comes under the heading of very Public Lavatory indeed – especially when the light's on.

Downstairs the mirrored pale blue dining room is elegant – and *full*. There are two sorts of menu – an à la carte and a table d'hôte that appeals because of its simplicity. Mr Foster bustles about taking orders, a somewhat dreamy look on his face. His wife Sarah appears and gives me a goats' cheese salad. 'But I ordered...'

'Have I got it wrong?' she asks, vexed. 'Usually I just know...'

'But how?'

'Well, ladies always prefer healthy food like goat's cheese,' she says some-what mysteriously. This makes me laugh and I dive contentedly into no doubt unhealthy crab and sweetcorn pancake. 'Just the right amount of dressing,' says my husband appreciatively of his salad. Bet my pancake's better.

A couple of Americans sit at the next table. Well, there would be American visitors in Rye, wouldn't there? Wrong. They live round the corner. 'Which side is your room?' he asks.

'At the back.'

'Ah,' he says, 'you want to get up at five and the sun'll be pouring in...the view's just inspirational.'

They leave and I buttonhole Mr Foster. 'Is your wife doing the cooking?'

'Yes,' he says.

'But she looks so calm!'

'Then she must be a very good actress indeed...' he growls.

For my main course I choose grilled lamb cutlets with rosemary, which arrive pinkly cooked minus fatty bits – while my husband has a pork, ginger and orange dish. 'Can't taste the ginger,' he says, 'but it's nice and sharp.'

Afterwards we move our chairs to the window and order coffee. Everyone else has left. What a peaceful room this is. But where's our coffee? 'Mmm,' I say. 'Have you – er – forgotten...?' Nice Mr Foster looks stricken. 'I'm so sorry. I remembered to make it...and then I put it away.'

Now for a brisk walk around Rye's quiet little streets. Back for a spot of TV and so to bed. It doesn't take much lying down to tell that the bed's not brilliant and the pillows on the lumpy side. Yes, we are up at five. Try keeping the sun *out.*

Now after such a delicious and reasonable dinner, we have high hopes of breakfast. The bowls of brown and white sugar, and one of dark chunky marmalade, look promising...and then we get less-than-best OJ, packet butter, hard poached and crumbly scrambled egg. Now I've said it before and I'll say it again. A hotel can do a brilliant evening meal but let the side down at breakfast. If the chef's having time off, I can understand, but here this isn't the case. The Fosters are nice people, though, and their hotel has a warm and welcoming feel.

'Many of the points made have been taken on board and changes made as appropriate. Now thick blind in Loo with View! One v. large lady arrived from Bath clutching your article. Booked for one night and stayed five in the room you had. She obviously liked the view.'

The Old Vicarage Hotel,

East Street,
Rye,
East Sussex TN31 7JY.
Tel/Fax: (01797) 225131.
Mrs Sarah Foster.
Location: in the centre of Rye.
Open: February–December.
Rooms: 4. 2 twin/double, 2 four-poster (£56–£84), all ensuite. Single in double (as above).
Restaurant: open for dinner 6.45–9pm.
Chef: Sarah Foster. Table d'hôte £12.95.
Wine List: mainly European, some Australian, from £9.15.
Children: yes.
Dogs: yes.
Smoking: if you wish.
And Also: antique and coffee shops, medieval town walk, the Cathedral of the Marsh, bird watching.

St Margaret's at Cliffe, Kent
WALLETT'S COURT

Wallett's Court near Dover – handy for the ferry – has a 'special atmosphere', or so it says in its brochure. There's also a quote from a chap called Sir John Neale: 'The Elizabethans indulged in pleasures as if they were to die tomorrow, and built as if they were to live forever.' I'll enlighten you. This 'aptly describes the historic house and the experience of staying and dining there.'

The things hoteliers say. But it's welcome low-key stuff all the same. Many hotels cannot resist serving up extravagant verbiage and then, when you get there, they are empty – though maybe one should not judge them during the skint-after-Christmas period.

But Wallett's Court is far from empty. No apologetic: 'Well, it's our quiet time you know...' January is bustin' out all over in the drawing room with family parties and lovey-dovey couples. Over by the inglenook fireplace a Prince Charles lookalike holds forth in an accent that's not *quite* Royal while, sunk into a velvet chair by the gleaming Steinway, an elderly gentleman harrumphs at the pretty waitress in navy-and-white coin-dotted blouse: 'Scotch and no water please.'

Wallett's Court is a charming old Kent manor house with rough brick walls, beams, stripped doors, gnarled banisters and uneven stairs. Our room has an antique wooden bed covered with a patterned blanket and a pair of armchairs in front of the brick fireplace for watching television. Even better, the warmth hits you, none of this 'We've only just turned the heating on' lark.

In the dining room, as elsewhere, the lighting is also low-key. Chef/proprietor Chris Oakley serves a gourmet dinner on Saturday nights and everyone is dressed up. There's a sense of occasion but no pomposity. A couple of tables even have second sittings.

Having perused Mr Oakley's bearded photograph and credentials that hang in the drawing room, we now know that he used to work with the Roux Brothers. His five-course dinner at £25 is a most pleasant experience and includes a choice of starters, followed by a slice of Hebridean salmon in a cucumber and basil sauce, with Orchard sorbet, tasting of apple, squeezed in before a choice of main courses. Here, breast of Barbary duck accompanied by a caramelized orange and port wine sauce is top of the pops. Puddings arrive on a tray and are described by rote – always a faintly embarrassing experience – by the coin-dotted waitress.

Early next morning – well before eight – I peer out of the window at the peaceful manicured garden and church opposite. Cars are pulling up and there's a soothing sight of elderly ladies hurrying in for a good pray.

There are quite a few people around for breakfast, served by Mrs Oakley. A Canadian declares in a loud voice he is 'enamoured by this place' though I wouldn't be enamoured if *I* were his girlfriend and he beat *me* to the best seat and sat himself down first.

Now we pump Mrs Oakley for a few relevant details as she brings scrambled egg and bacon and good strong coffee. 'Didn't know you had another dining room?'

'Oh, we use that when we have a big party, then they can all make as much noise as they like.' Through the window we spot the rotund Mr Oakley – he couldn't be anything other than a chef – returning from a game of tennis. 'He always plays on Sundays – even in the snow. Then they use yellow balls...'

And has Wallett's Court *really* got a special atmosphere? Oh yes. Lovely house, good food, nice people. Any criticisms? We-e-ll ...apart from the usual recalcitrant shower, there's a personal thing. I'm allergic to brass rubbings and cute little lace sachets hanging in unexpected places. Other people may love them.

'Since your visit,' writes Chris Oakley, 'we have built a large conservatory looking out across the fields, for use as breakfast room, restaurant overspill, afternoon tea and coffee during the summer.'

Wallett's Court,

St Margarets at Cliffe,
Dover,
Kent CT15 6EW.
Tel: (01304) 852424.
Fax: (01304) 853430.
Chris and Lea Oakley.
Location: 5 minutes from Dover docks.
Open: all year except Christmas/New Year.
Rooms: 11. 9 twin/double (£50–£70), 2 family rooms (£60–£80), all ensuite. Single in double (£40–£60). 2 ground-floor rooms.
Restaurant: open for dinner from 7–9pm.
Chef: Christopher Oakley. Table d'hôte £20–£25.
Wine List: mainly French, also Australian and English, from £8.75.
Children: yes.
Dogs: no.
Smoking: not in dining room.
And Also: tennis courts. at hotel Dover Castle nearby.

Salisbury, Wiltshire
THE NEW INN & OLD HOUSE RESTAURANT

When I telephone to book a room at the New Inn, they neglect to mention the riveting fact we're about to set foot in Britain's Healthiest Pub.

Elucidation comes upon arrival at this timbered 15th-century building in the middle of town. The historic epistle is carelessly chalked on a blackboard parked on the pavement: 'Treat Your Partner, Family & Friends To The Rare & Unique Experience Of Enjoying Healthy Eating And Drinking In A Healthy Atmosphere Completely Smoke Free.'

'Blimey' is my startled reaction. 'I've never been in a pub without smoke. Can't imagine what it will be like.'

'Different,' says my husband, non-smoker and man of few if pithy words.

In we go. Here's a smiling woman emerging from behind her smoke-free bar dressed exotically in a flowing garment, Tibetan lion dog at her heels. She, it transpires, is Maggie Spicer. 'Your dog's got that just-groomed look,' we comment. 'No, no, she *needs* grooming.'

Maggie takes us out into the street again and into the next-door building. The New Inn consists of three buildings: the building with rooms; the building with pub; the building with Old House restaurant. 'February 1994 will be the fifth anniversary of our smoke-free policy,' Maggie mentions *en passant.*

Climbing up a winding staircase, we arrive in a room with a view. Through uncurtained windows, the floodlit Salisbury Cathedral appears so close you could almost reach out and touch. 'It looks like a stage set.'

'But it's *real.*' says Maggie.

We admire the craftsman-made four-poster with pretty drapes. None of your knocked-up rubbish in *this* pretty attic room. But soon we're discovering how annoying it is that the basin and vanitory unit are in the bedroom rather than bathroom. I want a bath. In I get. Oh. Where's the soap? In the other room, silly. Towel? Ditto. Bath bubbles? They've forgotten all about *those.* If only we were a more organized couple...

Now we can't wait to get downstairs. How many stylishly decorated traditional bars do you find? This is one. Even the pub carpet's pleasing. There is a fire, attractive covers on the oak pews and the lighting's just right.

Alas, we can't hang around – we've an appointment in a nearby village. 'When's the latest we can eat?' we ask. 'As long as you're back by ten,' says proprietor John, adding the restaurant's closed 'because it's January. Why not give us your order now,' he suggests. 'If you want trout, I'll dangle my rod...' *Such* an obliging man.

No, no, we can't send him out fishing this time of night. Dashing back late, we tuck into huge platters of pheasant casserole and duck breast with honey, and drink a Petit Chablis 'with a lovely Chardonnay nose'. 'I'm *so* glad I didn't order a starter,' I mutter. 'This is definitely real pheasant – here's a bit of lead shot,' replies my husband.

Across the room a group of young girl musicians, complete with instruments larger than they are, sip their drinks. Les, the barman, offers us apple pie with double cream. 'Would you like ice-cream as well?'

'Oh *no* – just cream.' All good filling pub grub.

The lighting in the bedroom isn't conducive to harmony. I lose out over the one bedside light, but smile to myself when he's forced to hold it like a torch in order to read.

Looking out next morning, how we wish it was summer and we could breakfast in the garden. Instead, John Spicer leads us to a small bar at the back where he plies us with coffee and conversation. There's something *very* nice about being in a pub with no smoke.

'We're also geared towards healthy eating,' says John Spicer. 'Even if it's only fish and chips, it won't be running with grease.'

The New Inn and Old House Restaurant,

41–49 New Street,
Salisbury,
Wiltshire SP1 2PH.
Tel: (01722) 327679.
John and Maggie Spicer & Sons.
Location: in the centre of city.
Open: all year.
Rooms: 6. 6 double (£45–£65), 3 ensuite. Single in double (£25–£35).
Restaurant: open for dinner from 7–9.30pm, bar meals available.
Chef: John Spicer. A la carte, average £12.
Wine List: 30 wines including good Burgundies and Chablis, from £6.95.
Children: yes.
Dogs: yes.
Smoking: good heavens no.
And Also: delightful garden.

THE PHEASANT

Here's a letter from a Somerset reader: 'I don't know much about this establishment...' it begins. Now comes the cryptic bit: 'but I think the Proprietor would definitely give you scope for your particular brand of journalism. Happy New Year.'

To you too, Mr S————. I telephone The Pheasant. A chummy Italian voice informs me 'e's zo, *zo* sorry, zey are fully booked. Late August I try again. This time zey 'ava very nice room. 'We 'ava very good restaurant too.'

Shooting down to Somerset on a fine Friday night, I assume The Pheasant to be a wee country inn. No, no, no. We find an immaculate 17th-century converted stone farmhouse surrounded by a lovingly tended, landscaped garden. On the terrace outside are smart pots of flowers and umbrella-ed tables – now I twig why our room costs £70. The welcoming girl at reception adds that we've got a four-poster: 'It's beautiful,' she says reverently.

And it *is:* the room's small, but with red-upholstered armchairs; elegant polished wood furniture; a green-painted butler's tray for tea and coffee things; designer fabrics; brass bathroom fittings. Are we in Knightsbridge?

Nipping out for a pre-dinner walk, we get into conversation with the proprietor's English wife who's wielding a hose. 'We've been here thirteen years,' she says. 'It's taken us ten to train our suppliers. Now they know that when we specify 8oz fillet steaks, they

must all be *exactly* the same, not some thick, some thin...'

In the cosy beamed bar we meet Ze Proprietor Himself, resplendent in blue-and-red striped suit with yellow silk hanky tucked in his breast pocket. 'Of course I've got Punt e Mes,' he growls. 'It ees my favoureet drink. You want it like in Italy?'

'Of course,' says my husband, who's never got over a weekend in Rome. 'Very good,' he pronounces happily.

We've already peeped into the dining room – intimate's the word – and noted the pink candles, mahogany tables, upholstered chairs and window seats. Now we're handed traditional-style Italian menus – ie very long – to pore over.

For starters, I choose smoked salmon and my husband an aubergine and mozzarella dish. 'Hot and herby,' he says, smacking his lips. But why has he picked Provençal prawns and rice for his main course when it's French, not Italian? 'Testing, testing,' he replies, frowning over what he considers a 'rather pedestrian sauce'. Alas, my rack of lamb, prettily presented with frilly crowns, is too fatty for my taste. I *hate* leaving food. Maybe we should have stuck to pasta.

Across the room a noisy group of Midlanders is sizing up the homemade-pudding trolley: coffee and walnut meringue; fresh strawberries; pineapple cheesecake; pear and chocolate gateau; cherry, chocolate and something or other. The waitress pauses for breath.

'Could you repeat all that?' says one wag and they all fall about.

We fall about over the strong Italian coffee, accompanied by Amaretti biscuits: 'Needs a knife and fork, just as it should be,' observes my husband. What's more, he *sleeps* instead of pacing about half the night – must be the cotton sheets, merino wool blanket and sink-into pillows.

Now, as regular readers may know, this man's got a degree in scrambled egg. Next morning's verdict? 'Hmmm...it's like egg custard.' Oh dear.

Pinging the bell to settle up, our sunny *signor* emerges. He shows us his sparkling kitchen – 'My kitchen is alwayz open' – and reveals how he used to be in the London hotel business: 'Zen one day I thought how wonderful not to have a boss any more, and came down here. *Zen* I discover ze bank manager, ze VAT man...and my wife.'

'We now ask how clients like their scrambled eggs!' chuckles Edmondo Paolini, who tells me his restaurant has changed to peach-bloom table cloths and napkins to 'give additional elegance'.

The Pheasant,
Water Street,
Seavington St Mary,
Ilminster,
Somerset TA19 0QH.
Tel: (01460) 240502.
Fax: (01460) 242388.
Edmondo and Jacqueline Paolini.
Location: nr Ilminster.
Open: all year.
Rooms: 8. 8 twin/double (£70), all ensuite. Single in double (£50).
Restaurant: open for dinner from 7.30–9.30pm.
Chef: Edmondo Paolini. Large à la carte, average £23.
Wine List: large selection of Italian wines supplied by Enotria Wine, from £6.95.
Children: yes.
Dogs: yes.
Smoking: limited.
And Also: the landscaped Pheasant gardens tended by Mrs Paolini, the Fleet Air Arm Museum at Yeovilton, Cricket St Thomas Wild Life Park, stately homes.

BOWLISH HOUSE

The owner of Bowlish House greets us warmly. 'You must be the Browns.'

So friendly is Mr Bob Morley we feel we ought to own up right away to being The Browns – after all, no hotelier likes mixing up the guests' names. 'Er – actually – we're not the Browns,' we admit apologetically at last. He seems amazed. 'Forgive me. Today is turning into a bit of a disaster...' he adds somewhat mysteriously.

It transpires there have been cancellations, including the Browns. Well, I shall stick my neck out at once and say I bet the Browns didn't have half as good a dinner as we did, *or* as large a bath, *or* a loo with a view of the pub.

Just as it dawns on us that the pub has an equally good view of the Bowlish House loo, Mr Morley has carried our bags upstairs and is demonstrating how the bathroom shutters work. 'Some people think they're just for decoration,' he says. Gosh. How thick 'some people' are.

Bowlish House is a classic Grade II house built in the mid 1700s complete with Palladian frontage. To denote its age and grace, it has lovely creaky floors and *of course* the shutters work.

Our bedroom is comfortable, homely even, and is a pleasing room to be in. There are cushioned window seats, a dark chest of drawers and wardrobe, quilted headboard, bedside lights and not just one but *two* clocks. Brilliant. It's still a mystery to me why so few hotel rooms have clocks. Nothing is worse than waking in the wee small

hours and wondering whether it's two, three or even four o'clock.

I also like the fact that this room is generously equipped with large bath towels and plenty of bath bubbles, tissues etc. Not that one uses all of these things – it is the attitude that counts.

Swanning forth later, we pause to admire the decorative window halfway down the wood-panelled staircase. Stepping across the polished flagstoned hall we find a snug bar furnished with pink armchairs and Mr Morley.

He waves his arm in welcome. 'What a nice room,' we say, admiring the section of Mendip lead drainpipe on the mantelpiece. 'It carries the crest of the original owners,' Mr Morley beams. 'We specialize in decayed elegance here.' He hands us nuts, olives and a menu.

The dining room leads out into a conservatory. Family portraits – not Mr Morley's family – gaze down at the white-clothed tables and gleaming silver candlesticks. Although only we and one other couple are dining, we notice that candles on all tables have been lit. A nice touch. 'More cosy,' declares Mr Morley.

The food – by Linda Morley – is delicious. For example: lettuce, apple and mint soup and 'little parcels' of shredded vegetables with sweet and sour sauce. 'That sauce *certainly* didn't come from a bottle,' exclaims my husband. To follow, rack of lamb – pink and perfect – and chicken with a

Provençal sauce. In addition to the separate dishes of crisply cooked vegetables, we are brought a bowl of dauphinoise potato. What a treat.

From the four choices of both red and white house wine, all at £7.50 and all from different countries, we choose an Australian Semillion Chardonnay. Here's to The Browns. For once there's no muzak but we both agree that the right kind of music would add to – not detract from – the atmosphere.

Next morning we discover that Mr Morley is a Yorkshireman – 'midway between Dewsbury and Wakefield' – and that breakfast is treated as reverently as dinner. A cooked breakfast costs £3.50 extra, but who needs bacon and eggs when there's freshly squeezed orange juice, cereal, muesli, yoghurt, toast – and just-cooked muffins. Why muffins? 'We search around for interesting things to give our guests,' explains our dedicated host. 'Another weekend you might get drop scones instead...' Those Browns don't know what they missed.

'Everyone keeps booking in under the name of Brown,' grumbles Bob Morley. Cheering up, he adds: 'Now that we know you, please visit again – other people's reminiscences about memorable meals and hotels are always of interest. You've probably guessed that when not working, our hobby is eating out!'

Bowlish House,

Wells Road,
Shepton Mallet,
Somerset BA4 5JD.
Tel: (01749) 342022.
Bob and Linda Morley.
Location: on the outskirts of town.
Open: all year.
Rooms: 3. 3 twin/double (£48), all ensuite. Single in double (£48).
Restaurant: open for dinner 7–9.30pm.
Chef: Linda Morley. Table d'hôte, £22.50. Cooked breakfast £3.50.
Wine List: carefully chosen, including 10 *Good Food Guide*-recommended house wines, from £8.25.
Children: yes.
Dogs: yes (bedroom only).
Smoking: discouraged in restaurant.
And Also: Wells, Cheddar Gorge, Longleat, Bath are no more than a 30-minute drive away.

The entrance hall of the Crown Hotel in Southwold has a wooden floor undesecrated by rugs, an old-fashioned radiator, chunky iron umbrella stand and swoosh of dried flowers. It's not a bit like the hall of a proper hotel – but, then, the Crown is a cross between hotel and pub.

Collapsing at the reception desk, late, hungry and fed-up with driving – Suffolk's always further than I remember – I'm warmly greeted by a girl who, at my mere ping on the bell, has executed the sort of graceful sprint in my direction that demands applause.

'Is the hotel full?' I ask, remembering the earnest request when booking that I should be sure to confirm on the day itself. 'Yes, we're full every weekend, even during the winter,' she replies proudly.

Upstairs we march, right to the top, chatting all the way. My room is a pleasant little abode, nothing too fancy, with two pink Indian cotton-bedspreaded beds and a bathroom with a bidet. For all this I'm being charged £48, instead of £58 if there'd been two of us. I rather like being on my own and choosing the best bed.

Except it's only minutes before I'm shooting downstairs to the bar where the babble is inviting, the clientele largely jean-clad and the walls a cheerful crackle-glazed yellow. Sitting myself down at one of the long wooden tables, I savour the scene and am handed a menu that seems particularly suitable for a lone female, or lone anyone come to that, because it includes a large recommended 'wine by the glass' selection. Perhaps I shouldn't be surprised – The Crown does, after all, belong to Adnams, brewers and wine merchants. Anyway, what a good wheeze. 'A glass of the rosé (1990 Chateau Thieuley, Bordeaux Clairet, "dry but full of flavour") please...'

Soon I'm being beckoned into the equally unpretentious restaurant next door. The world and his best friend are here tonight. At the next table (I speculate) is a group that's got to be mother, father, son and daughter-in-law. On my other side a couple gaze passionately into each other's eyes. Alarmed, I order a cooling starter – Galia melon filled with champagne sorbet – followed by a steamed fillet of turbot Andalusian (whatever that means) and a glass of 1984 Mount Pleasant, Elizabeth Semillion, to accompany it.

Well. You don't get bored at The Crown. 'Had a good snort, dear?' asks the father figure as his lady wife returns from a protracted visit to the loo. *Really.* But my giggle changes to disbelief when the Jeffrey Archer lookalike across the room suddenly dons a pair of those half-moon specs so favoured by the Krug-quaffing Lord.

The waitress – Sue – has a lovely cackle and is very nice to me. 'We're so full we've even put two breakfasts in the bar tomorrow,' she confides. 'But I've put you at the table in the window. It's nice for "Ones" to look out...' Thanking her, I ask if they get many 'Ones'. 'We had five last week.

'Course, most of them are men. They've got business in Lowestoft, but much prefer to stay here.'

I think I'd describe dinner as upmarket pub grub uplifted by the carefully chosen wines. But breakfast is *brilliant:* a rare glass of freshly squeezed OJ, lots of strong coffee and, if I were starving (I'm not), buckwheat pancakes with maple syrup or a Crown kipper.

But I forget to extol the merits of my plain little room which, at first glance, had seemed a mite, well, plain but definitely grew on me when I discovered the radiator threw out comforting blasts of heat, that the bath towels were enormous and the bed was extremely comfy. Dear me. I think I'm in danger of being accused of having written a rave review.

'Your review of The Crown has given great pleasure to the staff, especially Sue, your waitress,' writes Simon Loftus, boss of Adnams. 'I am delighted because you didn't, as others have done, raise expectations which we are unable to fulfil or damn us for shortcomings which might be questioned at The Savoy but not at an informal pub with rooms in Southwold!'

I also got this curious missive, presumably from someone who was staying at the time: 'Were you,' he asks, 'the slightly overwarm large lady in the far corner of the dining room sniffing at her glass of rosé or were you the Twiggy figure enjoying her sorbet in the other corner? Actually I couldn't care less, so long as you continue to entertain me.'

The Crown Hotel,
90 High Street,
Southwold,
Suffolk IP18 6DP.
Tel: (01502) 722275.
Fax: (01502) 724222.
Adnam & Co Plc.
Location: in the centre of town.
Open: all year, except 1st week January.
Rooms: 12. 2 single (£38), 9 twin/double (7 ensuite, 2 with private bathroom) (£58), 1 family room ensuite (£82). Single in double (£48).
Restaurant: open for dinner at 7.30–9.30pm.
Chef: Andrew Mulliss. Table d'hôte £17.25–£19.25.
Wine List: around 300 wines from Adnams Wine Merchants, from £6.95, 20 wines by the glass.
Children: yes.
Dogs: no.
Smoking: not in restaurant.
And Also: fishing, golf, tennis, the sea.

How nice to find an establishment that isn't flaunting this thing called a brochure. Brochures tell you how marvellous a place is when half the time it's not. Brochures hoick up the prices. Brochures list how many bedrooms, the names of each one and, more predictably, how hard the owners have worked to transform their 17th-century wreck into the wonderful, welcoming haven from the stresses of the '90s it is today.

At the ancient Angel Inn, there are no such frills – simply a manager who modestly describes himself as 'general factotum'. He's also proud Dad and the Angel his baby. Getting out the album of 'childhood' photographs, he launches into the story of his Angel in all its various stages of babyhood: 'There was a wall here, but we knocked it down. See that door over there, the floors were so uneven that...' And when asked the ten-dollar question: 'Have you a brochure?' he replies with a smile and a poem: 'When looking back on your stay at The Angel, it's the memories in your head that are the brochure...' There no reply to *that*.

The Angel Inn hotel and restaurant stands on a crossroads in a village on the borders of Suffolk and Essex. Upon our arrival, we're jetted up the narrow staircase – no signing in or being asked for deposits or credit cards – that leads onto a gallery overlooking a raftered, high-ceilinged dining room with brick walls, old-style stove and tables with pink cloths and carnations on them. I register how smart The Angel Inn is.

Our tiny room, unlike some brochured and grander places, avoids the naff with cobalt blue paintwork, lacy bedspread and a whet-your-appetite menu tucked thoughtfully into a green folder on the bedside table.

Food is a feature of The Angel. People drive in from neighbouring villages dressed up for a Saturday night out. They expect the works. They can eat in the bar or in the restaurant. Both are packed. One girl, part of a family party, is dressed in black-and-white houndstooth jacket and black bowler hat as she stuffs her face.

We sip our drinks and wait for the menu. Are they too busy to notice us? At 9pm we go into the dining room – not, alas, the lovely high-ceilinged one, but the room next door where we sit by the window and watch the headlamps coming round the corner.

Food is on the tricksy dicksy side, but well and professionally done judging by the dishes that keep arriving at other tables. We say no to things like 'quails' eggs presented on a nest of Greek katifi pastry upon a bed of salad leaf with a feta cheese and light herb mayonnaise' and choose the simpler things of life like grilled fish and medium-rare steak. Appetizers garnished with parsley are laid in front of us – very nice too – though the vegetables that accompany our fish and well-done steak are swimming in butter.

Pudding time produces a somewhat unusual method of presentation with model puddings on a tray. When the clingfilm is lifted, the merits of each pansy-decorated confection is pointed out. Pansies have such friendly faces, I can't bear to eat mine.

Meanwhile our friend, the manager, regales us with further Angel stories. 'I came here five years ago to help out,' he says, 'and I'm still here...'

Breakfast is not nearly as polished a performance as dinner. There are no spoons laid on any of the tables – ever eaten Weetabix with a teaspoon? – and a pretty girl in flowing black clothes exudes an air of panic as she hurtles from table to table. The one small bowl of sugar sits on a side table and the English, being so English, resignedly get up, borrow it and return it. What a farce. The whole arrangement, or lack of it, cries out for a help-yourself sideboard crammed with cereal, fruit, juices and milk. Having said that, the pristine Angel Inn pleases many people (including me) and the manager is better value than any brochure.

'Hopefully we've improved the breakfast service!' reports The Angel Inn.

The Angel Inn,

Stoke by Nayland
Suffolk CO6 4SA.
Tel: (01206) 263245.
Fax: (01206) 37324.
P.G. Smith and Richard E. Wright.
Location: halfway between Colchester and Sudbury.
Open: all year except Christmas and Boxing Day.
Rooms: 6. 6 twin/double (£57.50), all ensuite. Single in double (£44).
Restaurant: open for dinner from 6.30–9pm.
Chef: Mark Johnson. Large à la carte menu, average £15.50.
Wine List: international, from £7.30.
Children: yes, over 8.
Dogs: no.
Smoking: feel free.
And Also: fishing, golf, the villages of Essex and Suffolk.

Strachur, Argyll
CREGGANS INN

Arriving at Creggans Inn around six, we're asked to wait 'a wee while'. The receptionist, it seems, is 'just performing the evening ceremony of lowering the flag of St Andrew'. The *what?* We belt across the road to investigate. Ah. Now all's clear. The flagpole on the banks of Loch Fyne bears the inscription: 'Mary, Queen of Scots landed here.' They're keen on history – and flags – in Argyll.

And in the conservatory reception area, we're reminded that Creggans is owned by Sir Fitzroy and Lady Maclean: a pile of His (history) and Hers (cookery) books sits on the table. 'I'll take ye to your room,' says the versatile receptionist.

'Will we meet Sir Fitzroy later?'

'Och, no,' she says. 'He's in Bosnia.'

Our freshly painted room has vast, enchanted views of loch and hills. Dutifully perusing the bumph instead, I get the drift of Creggans in one word: *friendliness.* 'We like our guests to meet before dinner to discuss their day over a drink in one of our bars...' it says.

Try and stop us. After hot baths – no problems in this no-nonsense but efficient bathroom – we sally downstairs. Should I, in the interests of research, try a wee dram of malt? But no: I don't fancy whisky. 'Campari and orange, please,' and how nice that the barman goes to such trouble to find a fresh orange slice to accompany it.

The bar is now full: over there is a young man in a wheelchair and his attentive female companion; a couple of elderly ladies: 'Mother and daughter,' I decide. And apart from the woman – from Wiltshire, at a guess – and her two well-brought-up daughters, there are only soft Scottish voices to be heard.

Studying the menu, yes, it *is,* as promised, different. 'Lady Maclean has collected literally thousands of recipes from all over the world and, though this influences our cuisine, what Creggans aims at is simple food perfectly cooked.' My sentiments too.

In the brochure, the restaurant is described as Victorian and, although decorated with rose wallpaper and red velvet curtains, to me, it has an old-fashioned tearoom air. We're shown to a corner table and watch the two tartan-waistcoated waitresses dashing about. We've ordered two half bottles of wine: one red, one white – everyone's happy. Mmmm. I haven't eaten all day and am *hungry.*

Just as well. 'Can this really be a starter?' I gasp as the seafood pancake is put before me. Not only *is* it, but I manage it all. 'This is a wonderfully strongly flavoured sauce,' I say, mopping up what's left with bread.

Now if my starter's generous, my husband nearly faints at the sight of his huge plateful of sirloin of beef. 'Carnivore,' I mutter. 'I know,' he says, looking embarrassed. Adopting a manful air, he wolfs the lot. Trolley puddings are made in the kitchen and are creamy and rich.

Oh dear, how embarrassing, I manage to knock my glass of Gerwürztraminer into a bowl of brown sugar. 'I'm very sorry,' I confess to the nice head waiter. 'I suppose the chef could make it into a pudding,' he says, regarding it doubtfully.

In *usual* places, you get chocolates with your coffee. Here, it's fudge and my husband pinches most of it. 'Not good for you,' is his response.

We're woken early by someone in the room above. As befits an old inn, there are creaky floors you see. Never mind, let's go for a walk in readiness for real Highland porridge served in wooden bowls with a horn spoon. '*Now* I know why I didn't have porridge,' says the girl at the next table, grinning. No porridge for me either, I wimpishly opt for Lady Maclean's prunes soaked in China tea and very good they are too.

Says chef/manager Jean-Pierre Puech: 'The day your article came out, the pastry chef made a hot banana pudding with demerara sugar on top. Said one guest: "Oh, I suppose that's the leftover from the Gerwürztraminer of Paddy Burt."'

Creggans Inn,

Strachur,
Argyll PA27 8BX.
Tel: (0136986) 279.
Fax: (0136986) 637.
Sir Fitzroy and Lady Maclean.
Location: on the A815 at Strachur.
Open: all year.
Rooms: 21. 4 single (£49.50), 17 twin/double (£98), most ensuite. Single in double (as above). 1 ground-floor room.
Restaurant: open for dinner 7–9pm.
Chef/Manager: Jean-Pierre Puech. Table d'hôte £18.50.
Wine List: award-winning, from £10.95.
Children: yes.
Dogs: yes.
Smoking: not in restaurant.
And Also: sea and freshwater loch fishing, bathing from hotel beach, pony trekking, golf and bowling, private woodland walk.

Swaffham, Norfolk
STRATTONS HOTEL

A reader wrote suggesting that I should visit Strattons. 'The atmosphere's unique,' she says.

Uniqueness being rare, I cautiously get on the phone and suss out the merits of the various rooms with owner Mr Scott. These have names like The Venetian, The Louis, The Rosewood Room – and *all*, according to Mr Scott, are unique. Eventually I book the Cottage Suite, a room that won't object to my calling it an attic.

But unique? Let's begin at the beginning. To find Stratton House, we drive down a clearly signposted lane off the marketplace, just wide enough to take a car. Suddenly, here we are, in an unexpected country setting with a lawn, a circular gravelled driveway, ancient trees and a view of the church.

The house itself is Grade II Queen Anne with a Victorian addition. As we enter the front door via stone steps flanked with iron railings, we can see red candles flickering on dining tables in the semi-basement area known, in days gone by, as The Rustic. Now it's The Rustic Restaurant.

To those who like cats, the next thing that appeals is the two cosy baskets sitting side by side in the hall. Unoccupied of course – their owners prefer the drawing room armchairs. Then there's Mr Scott himself. He's pretty unique. 'Hi, I'm Les,' he grins, grabbing our bags and personally delivering them and us to the attic room. Suddenly he looks worried. 'You can have another room if you prefer,' he offers. 'This one hasn't a bath, only a shower...'

'Only a shower' or not, *I* think the Cottage Suite is ace – though, being curious, we accept his offer to inspect a couple of the other available rooms. We find they are elegantly furnished with a designer's touch and wonderful antique beds – where *did* they find them? – and furniture. The sort of rooms, in fact, that make me want to go home and throw everything out.

Downstairs, there's a drawing room with pine double doors that interconnect with a similar room. Both have Chinese carpets, pine floorboards and lots of comfortable chairs and sofas. The windows are decked out in lace and flowery curtains. Pottery cats abound, peeping at you from bookcase, mantelpiece and hall. There are paintings and a photograph of the Scotts' very modern young daughter in an antique frame. Les brings us the drinks we've ordered – 'I'm no barman,' he quips – and my goodness they're stiff. He tells us that his wife Vanessa supervises the kitchen and brings us menus. 'Everything is *freshly cooked*,' he assures us.

We find the menu a mite over-elaborate, with not enough variation between the various dishes. What's more, the food takes a while to arrive and, once again, we're reminded this is because everything is 'freshly cooked'. The crunch comes when my husband chooses a banana and rum concoction for pudding and the waitress warns: 'It might take a few minutes because...'

'It's *freshly* cooked,' says my husband, dead on cue.

Waking up in the Cottage Suite takes me back to childhood and the poem I learned at school: 'I remember, I remember, the house where I was born. The little window where the sun came peeping in at morn.' Except this room has more going for it than most childhood rooms, with its tray for tea, jug of milk with clingfilm on top, pretty flowered bedcovers, brass and iron beds, pink-washed walls and raftered sloping ceiling.

Next morning we discover the Scotts' secret – they met as art students. Breakfast *certainly* resembles a still life: crisp white damask cloth, a jug of red tulips, bowls of butter and three different homemade preserves. The care and attention the Scotts lavish on their guests is laudable. There may, however, be some people who find this unique blend of elegant surroundings and informality difficult to reconcile.

When this piece appeared, I received an oh-my-God letter from Vanessa. 'You didn't mention it, but what did you think of the Siamese cat that helped itself to the remains of the cream jug and the little girl who gravely explained: 'Daddy would kick him up the bum if he knew.'?' It made our stay, Vanessa!

'My food's no longer elaborate,' she says. 'My philosophy is to use all the wonderful food produced around us: fish, beef, pork, lamb, poultry; stone-ground flour for our oatcakes, pastries and breads; vegetables and herbs from my father's garden.'

Strattons Hotel,

4 Ash Close,
Swaffham,
Norfolk PE37 7NH.
Tel/Fax: (01760) 723845.
Les and Vanessa Scott
Location: just off the marketplace, behind shops.
Open: all year.
Bedchambers: 7. Antique beds, modern mattresses. 1 single (£52), 5 twin/double (£70–£80), 1 family room (£80), all ensuite. Single in double (£53–£60).
Restaurant: open for dinner from 7pm.
Chef: Vanessa Scott. Table d'hôte £22.50.
Wine List: handwritten, illustrated, innovative, from £8.
Children: yes.
Dogs: yes.
Smoking: in one half of drawing room only.
And Also: the lonely Norfolk coastline, villages, antique shops.

$\mathcal{T}$*enterden, Kent*
LITTLE SILVER COUNTRY HOTEL

Now here's an amazing place. The cutely named Little Silver Country Hotel is the 'baby' of two ladies – Dorothy Lawson and Rosemary Frith – who, if you ask (and even if you don't) will be delighted to go into blow-by-blow detail about the hard labour involved in the creation of their dream country hotel.

Unusually, on this occasion, I am staying as guest of the English Tourist Board along with a group of other journalists. Before dinner, we do the obligatory tour of the bedrooms. 'This one's for you; this for you...' And, how embarrassing, when we reach the biggest room, the one with the four-poster and the jacuzzi: 'This one's for you,' says Rosemary, or is it Dorothy, pointing in *my* direction.

But, as I soon discover, these two indefatigable ladies leave nothing to chance. The Adventures of Dorothy and Rosemary – all three single-space pages of them – are neatly tucked into a folder on the table in my plush room and are perhaps intended as light bedside reading.

In 1986, I read, these nursery school teachers, both widows, fell in love with this neglected Tudor house *circa* 1935. 'We wanted a country house hotel which would be special. As soon as we saw Little Silver, we knew it was for us,' says Rosemary or is it Dorothy.

When they arrived, they say, the place was gloomy, dark, dull, dank, dreary, desolate. The building works that ensued are lovingly recorded. Walls were knocked down, loos

removed, the garage turned into the dining room, a conservatory and new wing added. And in 1990, the *pièce de résistance* was completed: a reception and conference room called Kent Hall designed to resemble an oasthouse. 'We are fully booked on Saturdays for weddings for the next eighteen months,' they say proudly.

The result of their Herculean endeavours is a superbly comfortable and homely hotel where absolutely everything has been thought of and more besides. There are facilities for disabled guests too: 'In fact, all special needs are catered for,' chorus these two awe-inspiring ex-nursery school teachers

Not everyone will warm to the elaborate whirly 'fan' effects on many of the ceilings or some of the whimsical attention to detail, but you'd have to be a people-hater not to warm to Dorothy and Rosemary's devotion to their hotel and to each other.

Rosemary and Dorothy have plans for the garden too, of the 'we'll put a pond there and move that flowerbed there' variety. I can't help thinking it's a pity to change for the sake of change and that maybe they should simply enjoy the fruits of their labours.

Dinner is served by a bevy of local girls – ask Dorothy or is it Rosemary – and they'll tell you how each one came to work at Little Silver. They're all one big happy family here it seems.

I choose honeydew melon boats garnished with fruit and served with a glass of emerald-green Midori liqueur from Japan – new to me – followed by a pleasant salmon en croute and veg. Or I *could* have had fillets of lemon sole garnished with prawns in a white sauce or pieces of venison served with mushrooms in a red wine sauce. Wine comes from local Biddenden Manor and costs £8.25.

Afterwards we retire to the sitting room for a choice of seven liqueur coffees and Amber, the cocker spaniel, bounds in and does her party pieces in exchange for chocolate drops.

Everyone wants to know how I like my jacuzzi. I reply that it must have been designed by a devotee of Kama Sutra. Suddenly there's excited talk of a jacuzzi party. No, thank you. Although I'm not large, there is definitely room for only one in that jacuzzi. Rosemary and/or Dorothy firmly nod their heads. Little Silver is just not that class of hotel.

For The Further Adventures of Dorothy and Rosemary, read on: 'The new pond has now been enhanced with four waterfalls, lit at dusk. The bedrooms have been upgraded and the sitting room is now 40ft long.' As for the hotel sign, it has become 'something rather grand'.

'Nominated by Mr Fred Cubbage 1992 for 'England for Excellence Award', reached final six in England.'

You have to hand it to them. As a Belgian gentleman wrote in their guest book: 'To obtain the standards that you have created, you two ladies must have learnt to sleep very quickly.'

Little Silver Country Hotel,

Ashlord Road,
St Michael's,
Tenterden,
Kent TN30 6SP.
Tel: (01233) 850321.
Fax: (01233) 850647.
Dorothy Lawson and Rosemary Frith.
Location: in the Weald of Kent.
Open: all year.
Rooms: 10. 9 twin/ double (£80–£95), 1 four-poster (£100) all ensuite. Single in double (from £60).
Restaurant: open for dinner from 7–10pm.
Chef: Rosemary Frith. Table d'hôte £14, also à la carte.
Wine List: short but varied, from £8.80.
Children: yes.
Dogs: by strict arrangement:
Smoking: feel free.
And Also: golf, the Whitbread Hop Farm, the Tenterden clay pigeon shooting ranch.

*T*hornton le Fylde, Lancashire
THE RIVER HOUSE HOTEL & RESTAURANT

From beneath the front door of the somewhat grandly titled The River House Country House Hotel and Restaurant, a piece of rope is hanging out over the step. Pushing open the door we find the other end attached to an elderly, sleeping labrador complete with Don't Disturb notice (I speak metaphorically). Step over him and, further down the hall, a small, impish dog of the shaggy variety is enthusiastically causing a riot to break out among a motley selection of pussy cats. Call this a hotel? Good gracious. A friendly zoo more likely.

In the midst of this fraças, a hearty chap in jeans is bidding farewell to, and taking money from, what appear to be departing luncheon guests. Meet proprietor Bill Scott. Oh dear. As soon as he discovers who we are, he starts barking too: '*But you're not supposed to be here till six...*' Snap, snap.

He's right (I imagine he always is) because, amazingly, locating The River House at Skippool Creek had been no trouble at all – though on a drizzly autumn afternoon we could be forgiven for thinking Skippool Creek a depressing sort of place. The tide is out and the main impression is of rickety landing stages, yachts and mud.

What, then, is the attraction of The River House – not *quite* in the middle of nowhere, but almost – a medium-sized detached 1830 villa with conservatory and rain-sodden garden? The answer's got to be the lure of the rich and powerful. There isn't yet a blue plaque that says Sir Edward Heath, Sir Robin Day and Co are habitués here, but what, in fact, this hotel is famous for is being crammed to the gills with politicians and journalists at conference times. I can picture Mr Scott being buddies with them all: 'One evening I had *nine* Cabinet ministers at dinner,' he says.

By now, I'm happy to say, he has stopped barking and is positively cheerful as he grabs our bags with great energy and hurtles us up a staircase hung with water colours and cupboards stuffed with family china to the Pink Room. He flings open the door with pride. As well he might. No common or garden hotel room, this.

Furnished with French mahogany wardrobe and dressing table, a huge bed with pink velvet curtains, *and* an antique wireless set, it is both splendid and eccentric. Through the window is a view of the estuary. On the dressing table, silver-backed brushes and mirror. On the window sill, a stone painted with the words: 'Guests are requested to vacate their rooms by 12 noon.' And in the brochure, a few words reminding us that we will be 'treated as individuals not as room numbers' and that 'to invite a person into your house is to take charge of their happiness for as long as they are under your roof.' It's stirring stuff.

Handing us a key, Mr Scott explains that the bathroom is across the corridor. 'Make sure you lock the door,' he instructs. 'If you don't, *others* will use it.'

If we think the bedroom is a touch unusual, we are obviously being tiresomely conventional. Perhaps the best way to describe the not inconsiderably sized bathroom is to say it's meant for partying in: a vast bath, with wooden 'hooded' shower – no fakes these – a flower-decorated loo and wash basin. Better still, blasts of hot air from myriad pipes. Some might think the bathroom a little too full of hot air.

Downstairs we pass a dogs' sitting room with two occupants watching television. Over drinks in the snug bar next door, Mr Scott – a raconteur, you may have gathered – regales his guests with stories of his four wives and the sad story of how he was conned by two of them. His present one isn't around, though he declines to say why, preferring to launch into the culinary delights to come. 'Try the scallops,' he orders me. I wouldn't dare refuse, and they are excellent, though the lamb to follow is a trifle overdone for my taste, ditto my husband's monkfish.

After a deliciously sticky toffee pudding, we retire to the romantically lit conservatory for coffee and to ponder over the boss's plea that he hopes we won't want breakfast too early because he 'just hates getting up...'

'I've added another bedroom since you were here,' says Bill Scott, for once lost for further words.

The River House Hotel and Restaurant,

Skippool Creek,
Thornton le Fylde,
Blackpool,
Lancashire FY5 5LF.
Tel: (01253) 883497.
Fax: (01253) 892083.
Bill Scott.
Location: 4 miles from Blackpool.
Open: all year.
Rooms: 5. 1 single (£50), 4 double (£80), not all ensuite. Single in double (£65).
Restaurant: from 7pm.
Chef: Bill Scott. Table d'hôte £18.50. Also à la carte.
Wine List: versatile, from £11.30.
Children: yes.
Dogs: yes.
Smoking: feel free.
And Also: golf; clay pigeon shooting parties for 10 or more can be arranged; also duck shooting parties for 8.

$\mathcal{T}$intagel, *Cornwall*
TREBREA LODGE

On the Tintagel road, at Trenale, a shy sign announces Trebrea Lodge. As we whizz into the circular driveway of this striking Cornish manor house, the front door swings open. There stands a blue-striped-aproned figure, bathed in golden light. It's Sean the Chef.

'Are you the ——s?' he enquires cheerfully, marching us up a steep attic staircase to a dolls' house bedroom. 'Shall we do the grand tour now?' he asks next. Grand what? Oh, if you insist. Dumping our bags, we streak down in hot pursuit of *le petit Sean* to the 'Snug'. It's well named: fire, smudgy pink walls, honesty bar, squashy chairs, elderly sofas, books, games, piles of *Country Life*.

In the oak-panelled dining room, he points out our corner table and brrrms through the set menu: 'If there's anything you don't like, you can let us know now.' Quick march. Up the grand main staircase, lined with stately portraits, to the elegant first-floor drawing room. Back to our attic. It's all go at Trebrea Lodge.

Now we've a moment to discover the two glasses of sherry and a Welcome to Trebrea Lodge note. There are flowers, too, and the lamps are lit. How very pampering. Then the phone rings and we learn our senior cat's been rushed off for an emergency op. 'He may not get better. I wouldn't want you to come home and find only *two* pussy cats,' explains our daughter mournfully.

Ardour dampened, we return to the Snug and help ourselves to more sooth-ing drinks while sussing out the fellow punters. 'That lot's media,' I exclaim. 'What do you expect? They're from Barnes,' retorts my husband.

It's the week between Christmas and New Year and the atmosphere's jolly. At eight we're summoned for dinner: starched white cloths, candles and full house.

Perhaps it would have been nice, we reflect, to have been told, when booking, that it was a no-choice menu – after all, we might have been cele-brating. But I'm not moaning. The simple farmhouse food is served with all the ceremony of a six-course à la carte *and* a smile. John Charlick, partner of Sean, is the perfect host – so *simpatico* we tell him the story of the injured cat.

We begin with a creamy cauliflower soup, followed by homely boeuf bour-guignon. Tantalizing sounds of bom-di-bom thirties music drift from the kitchen. 'Pity they keep it to them-selves, otherwise we could all be foxtrotting between courses,' I say. Now we encounter a cheese called called Yarg: 'Made locally by a family called Gray,' says John, straight-faced. Geddit?

Off I go to telephone. The cat's OK! So I can manage loganberry pot with clear conscience: 'Like crème brulée, without the brulée,' says John helpfully.

If the dining room's magic, the Snug isn't as snug as it could be. The best bits, next to the fire, are bagged. So we try the upstairs drawing room where they're noisily playing Trivial Pursuit. Shall we join in? No one asks.

In our room we discover a doll-sized bath and a mirror for midgets even midgeter than me. But I quibble and, in the morning, pulling back the curtains, I can see the sea.

Breakfast's pure country house party – if only I had my camera. The serving table is laid with spanking white cloth, with two brass lamps with red shades on either side. Sean is lovingly laying out dishes of tomatoes, bacon, sausage and scrambled egg on the hotplate.

Red and brown sauces look smug in bowls. Hot plates, in relays, are discreetly brought in and, each time the kitchen door opens, snatches of 'The Marriage of Figaro' float out. There's also fruit, muesli, cereal. The orange juice is fresh and the coffee strong. They know how to do things, these boys... *and* they ask after the cat.

'Your article is the first thing we read over breakfast,' writes John Charlick. 'On that Saturday morning I handed Sean the Weekend section and said 'where is it this week?' He was already choking by then...'

Trebrea Lodge,

Trenale,
nr Tintagel,
Cornwall PL34 0HR.
Tel: (01840) 770410.
John Charlick and Sean Devlin.
Location: just off Tintagel–Boscastle road.
Open: all year.
Rooms: 7. 7 twin/double (£58–£72), all ensuite. Single in double (£45).
Restaurant: open for dinner at 8pm.
Chef: Sean Devlin. Table d'hôte £15.75.
Wine List: short but carefully chosen, from £8.25.
Children: yes, over 5.
Dogs: by arrangement.
Smoking: in 1 public room only.
And Also: views over open fields to the Atlantic, less than a mile away. Tintagel Island and its 12th-century castle ruins is nearby.

$\mathcal{T}$wo Bridges, Dartmoor, Devon
PRINCE HALL HOTEL

'You're going to the wedding?' asks Mrs Denat, proprietor of Prince Hall Hotel. 'No,' I murmur, surprised. 'Oh? Everyone else is...which is why we are *fully booked.*'

We may not be wedding guests, but we still want to get a foot in the door of this small hotel in the middle of Dartmoor so highly recommended by my friend Karen's mother. Huh. It's always fully booked. I feel quite cross.

Oh good, it shows! 'Hang on... I've got a twin-bedded room! Someone's cancelled. Will that be all right?'

'Perfect,' I purr.

Not purring quite so loudly by the time we arrive – having overshot the hotel by twenty miles and it's all my fault – we're delighted to find ourselves in such a snug old stone house. Our helpful hostess tries to seize both our bags and march them upstairs. 'No, no,' we cry, horrified – mine's full of books for goodness sake.

Talking of books: a tome in our pale pink attic room hints of Royal connections: in 1936, the Prince of Wales, Mrs Simpson and a string of Arab horses were here. Good heavens. Whatever next? 'Next,' says my husband, 'get your nose out of that book and come down and meet all those wedding guests.'

Drawing Room Number One, with fantastic moorland view, is fully booked by a snoring, stretched-out labrador; the other with equally fantastic view by...wedding guests? Yes, yes. That lot over there are definitely wedding-ish: mother, father, a couple of large teenage boys, daughter, son-in-law, granddaughter. Even better, they're all on speaking terms.

Flitting about like a moth, Mrs Denat dispenses drinks. 'I'm thirsty, what's in there?' asks my husband, peering at the pump handle on the bar. 'A very nice lager. Try some,' she offers. 'Mmmm... yes, please.' Now *we* pump Mrs Denat. 'My husband, Jean-Claude, is French and he does the cooking,' she confides. 'He's a bit shy, so he thinks *he's* got the best job, while I think I have...' Now she shows us the wine list and we choose a Pouilly Fumé described as having 'a gunmetal and gooseberry flavour'.

'Is that your husband's description?'

'Probably our wine merchant's, though my husband *always* alters anything he thinks isn't right.'

Soon every single chair in the room is occupied and there's a comforting pre-dinner hum of conversation. What a great atmosphere this hotel has. It's not just the people factor, it's the books and games on the shelves and the fact one can imagine being marooned here on a wild wet night, listening out for the Hound of the Baskervilles and playing draughts. 'Your table's ready,' says Mrs Denat.

The restaurant has stone walls, pink cloths, soft lighting. We watch, fascinated, as our neighbours demolish piles of garlicky mussels. We remember Mrs Denat's words: 'Our portions are generous.'

$\mathcal{T}$wo Bridges, Dartmoor, Devon

I get a mite confused about Red Sea Bream – 'It can't have come from the Red Sea surely?' – or is it red Sea Bream? Does it matter? Served with capers and crisply cooked vegetables, it's very good indeed. 'My rabbit, with dark brown sauce, is done the *French* way,' explains my husband foodily. Oh, really? We listen in at the next table. Our neighbour has progressed from mussels to a 'very tender piece of steak' and a 'very ripe piece of Camembert'. Satisfied customers indeed.

Our womb like room has a Wendy House wardrobe specially designed for insomniacs to crawl into during the wee small hours with book and storm torch provided. As for breakfast, there's a vast selection of cereals, fruit and yoghurt laid out, plus the full English works.

Congrats the Denats! Hotels may be having a hard time, but again and again I notice that those who offer good value and treat their guests as if they *really* care about them are the ones who seem to be doing well.

'It's so peaceful here, even on Bank holidays...' sighs Mrs Denat.

Prince Hall Hotel,

Two Bridges,
Devon PL20 6SA.
Tel: (01822) 890403.
Fax: (01822) 890676.
Jean-Claude and Tessa Denat.
Location: on the B3357 road, 1 mile from Two Bridges.
Open: all year except mid December–mid January.
Rooms: 8. 1 single (£47.50), 7 twin/double (£95–£105), all ensuite. Single in double (£50.50–£55.50). These prices include dinner and are reduced depending on length of stay.
Restaurant: open for dinner from 7–8.30pm.
Chef: Jean-Claude Denat. Table d'hôte £19.50 (included in room rate).
Wine List: mainly French, from £7.50.
Children: tolerated when controlled by parents.
Dogs: yes.
Smoking: not in dining room.
And Also: fishing (April–September) at hotel. Clay pigeon shooting and golf nearby.

ℐUckfield, *East Sussex*
HOOKE HALL

Some people assume hotel reviewing to be an endless series of treats. But when (as sometimes happens) you find yourself stuck in a room where the heating doesn't work, the proprietor's obnoxious and the food's foul, you long to be at home.

Which is why we're only half convinced by the inviting sight of Hooke Hall, a subtly floodlit Queen Anne house in High Street, Uckfield. 'Looks promising,' murmurs my husband. 'We've said that before,' I remind him.

Turning into the car park at the back, us doubters encounter a man emerging from the shadows. The owner perhaps? Psst...he vanishes. 'Funny – I thought he'd come to greet us!' My husband has a better idea: 'Maybe he's done a Basil Fawlty and sneaked out to buy his guests' dinner from another restaurant.'

Going round the front, we ring the bell of the smart dark-green front door, complete with brass whatnots. We are let in by a smiling woman. 'Clearly you're staying,' she says. 'I'll fetch the owner.' After a longish wait, a pretty woman in a pinny appears. 'Sorry to have kept you waiting – my husband's just popped out.' Oh? We exchange glances. 'I'll take you up...'

This place is clever. It manages to be smart yet homely. In the hall sits an antique pram full of plants and dried flowers. Beyond the glass door leading to the stairs lurks a tall, weird tribal sculpture.

Up the wide staircase we go. The landing at the top contains plants, flowers, oil paintings, an antique piano and a leather-topped desk lit by a lamp. Our room is quite sumptuous – it even has a mini bar, unusual in a small (nine-room) hotel. Still chatting, the woman bustles about, turning down the bed, drawing curtains. 'We'll see you for dinner shortly,' she smiles.

Downstairs, we wander into the small drawing room and sit in front of the fire. From the dining room beyond comes a buzz of voices. In saunters The Man Who Vanished. 'Sorry I wasn't around to greet you. I had to slip out and do a little panic buying,' he says. We fall about.

Choosing from his cheerfully unpretentious table d'hôte menu (with choices) at £22.50, I'm forced to go easy because of a temporary filling. So instead of something chewy like rack of lamb, I decide on eggs Florentine followed by skate wing with capers. 'I'll have the autumn salad,' says my husband, 'and the beef.'

The smallish dining room – given a confident air with important curtains and handsome pieces of antique furniture – is full. Our host, who wanders, chatting, from table to table, has such a delightful giggle he makes us feel that running a hotel is something not to be taken too seriously. Except he *does* take it seriously: the food, cooked by his wife, is delicious, unpretentious and presented with flair; the ambience is great; and the key word is style.

Afterwards we sink into a – I mean, *the* – sofa in the drawing room.

Suppose everybody wanted their coffee in here? They'd be unlucky wouldn't they. Once again, our genial host swans through. 'How long has the hotel been open?' we want to know. 'Six years,' he tells us, adding that his wife runs her own interior design business from an office at the back.

Inexplicably, he gets on to the tricky subject of hotel inspectors. 'These days you never know who's coming through the door,' he remarks darkly. 'I'm afraid I always regard the lone guest with suspicion.' Good. That lets me off the hook(e).

In bustles the jolly lady who let us in and waited at table. She suggests we have breakfast in our room. Why not? This column *is* 'Room Service' after all. And the RS breakfast is well thought out, with white cloth, blue-and-white china, toast, croissants, strong coffee and elegant scrambled egg. The only problem is that she arrives when my husband's still in the bath, which is in an uncurtained alcove rather than separate room. Men have no panache. This one stops singing at once and I never saw anyone leap out of a bath so quickly and hide in bed.

Anyway, we're agreed. Here's a hotel that restores the hotel reviewer's faith. Though I rather fear the proprietor's faith in guests who arrive à *deux* may be rudely shattered.

'Juliet's cooking continues for private parties,' writes Alister Percy, 'but we now have two Italian chefs.' The menu certainly has an Italian bias, but how sad that the new regime means Mr

Hooke Hall,

250 High Street,
Uckfield,
East Sussex TN22 1EN.
Tel: (01825) 761578.
Fax: (01825) 768025.
Juliet and Alister Percy.
Location: in middle of High Street.
Open: all year, except Christmas–New Year's Eve.
Rooms: 9. 9 twin/double (£55–£110), all ensuite. Single in double (from £37.50).
Restaurant: open for dinner 7.15–9.15pm.
Chefs: Mutele Pavanello and Silvano Sambetia. A la carte, average £15–£18. Continental breakfast £4.50, cooked £6.50.
Wine List: mainly Italian, from £8.75.
Children: yes.
Dogs: no.
Smoking: we'd rather you didn't.
And Also: walking and riding in Ashdown Forest. 15 minutes Glyndebourne.

Percy will no longer be caught skulking in the bushes on his way out for a panic buy. The restaurant may be different, but the people in charge are the same. Over and over again, I find that what makes a hotel special is its owners. Of course the converse also applies.

ᵁlingswick, Hereford and Worcester
THE STEPPES COUNTRY HOUSE HOTEL

Driving into the side entrance of The Steppes, a small 17th-century country house hotel near Hereford, we nearly flatten an anxious-looking man in close-fitting red shirt and dark bow tie. 'Mr and Mrs...? Ah, good,' he says, looking intensely relieved.

This must be our host, solicitor Henry Howland. While it's lovely to feel so wanted, there's also the distinct impression we may have offended. Glancing at his watch he says: 'We are *just serving dinner.*'

Oh dear. We are fifteen minutes late. Feeling like naughty children, we trail behind him into our room in a restored barn. Issuing a few brisk instructions on where to find everything, he beetles towards the door. 'We'll be along in about ten minutes,' I chirrup politely.

He whips round. 'Oh, please make it less than that. We are *just serving dinner.*'

Glancing down at my tee-shirt and shorts with frayed edges, I register how inappropriate these look compared with Mr Howland's bow tie. 'But we must change first.'

'Come as you are.'

This puts us in flippant mood. Posh clothes are donned in two minutes flat. We hurry to the house and dining room where the centre table for two is conspicuously unoccupied.

A sudden hush descends. Impossible not to notice that the other guests are of a certain age (or beyond) and that they are giving us the onceover. One man with his back to our table even turns and treats us to a long, hard stare. Do we look funny? Suddenly we realize. They've been kept waiting for their tucker until we turn up.

The dining room is very Herefordshire farmhouse: inglenook fireplace with horse brasses, low beamed ceiling, a black and terracotta tiled floor laid with rugs. Bunches of dried hops, corn dollies and a horse's tail – or is it a scalp? – hang from the beams. Mr Howland, meanwhile, bustles around while his wife (we presume) slaves over the hot stove. With a flourish, he presents the menus. As we deliberate the merits of rosti or Herefordshire gammon in puff pastry or cabbage and apple casserole, menus are abruptly removed and bowls of gazpacho set in front of us.

As for choice, the penny drops. There isn't any. All three dishes arrive at the same time and are part of the main course. (The Steppes serve a set menu unless you have chosen from the à la carte by 10 am that morning.)

Fair enough. Except we find the combination of strongly flavoured dishes too much for us. 'There's more pastry than Herefordshire gammon,' I murmur, keeping my voice well down.

Afterwards we commute to the cellar bar where help-yourself coffee awaits. Mr Howland is brandishing menus again and making cheery remarks like 'Contemplate your breakfast.' Oh no, we groan. The pudding – a rich syllabub – has knocked us for six.

Now he's advancing in our direction. 'Nothing cooked for us. And what time is breakfast?'

'At nine.'

'You mean, *from* nine?'

'No, at nine.'

We decide to go to bed and watch TV. Our room is imaginatively decorated with dried hops, dried and artificial flowers, corn dollies, a beribboned straw hat and, above the red buttoned bedhead, a pair of cornucopia bulging with dried flowers and ears of wheat. There are are two pink velvety chairs and a pinkish sculptured carpet. In the bathroom a bidet and – unusually in my experience – an efficient shower. All very nice.

Yet when I stay in a hotel I like to relax. I like to leave rules and regulations behind. And I particularly like to feel the hotel is run for *my* – the guest's – convenience rather than the owners.

The Howlands thought my review most unfair and said so. Would they want to be in this book? Perhaps not. But lo! 'We have finished restoring the timber-framed barn where guests are now accommodated,' writes Tricia Howland. 'We have also created a proper sitting room – no longer any need to greet guests in the drive! Breakfast is now available between 7am and 10am and guests aren't asked the evening before what they want, although many of the unusual items (The Steppes is famous for its breakfasts) do require ordering in advance – but by form. Dinner is now available between 7.30pm and 9pm.

'Now I'm sure you're always interested to know how your 'victims' have fared

---

The Steppes Country House Hotel,

Ullingswick,
Hereford and Worcester HR1 3JG.
Tel: (01432) 820424.
Henry and Tricia Howland.
Location: off the A417 Gloucester–Leominster road.
Open: almost all year -ask!
Rooms: 6. 6 twin/double (£75), all ensuite. Single in double (£47.50).
Restaurant: dinner served between 7.30–9pm.
Chef: Tricia Howland. Cordon Bleu table d'hôte £22.50.
Wine List: international, carefully selected, from £7.
Children: yes, over 10.
Dogs: yes.
Smoking: not in bar or dining room.
And Also: delightful gardens. Table d'hôte gourmet dinner B&B packages – please enquire. (Payment by credit card may attract a 5% handling charge.)

---

since your visit. This year (1994) we are Which? County Hotel of the Year, awarded in view of the 'good-natured hosts' quality of care'. And – our biggest accolade – Heart of England winner of the Logis Regional Cuisine Competition – judged by Albert Roux. PS: You will also be pleased to hear that Henry has afforded himself a new shirt!'

Ah, but what about that bow tie? Congratulations!

THE LAKE ISLE

How worrying when smart friends say please can they come on the next hotel expedition and are prepared to pay for the pleasure.

Worrying? It's the apology factor. How mortifying to show off England to sophisticated Sydneysiders only to find the carefully chosen country hotel has unwelcoming proprietors and smells of stale biscuit tin...and that the idyllic inn we confidently take Mother-in-Law to boasts a pongy Gents' right next to the dining room.

Is there something about taking guests that invites disaster? On this occasion, I check out heaps of hotels. The Lake Isle (Uppingham, not Innisfree) sounds promising. 'Yes, I can do two rooms,' says the proprietor, 'though, being Friday, our main restaurant's fully booked. I can, however, offer you dinner in our small dining room upstairs...' She extols the virtues of dining in this room, how quiet it is. How boring – *we* go out to dinner to watch other people. 'But why don't I hold the rooms until three by which time you'll have had a chance to talk to your friends?' she wheedles. Oh, why not. Just in case.

Soon she's calling me back. 'A couple wants to book one of your rooms...' she announces. Oh yeah? 'My friends don't fancy eating in the upstairs room,' I reply smoothly, 'so we'll have to let the bookings go.'

Vrooom. Now it seems she can rearrange the tables in the main dining room. '£85, three-course dinner, bed

and breakfast for two,' she says. The price clinches it. 'We'll be there seven-thirty or eight,' I promise optimistically. ('And I suppose we'll appear in your column as 'stroppy friends',' complains my suspicious friend.)

Well, there has to be a problem, and it's queues on the A1. I phone the Lake Isle. 'We're on our way, we're very hungry...but we won't make it until at least nine-thirty.' The welcome's still warm. 'Don't worry, don't hurry. We just look forward to seeing you...'

What bliss to see *them*. Slinging the car in the Lake Isle's private space just off Uppingham's prosperous High Street, we hurry into a small, softly lit bar with crackling fire. The proprietor whisks us smartly upstairs to dear little rooms with fruit, flowers, exotic teas, homemade biscuits, jugs of chilled water, trouser presses, carafes of sherry. It's so warm I even find myself turning the heating *down*. 'Not well, dear?' enquires my husband.

In the bar, drinks and menus are accompanied by tasty appetizers. Two wine lists are offered: one short, inexpensive and everyday, the other for wine buffs. 'You've a market for these kind of wines?'

'You'd be *surprised*,' says our hostess.

The packed restaurant has a dresser, a splendid collection of antique polished pine tables and cheery, dashing-about waiters in zappy waistcoats. Food is enjoyable rather than memorable, though I do recall some excellent home made soup, a choice of three main courses – venison, lamb and halibut – and lovely crisp vegetables.

I also remember falling for a sensational pudding made of clementine, orange marmalade, orange juice and Cointreau. Over coffee and mince pies, we watch the cabaret performed by a large table of merrymakers with a wag called Brian leaping maniacally up and down banging on about That Treaty. 'Ma-a-a-stricht, Ma-a-a-stricht,' the others baa.

Although our friends have impeccable manners, this time I know they really mean it when they praise the Lake Isle's lovely atmosphere, the comfortable bed, the freshly squeezed breakfast OJ. *Such* a relief not to have to apologize for a single thing...Except walking through the courtyard on the way to the car, I happen to look up. It seems they could think of no better way of keeping their window open during the night than with one of the oranges thoughtfully provided by the owners.

'It amuses Mr Williams, one of our customers, to come into the restaurant and announce he is Paddy Burt,' says Claire Whitfield. 'It would make his day if his name was in print – it might also shut him up once and for all. Kind regards.'

The Lake Isle,
16 High Street East,
Uppingham,
Leicestershire LE15 9PZ.
Tel/Fax: (01572) 822951.
David and Claire Whitfield.
Location: in the centre of town.
Open: all year.
Rooms: 12. 1 single (£50), 9 twin/double (£70), 2 suites (£90), all ensuite. Single in double (£50).
Restaurant: open for dinner 7–10pm.
Chef: David Whitfield. Table d'hôte £21–£24.
Wine List: wide selection, lots of half bottles, from £8.95.
Children: yes.
Dogs: yes.
Smoking: all we ask is consideration for others.
And Also: elegant upstairs drawing room, Uppingham School, Rutland Water, antique shops, old book shops, art galleries. Special wine evenings four times a year – please enquire.

Wareham, Dorset
THE PRIORY HOTEL

In Dorset – in sunny January – I rashly decide I've found the perfect hotel: a 16th-century converted priory on the banks of the River Frome. Perfect? Don't get carried away now.

Putting cautious noses round the door we encounter the manager. To these casual visitors (who may never return) he's *politesse* itself. 'It will be my pleasure to show you round.'

In fact the pleasure is ours. First he ushers us into the large drawing room, where a pianist plays on Saturday nights, and then whips us down for a quick look at the elegant Abbots Cellar restaurant. Next we trip across the gardens to the recently converted boathouse. Annexe may be a dirty word in some hotels, but not this one. He shows us 'Mallard', a luxurious room with four-poster, whirlpool bath and its own private balcony and, down-stairs, two beautiful suites – 'Heron' and 'Swan' – both of which have doors that open onto the river bank.

We thank him warmly. Back in the car I write in my notebook for future reference: the Priory Hotel, Wareham, Dorset. But how sad. When we return at the end of June for a test visit, it's raining cats and dogs. Unlike Gene Kelly (who had the benefit of a large umbrella) we are not in singing mood. We'd had foolish visions of wandering in the wonderful gardens and breakfast-ing on the verandah-ed terrace with its view of the river. No chance.

We are welcomed this time – and I mean just that – by another man who escorts us up to our attic room which, at £95 for two, is one of their cheapest. Would we like a drink, he enquires: 'Tea, coffee? Something stronger?' Tea would be nice. Five minutes later it – and biscuits – arrive.

From our window there's a wet view of fluttering doves, lawns, topiary, herbaceous borders, roses, shrubs and a few masts poking up through the trees. Inside, a bowl of fruit on the dressing table, vase of carnations, a folder containing menus. The bed has fluffy blue blankets and there's a blue velvet chair for watching TV. A big plus – the lighting is just right. Although small and decorated in slightly stuffy traditional style, the room adds up to comfort.

Downstairs the drawing room is full of family parties and one obvious honeymoon couple. We are disap-pointed to be allotted a table in the Greenwood Restaurant, not the more intimate Abbots Cellar, but never mind.

I choose orange juice for starters but it *is* freshly squeezed. My husband has smoked chicken with cherry tomatoes in 'a variety of leaves' dressed with walnut oil. Cream of broccoli soup with almonds is followed by a choice of main courses that arrive beneath silver covers. I always want to giggle when these are solemnly whipped off simulta-neously, but here the waiter joins in as well: 'This is lucky dip time, ' he grins.

Halibut with a light champagne cream sauce with grapes sounds over-fancy but isn't too rich. Puddings from the trolley – raspberry mousse and summer fruit pudding – are both pleasantly sharp.

After dinner we sink into chairs in the drawing room where, if it were not raining, French doors would be open to the scented garden. Half asleep, we listen to soothing jazz and Cole Porter on the piano.

The Priory turns out to be owned by brothers John and Stuart Turner. Settling the bill next morning, we encounter John who looks more West country farmer than hotelier. 'We'd love to come back and see the gardens one day,' we say. 'Please do,' he says. 'National Westminster Bank will welcome you with open arms...' What an agreeable man...what a happy hotel.

'Although you got our telephone number wrong in The Telegraph,' writes John Turner, 'by coincidence the number quoted was that of a member of my staff and she's still speaking to me!'

The Priory Hotel,

Church Green,
Wareham,
Dorset BH20 4ND.
Tel: (01929) 551666.
Fax: (01929) 554519.
John and Stuart Turner.
Location: near the church.
Open: all year.
Rooms: 19. 3 single (£70), 12 twin/double (£80–£160), single in double (£60–£95), 4 boathouse rooms and suites (£160–£185), single (£95–£105), all ensuite.
Restaurants: dinner served from 7.30–10pm.
Chef: Michael Rust. From £22–£26.50).
Wine List: truly international, from £8.50.
Children: no.
Dogs: no.
Smoking: if you must.
And Also: fishing in Garden Lake, boating on River Frome, five golf courses within 30 minutes drive.

We arrive at the peaceful Old Church Hotel on the shores of Ullswater in time for tea. Would we like a tray in the garden, asks a waitress in a black dress? Yes, we would.

On the lawns we encounter another tea-drinking couple, a retired lawyer and his wife admiring the lakeside view. The wife is nostalgic. She grew up near here, she says. This had once been a favourite hotel. She sniffs. 'Now it's full of fancy wallpaper and ensuites.'

Happily the lawns are not decorated with stripes. Nor is the car park – though, today, it boasts its own decoration in the form of a '70s Roller. Wonder who that belongs to? He's not hard to spot. Owners of such vehicles rarely are.

Our lawyer's wife is correct. Inside, the wallpaper's very fancy indeed. In fact, if it weren't for glorious view of lake and mountain, you could imagine yourself cosily ensconced in one of London's smart country house hotels.

But I've done my homework and know the reason why. Owner Maureen Whitemore has gone to town because she's a soft-furnishings expert and, for anyone wishing to learn interior decorating, runs courses throughout the year.

She has painted the hall a deep, confident red and complemented it with matching floral arrangements in huge vases. In one sitting room, bookcases and ceiling are deep pink to tone with curtains and paper. Over the top? Flamboyant? Yes – and it looks terrific.

One room – with the hotel television in it – is an exception. Maybe it's the 'before' room. More to the point perhaps, anyone who feels the need to watch TV when in such an idyllic spot – there are deliberately none in the bedrooms – deserves those fringed velvety chairs and sofas.

There are also nice country touches: the entrance mat that says and means Welcome; the cluttered porch with its paraphernalia of life jackets and oars for use with the hotel rowboat. Who could resist that rowboat? We decide to brush up our rowing skills before dinner, across the lake to the Sharrow Bay Hotel. The sun is setting. This is the life.

In the dining room we find ourselves parked next to Mr Rolls Royce and have the uncomfortable feeling he's listening to every word. Perhaps it's because the dining room is so quiet. *Everyone* is talking in whispers. A bit of Mozart would be nice. As the reverential hush becomes too much for me, I have a sudden fantasy of Mr RR running amok, scattering diners with a few choice swear words.

The food is classy stuff with plenty of alcoholic additions: for example, a sauté of lamb's liver with an orange and Dubonnet sauce; honey-baked Cumberland ham with mustard, cider and apples; roast boned duckling with sage stuffing and a port wine and damson sauce. The non-alcoholic brown bread and honey ice-cream is terrific. To follow there's an immaculate dish of cheese accompanied by black grapes and Old Church biscuits. House wine is offered in litres or half litres.

More alcoholic refreshment at breakfast time almost results in one tipsy hotel reviewer as fumes envelope her as she tests the Creamy Porridge Oats with Whisky and Demerara. Throwing caution to the winds, I then order smoked salmon and scrambled egg.

Upon leaving, we endeavour to draw the bearded Kevin Whitemore on the subject of his other guests. Who's the chap with the Roller? A '70s pop star aged beyond recognition? Go on, tell us. But his lips are sealed – it's good news for Mr and Mrs Smith.

The discreet Mr Whitemore does however let slip that one of the waiters is his Number One son. But when we proffer a tip for *all* the very professional staff, he looks embarrassed. 'We don't expect or encourage that,' he says. 'It's enough if people have enjoyed staying here.' Oh, we have, we have.

When this piece was published, Maureen Whitemore wrote me a letter: 'I don't know what originally brought you to our hotel, but we hope that, should you return, we will have maintained if not improved our standards, the worrying fact being that, should they have dropped, I know it will not go unnoticed.'

A second letter, prompted by news of this book, says: 'You will be pleased to know we no longer have those NAFF pink sofas... and, sadly, we do now have TVs in all rooms.'

The Old Church Hotel,

Watermillock,
Penrith,
Cumbria CA11 0JN.
Tel: (017684) 86204.
Fax: (017684) 86368.
Kevin and Maureen Whitemore.
Location: off A592, south of Pooley Bridge.
Open: April–October.
Rooms: 10. 10 twin/double (from £90–£150), all ensuite. Single in double (as above).
Restaurant: dinner served at 8pm.
Chef: Kevin Whitemore. Table d'hôte £26.
Wine List: French, German, New World, from £9.95.
Children: yes.
Dogs: not inside.
Smoking: not in dining room.
And Also: stunning lake views, row-boat, guided fell walking and rock climbing, pony trekking, fishing and golf. Comprehensive 2-day soft-furnishing courses are held regularly – please enquire.

*W*elwyn Garden City, Hertfordshire
TEWIN BURY FARM

Help. We're lost in wet, narrow, Hertfordshire lanes. We've crossed bridges that take us too far. 'Can you direct us to Tewin Bury Farm?' we cry, but even the taxi driver we ask gets it wrong. Blaming our guidebook whose directions don't quite match reality, we cross one more bridge (over the weeny River Mimram) and finally make it into a large muddy yard.

The last thing we expect to find just two miles from Welwyn Garden City is a real working farm. At first glance, though, and in the dark, Tewin Bury Farm isn't immediately promising. There's a handsome but seemingly deserted farmhouse, a farm shop, some outbuildings and a reception office that says 'We're Closed' and asks us to enquire at the restaurant next door.

Noise hits us when we open *that* door – now we know why there are so many cars parked outside. It's all deco-rated for Christmas in here, music's playing and there's just one table left – ours. The girl behind the bar is welcoming and businesslike. She's the one who'd persuaded me over the phone that 'the annexe rooms are much nicer than those in the house.'

'Follow me,' she says now, so we traipse along behind her along a covered cobbled path. (I wish all hotels had covered walkways to their annexe rooms.)

These rooms were once cowsheds, she tells us. Oh, really? The second surprise is to find that our room is not only warm and luxurious, but has been converted with taste and imagination. Sorry, Tewin Bury. Should I be so surprised? It's just that other farmhouses I've stayed in haven't majored on either of those.

Here, there's a pitched ceiling, beams and antique furniture that includes a handsome four-poster with wooden top and no naff trimmings. Hotels tend to make a great thing of their four-poster rooms, talking about them in almost reverential tones. This one's just *here* and taken for granted.

There *is* one thing missing, though: a bedside lamp for the other side of the bed. 'Sorry,' I grin at my husband. 'Don't be,' he says. 'I shall ask for one...'

After investigating the bathroom and admiring its antique brass accessories, marvelling at the vast selection of goodies including such unlikelies as comb, razor and underarm spray, we stroll along the path to the restaurant.

The cheerful atmosphere is infec-tious. Looking around, we guess most of the clientele to be local farmers. The room is huge, with much use being made of brick and rough-hewn beams. A brick chimney piece houses a kitchen range.

What to eat then? For starters we decide on homemade cucumber and mint soup and 'sliced and marinated salmon served with a ginger and Chablis dressing', followed by sautéed lamb's kidneys and chicken breast in a light curry sauce accompanied by a reasonably priced 'oakey' Australian

Chardonnay. We resist trolley puddings with names like lemon swirl.

'All delicious!' we tell the waitress. My husband asks about a bedside light. 'I'll find you one.' After consultation with the other girls, she pops into the next door room and emerges bearing a lamp. 'Shall I carry it for you?'

'No, no, we can manage.'

Now, I don't usually notice things like mattresses, but this one's particularly comfortable. And next morning we know we're on a *real* farm because outside our window a tractor trundles by.

Over breakfast we discover the story of Tewin Bury Farm, run by the Williams Family: 'We started in 1985 when my brother, Vaughan, got married,' says green-wellied farmer Ivor Williams, drinking his coffee.

'At first, we let a few rooms in the house and then decided to extend...' Now we meet Vaughan's wife, the glamorous Angie, who's decorated and designed, and hunted out the antique furniture.

So this genuine family-run farm is now a sophisticated farm hotel offering twelve rooms, conference facilities, a romantic 17th-century barn for weddings, a day's shooting. Guests can even walk the dog. This place is not just a surprise, it's a find.

'On the night you were here,' says Vaughan Williams, 'we were celebrating Angela's father's sixtieth birthday in London. No wonder the house looked deserted. It was! Thought you'd be pleased to know the 'muddy yard' is now a shingled car park...'

Tewin Bury Farm,

nr Welwyn,
Hertfordshire AL6 OJB.
Tel: (01438) 840793.
Fax: (01438) 840440.
Vaughan and Angela Williams.
Location: 2 miles from A1(M) – brochure includes map.
Open: all year.
Rooms: 16. 16 twin/double (including exec and four-posters) (£58.25–£65), single in double (£58.25), all ensuite.
Restaurant: open for dinner 7–9.30pm.
Chef: Colin King. Table d'hôte £11.95–£15.50.
Wine List: Tewin vineyard to New World, from £7.50.
Children: yes.
Dogs: yes, if good.
Smoking: not encouraged.
And Also: farm shop, trout fishing, shooting and clay pigeon shooting at farm, golf nearby.

Winchester, Hampshire
THE WYKEHAM ARMS

This ancient pub with rooms, tucked between Winchester's college and cathedral, boasts a brochure that's been designed with care and taste. The sort of brochure, in fact, that those of a sentimental slant of mind, like the couple who wrote in the Visitors' Book about it being their 'best anniversary ever' might even wish to frame.

So it's not surprising to learn then (it's all in the brochure) that The Wykeham Arms has acquired a collection of award-winning tags: Preferred Hotel in the south and south east of England (*Which Hotel Guide*); Pub of the Year (*Egon Ronay*); Wine Pub of the Year (*Good Pub Guide*) and Pub Caterer of the Year.

If all this isn't enough, proprietor Graeme Jameson has acquired a collection of his own: 'I specialize in Wykehamia, Nelson, Royalty and the military,' he announces briskly. Judging by his Royal Artillery tie, I suspect Mr Jameson was once part of the military himself. Certainly he runs his splendid and unique establishment with military precision – though I wouldn't like to be the person who wields the duster. The fruits of Mr Jameson's compulsive collecting habit are everywhere: pictures, bunches of dried hops and flowers dangling from the beams in the bar, hats and helmets, while as for tankards... 'I have almost a thousand of those,' barks Mr J. I'll take his word for it. They hang from every available space on walls and ceilings, enhanced by cunning lighting effects.

Mrs Jameson escorts us up the winding staircase to our attic room, beautifully kitted out in tones of brown, royal blue and cream. 'If you want anything, please let me know,' she says. A novel touch: the one armchair, smartly upholstered in blue velvet, is in the *bath*room, presumably for people who have a sudden urge to finish their book in the middle of the night without disturbing their partners.

Downstairs in one of the four inviting bars, we squeeze ourselves into a pair of school desks, complete with carved initials and inkwell holes, and order drinks. The staff, all young and exceptionally helpful, weave in and out of the mainly middle-class – though not middle-aged – crowd. But something funny's going on. No one's smoking. Then I spot the notice: 'please help us by not smoking in this area after 8pm on Friday and Saturday nights.'

Today's menu is chalked on a blackboard – the same whether you eat in the bar or dining room – and offers things like tomato and celeriac soup and coarse pâté with pine nuts for starters; pigeon breast or roast rack of lamb with dauphinoise potatoes to follow. There's just one snag. When booking, I had been told we'd better arrive in good time for dinner 'otherwise there won't be much choice...but if you arrive by seven-thirty you should be all right'.

And yes, we *are* all right. We edge our way to the dining room in the corner, until 1974 the College watchmaker's shop and now the

Watchmaker's Room. Here, a collection of old watches adorns the mantelpiece while, squashed into a corner, is a handsome grandfather clock. We have reserved a table for two. 'That's yours,' says the waitress, pointing. The candles flicker. We order a bottle of Chairman's white Burgundy (£12.95) from the short but to-the-point wine list and await our first courses – crab, ginger and sweet pepper strudel and tomato and carrot soup – with anticipation. But it seems it isn't exactly 'our' table because, shortly after the wine arrives, we're asked whether we would mind sharing it. It seems churlish to object.

'Bet those people whose anniversary was 'the greatest' didn't get another couple shoved onto *their* table,' I mutter to my husband. The food is great, but our neighbours have extremely loud voices. We can't compete. Deciding to forgo coffee, we step out for an explore around Winchester instead. When booking dinner *à deux* at the Wykeham Arms, be warned.

One *petit* as opposed to *grand* niggle: our room has one bedside table and lamp. Who's the lucky one to read then? We toss – I lose. And I can report that you need a very long arm indeed to reach the light switch halfway up the wall. They didn't tell me that in the brochure!

'I read your column regularly,' says Graeme Jameson, 'and am always brought up by my bootstraps if I think there is even half a whiff of compla-cency about me. Believe me, in a busy hostelry, it can be a creeping disease.'

The Wykeham Arms,

75 Kingsgate Street,
Winchester,
Hampshire SO23 9PE.
Tel: (01962) 853834.
Fax: (01962) 854411.
Graeme Jameson.
Location: between College and Cathedral.
Open: all year.
Rooms: 7. 7 twin/double (£75), all ensuite, single in double (£65).
Restaurant and Bar: open for dinner from 7.30pm.
Chef: Vanessa Booth. A la carte menu changes twice daily, average £16.
Wine List: mainly French and New World, from £10.95. 20 wines by the glass.
Children: yes, over 14.
Dogs: yes.
Smoking: not in bar.
And Also: close to the New Forest.

*W*interingham, *South Humberside*
WINTERINGHAM FIELDS

Annie Schwab likes nothing better than having the builders in. There's a zealot's gleam in her eye as she confides: 'The lovely thing about doing up a hotel is you can be *really* over the top.'

There are no prizes for guessing Mrs Schwab's favourite era. Queen Victoria reigns over us the minute we stroll through the door of Winteringham Fields Hotel. Would Her Majesty be at home, I wonder, in the palmy conservatory with its comfy old-fashioned antimacassared chairs and sofas? Would she be amused by the parlour with its fringed lamps and piano where a score of *The Mikado* is open ready to play? Would she smile graciously upon the plates, pictures, flowers, mirrors, lamps, screens, pelmets, firescreens, lacy cloths, glass domes et al? She ought. There's a fantastic atmosphere.

The brochure's already told us the house dates back to the 16th century and once belonged to the Marquis of Lincolnshire – there's no sign of *him*. 'Mind your head,' warns Annie, leading us along dark narrow passages with low ceilings and up the stairs to our small but perfectly formed room. After a day of driving we're knackered. We scatter newspapers around, have baths, leave our clothes on the floor and, all dressed up, scurry down to catch that Victorian feeling.

It's not hard. First, Annie shows off her just-decorated private dining room. 'Look,' she says, throwing open the door. 'When I bought that wallpaper,

the man in the shop said I was the only person who'd *ever* chosen it.'

'It's – um – eye catching,' I reply.

So is Germain, her husband, the chef/patron. In the conservatory, we're brought not one but *three* appetizers 'with the compliments of the chef'. If those appetizers are anything to go by, we're in for a feast.

The dining room is formal with white starchy cloths, gilded pillars with fleur de lys poking out of the tops and – *what?* – a large kitchen range. 'Was that already there?'

'No, we put it in...'

Now a bevy of waiters of the silently gliding variety take over our immediate future. There are three menus: a Menu Surprise, a Menu Epicurean and the à la carte. This place isn't cheap, but we already knew that. In the interests of research, we choose from the à la carte and, in particular, a confection of *mille feuille*, pan-fried scallops and langoustines which, delicious though it is, I live to regret. Why? While laying into a langoustine, I spill sauce all over the cloth and myself. 'Can't take you anywhere,' remarks my better half kindly.

But even he's impressed when, within seconds, as if by osmosis, a waiter appears with a bowl of water and a cloth, while another unobtrusively lays a folded napkin over the offending bit of cloth. Oh, it's beautifully executed. I'm not even made to feel a clumsy person who can't be taken anywhere.

The restaurant's full. At the next table is a couple who might just as well have Just Married signs all over them. Aaaah. Eating skate wings poached in cider garnished with samphire and fillet of lamb with a trio of cabbage, we comment on the JM's meagre appetites. What a waste. 'Not *quite* sure I like the sweetness of the cider with skate,' murmurs my husband – but he quibbles and he knows it.

After coffee in the softly lit conservatory, we creep upstairs. Opening the door, there's no mess. Someone's been in, turned back the bed, tidied us up. Even our clothes are put away. How *shaming.*

Even so, we've a little moan. Here's a room where everything's been thought of: flowers, fruit, mineral water, dressing gowns - but no *clock radio.* Sorry, two moans – my husband doesn't much like showers that dribble cold water all over him. Apart from that, we're two happy people...Made more so, I must add, by the personal attentions of Mr Schwab at breakfast. Not only does this man cook like an angel, he's a dish in himself.

'We have many restaurant critics and hotel inspectors visiting us throughout the year. All are supposed to be incognito but quite frankly they might just as well place a neon sign on their heads. One or two do slip through the net, as you did – I certainly wouldn't have been quite so gushing if I'd known you were a journalist...' says Annie Schwab.

Winteringham Fields,

Silver Street,
Winteringham,
South Humberside DN15 9PF.
Tel: (01724) 733096.
Fax: (01724) 733898.
Annie and Germain Schwab.
Location: on the crossroads, in centre of village.
Open: all year except 1st week August and 2 weeks at Christmas.
Rooms: 7. 7 twin/double/four-poster (£80–£95), all ensuite. Single in double (£60–£75). 3 ground-floor rooms.
Restaurant: dinner is served from 7.30–9.30pm.
Chef: Germain Schwab. Table d'hôte £27–£42.
Wine List: New World and Swiss, from £11. Cooked breakfast £7.
Children: yes.
Dogs: no.
Smoking: not in bedrooms or main restaurant.
And Also: Elsham Hall and Country Park, Normanby Hall, the historic town of Beverly.

$\mathcal{Y}$ork, North Yorkshire
THE GRANGE HOTEL

Alone in York on a business trip, merrily driving my hired car, I shoot past an elegant Regency hotel. Hang on. Isn't that The Grange, where I'm booked in tonight? It is! *Very* civilized it looks.

Returning later, I discover a car park right behind the hotel. How convenient. Zipping in through the back door and up a few stairs – voila! – I'm in a spacious reception area just as elegant as the exterior, with a flagged floor and Oriental rug.

A jolly chap whips me up a wide, iron-balustraded staircase to a first-floor room that dazzles with its display of floral extravaganza. He's eager to point out a second door in the bathroom marked 'Fire Exit – This door is Alarmed'. 'Take no notice,' he advises. 'We only put the alarm on when the room the other side is vacant. No one will burst in on you, I promise.'

I should hope not. And ten out of ten to The Grange because, having broken a nail opening the car boot, the first thing I spy in that bathroom is an emery board. Though I'm not quite as delirious when I realize there's no clock. How *do* people who've left their watches at home know what time it is?

My room's painted a crisp salmon pink and consists mostly of two twin beds pushed together. You sort of wiggle your way round. Two wigglers would be one too many and might lead to blows. Never mind. Room 17 is efficient, comfortable and warm.

Downstairs in the bar I get acquainted with the waiter/barman:

'The people I met today tell me your boss is a character,' I say.

'Oh yes, he is!'

'Will he be here tonight?'

'He usually pops in to see if we're behaving ourselves – he's a v*ery nice man* to work for,' he adds quickly.

In the dining room the order of the day is American couples past the first flush. On my corner table there's a vase of pinks and a pretty candlestick lamp. The deep yellow walls are decorated with equine water-colours in elaborate gilt frames. Some people might object to muzak in such an ostentatious setting, but *I* think there'd be a dreadful hush without it.

The waiter's most solicitous. When I refuse bread: 'Not *dieting*?' he politely enquires. My answer is that no dieter would choose a starter of Roquefort cheese soufflé with small blinis (just wonderful), followed by an equally mouth-watering breast of duck with spiced honey glaze. The crisp assortment of vegetables includes my favourite dauphinoise potatoes. A couple of departing Americans stop by my table: 'The food's so good here...'

'Would I like a pudding?' is my next predicament. Oh, he's persuasive, that one. 'Mmm...not sure.' But, yes, I do succumb and tulips of frozen prune parfait are brought to me in the handsome drawing room where, sitting by the window, I contentedly nosh on my own. Before going to bed I ask for a 7am wake-up call, but am wide-eyed much earlier in case they forget. They don't.

At breakfast I order grapefruit juice and coffee. 'Nothing else?' asks a different waiter. All this concern for the inner woman is touching. I explain about the big dinner the previous evening. In two twinks he's back. 'A few slices of melon, pineapple and strawberries?' he wheedles. Oh, twist my arm.

But the *real* twist comes when, breaking down the bill for *Telegraph* readers, I realize I've been undercharged. The single room rate of £88 bed and breakfast is correct, but the £28.30 dinner bill should be £37.55 (to include £10 for a half bottle of Chablis and £2 for camomile tea.)

When I telephone The Grange to point this out, Jeremy Cassel, the owner, does the gentlemanly thing: 'How really *sweet* of you to call,' he cries. 'I don't *think* I can charge you...but next time you're in York, do please introduce yourself, I'd just *love* to meet an honest soul.' Oh dear. And I gave him a false name.

'I'm delighted you enjoyed your stay,' writes Jeremy Cassel. **'I note your comment about the clock, but "The Jolly Chap" who whipped you up the stairs should also have shown you how the television works which has a clock incorporated within. Perhaps we can share a bottle of Chablis together, now that I know your preference?'**

The Grange Hotel,

Clifton,
York, North Yorkshire YO3 6AA.
Tel: (01904) 644744.
Fax: (01904) 612453.
Jeremy Cassel.
Location: 400 yards from City walls, on the A19 Thirsk road.
Open: all year.
Rooms: 30. 3 single (£87), 26 twin/double (£98–£140), 1 suite (£165), all ensuite. Single in double (£88). Some ground-floor rooms.
Restaurant: open for dinner from 7–10pm.
Chef: Christopher Falcus. Table d'hôte £19. Also cellar brasserie.
Wine List: reasonably priced, unusual, from £10.
Children: yes.
Dogs: yes.
Smoking: feel free.
And Also: wine weekends – please enquire. The Minster, the Jorvik, stately homes, the races.

INDEX (HOTELS)

The name of the hotel you are looking for...

Room Service

INDEX (COUNTIES)

Index (Counties)

INDEX (TOWNS)

The name of the town in which, or near where you would like to stay...

Air-cooled Volkswagens

Osprey Colour Series

AIR-COOLED

OLKSWAGENS

BEETLES
KARMANN GHIAS
TYPES 2 & 3

Colin Burnham

First published in 1986 by Osprey Publishing Limited
59 Grosvenor Street, London W1X 9DA
First reprint summer 1987
Second reprint spring 1988
Third reprint summer 1989

British Library Cataloguing in Publication Data

Burnham, Colin
  Air-cooled Volkswagens,
  1. Volkswagen automobile
  I. Title
  629.2'222   TL215.V6
ISBN 0-85045-733-5

Editor Tony Thacker
Design David Tarbutt

Printed in Hong Kong

Previous page The plate, *NOFATGY*, and the *wild*
sign on the wall in the background sum up the
California VW scene

Back cover Colin Burnham managed to capture
some of the elusive English sunshine in which to
photograph his own Cal-look '68 Bug

About the author
Colin Burnham is a freelance photojournalist
specializing in out-of-the-ordinary automotive
subjects. His passion for air-cooled Volkswagens
was born out of a close, though sometimes
frustrating, relationship with a 1963 Sunroof
Beetle whilst studying at art college. Since then he
has owned several VWs, the most notable being
his current Cal-look Bug, custom-built over a four-
year period. A former Technical Editor of
England's *Street Machine* magazine, Colin's work
appears regularly in several European and
American publications. He lives with his wife and
young son in North London.

Photography* and text by Colin Burnham

*Most of the photographs in this book were taken by the
author in Southern California, but he wishes to thank Jacky
Morel of *Nitro* magazine (France) and David Darby, Norman
Hodson and Roger Philips of *Custom Car* (England) for providing
the photos on the front cover and pages 32–33, 112, 113 and
114–115 – as well as the owners of all the extraordinary VWs
portrayed herein.

Front cover For once the sun shone in England at
least long enough for photographers Roger Philips
and Norman Hodson to assemble this collection of
Beetles, Ghias and a Type 3 owned from top to
bottom by Julian Reap, Rob Hendon, Tania
Pannell, Andy Barry, Gary Clift, El Ritchie and
Barry Cripps

Contents

Introduction

A small car at a small price for the ordinary working-class people in Europe. It was the dream of Ferdinand Porsche, an extremely talented, middle-aged Austrian car designer back in the early thirties. A dream which, through a complex set of circumstances related to Hitler's quest for power, eventually became the Volkswagen. The world's most successful car, with over 20 million sold during its 34 years of production in Germany.

Nowhere was the air-cooled VW more popular than in the USA, especially in the Golden State of California—a fact which has never been more evident than it is today. Whether you're cruising the highway or negotiating the supermarket parking lot, they're always there *en masse*. Young people love them. They're 'fun', they're 'cute', and they're cheap and simple to 'fix-up'. What's more, it's this intrinsic simplicity and omnipresence, coupled with an unseeming performance potential, which makes them the perfect basis for customizing. Literally tens of thousands of ageing VWs have undergone complete transformations in California in a myriad of different treatments. It is that fact which forms the basis of this book. I hope you enjoy it.

Colin Burnham
London, England

VW in the US

The first-ever shipment of Volkswagens to the United States arrived in New York in 1950. They were met with immediate disdain. The weird little car from Wolfsburg was well and truly tarnished with the memories of wartime press jibes about 'Hitler's car', and in one case a cartoon depicted the car with a machine-gun protruding through the windshield. It smelt of anything but luxury; its unorthodox appearance and mechanical design merely gave rise to suspicion, and its very approach to motoring was completely out of keeping with American trends. Only 352 sedans were sold in that first year, and its prospects within the world's largest car market looked altogether bleak.

By 1955 production in Europe had reached a

Above Any Beetle or air-cooled derivative, regardless of year, is an appreciating asset when in good, original condition. Consequently, there are an ever-increasing number of enthusiasts and collectors investing time and money in the restoration of VWs. And, in the case of earlier models, adorning them with genuine period accessories. This '60 Bug has that all-American 1950s flavour, but with European-style bumpers

staggering 1000 units a day, and VW had established an official US subsidiary called Volkswagen of America (VWoA), with its headquarters on Fifth Avenue. You'd think they couldn't have chosen a worse time—just when

Detroit was tooling-up to build some of its most outlandish, chrome-encrusted land yachts—but the 'Bug' was catching on, especially out in California. Residents of the Golden State have always gone for things that other Americans consider off-beat or zany, so it was only to be expected. Total sales for 1955 jumped four-fold over the previous year to 36,000, including 3000 Transporters. The future was looking promising for VW.

In contrast to the early post-war days in Europe when the then British Army-controlled factory was simply supplying cars to a continent suffering from an acute shortage of vehicles, the Volkswagen in America was having to prove itself to a discerning motoring public. Those liberal-minded citizens who chose to buy one soon developed admiration and respect for the little German car, and its reputation for reliability spread more by word of mouth than official exhortation, as advertising other than showroom sales literature was almost non-existent during the early years.

What had previously been looked upon as an insignificant threat to the US motoring giants was, by the late 1950s, taking on an increasingly menacing look. The fins-and-chrome craze was beginning to wane as American consumers began to awaken to this highly expensive, moreover ludicrous method of establishing their social status, and a more rational approach to motoring began to emerge. As did a Beetle black market, since the car's popularity had actually outstripped authorized dealer deliveries. Enterprising foreign agents shipped the cars through various ports in small numbers and distributed them to non-VW agents and used-car dealers.

In the spring of 1959, under the leadership of Carl Hahn in America, VW decided that the time had come to launch their first national advertising campaign. That autumn, Detroit's big three—Ford, GM and Chrysler—were to introduce their own brand of 'compact' car in an attempt to stem the growing flood of foreign cars that were reaching the USA (though unlike the Bug, many of these

Left Words fail when trying to describe this somewhat disguised 'wagon, suffice to say it's a regular attraction at California VW shows

early imports weren't really suited to operation in America, proving to be unreliable on long journeys and in extreme weather conditions). Hahn had recently arrived from Germany with the task of resisting this counter-attack. Finding a suitable advertising agency took him three months and involved him in meeting more than 4000 persuasive American ad men. The Beetle account was eventually awarded to the Doyle Dane Bernbach agency of New York, whose unusual but effective approach, not to mention integrity, impressed Hahn as much as it had such clients as Levis and El Al Airlines. The Volkswagen ads they produced through the 1960s and early 1970s literally changed the face of advertising—not just in America, but across the world—and they were undoubtedly one of the main contributory factors in VW's enormous success in the USA.

The copy, usually self-deprecating rather than self-congratulatory, spoke to the reader as though he was an intelligent friend, as opposed to a faceless consumer. It didn't promise a dream life or a rocket-ship ride, instead it suggested that the car buyer 'think small'. The Beetle was sincere. It was *real*. Buying one was a way of getting back to basics. The People's Car and Bus became icons for the 'flower power' generation that wanted to reverse the technological nightmare symbolized by the Detroit giants and later, more frighteningly, by Vietnam.

Within two years of the new home-produced compacts being launched, imported car sales in the US fell by almost 50 per cent—though VW sales were completely unscathed. In fact they improved, and in 1962 the company celebrated a total of one million units in the States, not counting the black market contingent. By the time Carl Hahn flew home to Germany in 1964, sales had almost tripled during his five-year stay, there was a highly organized distributor-dealer network right across North America, and VW had acquired almost 70 per cent of the foreign car market.

It is interesting to compare VW's progress in the 1960s against the changes within the domestic motor industry. While the Bug and its air-cooled relatives stayed faithful to Dr Porsche's pre-war formula, Detroit's so-called 'economy' cars soon began to flaunt more and more weight, bigger engines and 'sport trim' packages. Just as the Beetle was a symbol of sincerity, American cars became instant identity kits, an expression of where the driver 'was at'. Cars like the Riviera, Malibu and Monaco were so called to appeal to the man of leisure, while the hard-driving guys bought

machines like the Bonneville, Charger and Cobra. Each year's crop was a little bigger, a little more luxurious, and a little more powerful than the last. Yet still more and more consumers became fascinated by the staid little Bug, an anti-car by the standards of its day. Dependable, durable, faithful and thrifty—the Volkswagen was to the 1960s what Henry Ford's Model T had been to the teens—the beloved car of the *people*.

Annual sales in the USA peaked in 1968, with well over half a million Bugs, Buses, Type 3s and Karmann Ghias being sold that year. But sadly, sales of the ubiquitous Bug declined steadily thereafter. In the early 1970s, devaluation of the dollar and rising production costs meant that the

showroom price of a Volkswagen became noticeably inflated. This was followed by a general recession in the car market caused by the sharp rise in oil prices in 1973 and the subsequent influx of small, fuel-efficient cars—notably the water-cooled VW Rabbit. The curtain finally fell on the greatest act in motoring history on 19 January 1978, when the last People's Car came off the production line in Germany.

When Heinz Nordhoff (VW's first and longest-serving *Herr General Direktor*) made his first sales trip to the States in 1949, little could he have envisaged the day when Dr Porsche's creation would be seen on every freeway between New York and LA. The vehicle which had been thought

Above Not all California Bugs are rolling *objects d'art*. Many people still see them as the most cost-effective means of day-to-day transportation

of initially as nothing more than a joke on four wheels, became the country's biggest-selling small car and earned the respect of millions. Conquering the US car market was undoubtedly VW's finest achievement, and the evidence will certainly remain for many years to come. Long live the Bug!

Cal-look

The place is Huntington Beach, Southern California, just north of exclusive Newport Beach along the Pacific Coast Highway. It's the centre of SoCal surfing activity, a laid-back beach community lined with sky-high palm trees, multi-coloured surf shops and a variety of fast-food eateries. Where all the streets have names like Sunrise Drive and Seashell Boulevard, and the young summer residents are blonde, bronzed and predictably well proportioned. Certainly, it has all the ingredients of an imaginary Beach Boys movie, circa 1963. But then those all-important elements of West Coast imagery—the cars—are not perhaps what you might expect them to be.

What was once a territory ruled by hopped-up 'Woodies' and cut-down 'Deuce Coupés', is now the cruising ground for a relatively new breed of hot rod. They're brightly coloured, super-low and tricked-out in every department, yet they retain the shape that is familiar the world over. They have an in-built reputation for non-performance, even austerity, but many of these slick-looking examples can turn the quarter-mile quicker than a Ferrari. They're a young person's car, a 'cool' mode of transportation, and collectively they represent a multi-million dollar industry on the West Coast. They're called 'Cal-look' VWs.

Left This is the California-look for Volkswagens. It consists, most importantly, of a severe nose-down attitude that is usually gained by one of several commercially available lowering devices for the VW front end. Secondly, what little exterior trim there is must be removed (including the front indicators), and the resultant holes filled for a smoother overall appearance. Likewise the bumpers are relieved of their unsightly guards, or otherwise removed altogether and replaced by small, angled 'nerf bars'. Essentially, the idea is to make the simple Bug look even simpler, more understated. The all-important wheel selection is generally limited to the reproduction Empi eight-spoke, Porsche 911 five-spoke, or painted or chromed stock rims fitted with early-style Porsche hub caps. These are wrapped in skinny-section steel radials on the front, with 'fats' at the back. One-piece door windows are *de rigueur*, as are smooth window rubbers without the original trim groove. Finally, the look is always enhanced by a perfect paintjob, traditionally a fresh bright colour

15

Above The engine department is where the Cal-lookers really shine. Thanks to the developments within Midget, off-road and drag racing over the last 20 years, there is a vast range of speed equipment readily available for the flat-four. Hot street engines, like John Dean's super-clean 1776 cc, are normally based on the late-model 1600 case with dual-port cylinder heads. The 1600 can be enlarged to several different displacements by substituting larger diameter pistons and cylinders, and when these are used in conjunction with a 'stroker' crank, the figure can be increased even beyond 2.2 litres. The 1776 cc is a popular choice for the street, utilizing 90.5 mm pistons with the

stock 69 mm crank. High-revving engines require an eight-dowelled counter-weighted crank to survive for any length of time, and John's was balanced along with the Cima pistons, stock rods, lightened flywheel ($12\frac{1}{2}$ lb) and heavy duty clutch. Available camshafts range from mild to wild, and this builder's decision to go for a hot Engle 130 rod was based, as it should be, on the engine's radically-improved breathing capabilities. The dual-port heads incorporate big valves, heavy-duty rocker shafts and pushrods, and were hand-ported for the maximum possible flow. The fuel/air mix atomizes through a pair of giant Weber 48 carbs, while the exhaust gases pulsate through a

Fourtuned header with dual mufflers. Lubrication is also much improved thanks to a high-volume oil pump and full-flow external filtering, while a trick-looking 1950s fan-housing was modified to accept the much-acclaimed late-model offset cooler. The rebuilt transaxle features close-ratio third and fourth gears, a Super Diff and a heavy-duty side plate. With an estimated 150 hp on tap, John's drivetrain is an excellent representation of Cal-look motivation

Above With its bulbous nose and MacPherson strut front suspension, many Cal-look enthusiasts consider the Super Beetle to be an unsuitable basis for the treatment—but not Anaheim's John Dean. His '73 Super-looker was one of the first of its kind in SoCal, and, so John claims, the first to be painted in the now-popular shade of Porsche Raspberry. It has all the right ingredients, to be sure

Above John's *DUMPER* exemplifies the Cal-look stance: dumped-in-the-front and lowered a little at the rear. He brought the front down by shortening and modifying the original struts to incorporate the stock springs, although adjustable struts are now available. Rather than use late-model European bumpers with in-set turn signals, John installed his own custom 'signals within the bumper's recess. Highly-polished 6 x 15 in. Porsche alloys are encircled by 135/15 Michelins at the front and 185/70 Klebers at the rear

Right The Super Bug's slotted deck lid has been swapped for a smooth '69 item minus the licence plate light, and the rather applicable 'plate relocated to make the rear end appear smoother. Late-1960s tail-lights in place of the stock 'moon' assemblies do nothing to spoil the visual effect. No less than 14 coats of acrylic enamel were sprayed on the Bug's body

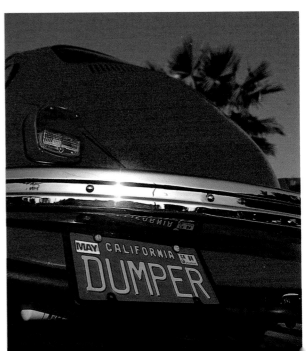

Above Inside, grey carpeting and a light grey velour headliner are contrasted with black vinyl and colourful cloth inserts on the door panels and Scheel front seats. The standard 'grab and guess' shifter was replaced by a short-throw, positive-gate Empi model, the steering wheel is a leather-rimmed three-spoke, and a tach now resides beneath the dash. The Cal-look is applied to all air-cooled VWs in California—check John's brother's Notchback in the Type 3 section of this book

Above 'Split window' is the term used to describe all Beetles manufactured before 1953, the year Volkswagen changed to a one-piece oval rear window. Splits are much sought-after—particularly the Sunroof model—because of their 'period' character. And since demand exceeds supply, more than one company are manufacturing split window roof sections in fibreglass to satisfy the desires of the less-fortunate Bug enthusiast. The owner of this lowered two-toner, however, has a real steel example with all its original trim firmly in place— what you might call a 'resto-looker'

Right Oval window Bugs are *neat*, and not all VW enthusiasts consider them too precious to modify. With their tiny little tail-lights, distinctly-formed deck lids and elongated air intakes, many consider them to be the perfect basis for the new-look Cal treatment. Whereas the demon rust has killed off the majority of vintage Volkswagens in Europe, there are still lots to be found in sunny California. This turquoise sedan is actually a '57 model, the year before VW made the rear window rectangular in shape, following the suggestion of a world-famous Italian car designer

20

Top left Todd Riley's low-down Looker is one of three cars that he owns. The others are a '63 Convertible Bug and a '65 Corvette, but Todd enjoys driving this Oval the most. He acquired the car back in 1983 from its original owner, and proceeded to 'look it' over the following six months. It now runs a heavy-breathing 1776 cc with all manner of go-faster goodies, and has turned the quarter-mile in just under 15 seconds. Its pan-scraping stance was achieved by cutting, turning and rewelding the centre section of both front torsion tubes, and relocating the rear trailing arms on the splined rear torsion bars. Shorter-length gas shocks are utilized. Todd has relieved the car of its hood and side trim, hood handle and quarter lights, and installed one-piece door windows, Cal-look rubbers, European bumper and, inside, a pair of low-slung Toyota Celica seats

Left The treatment of this '57 reflects Todd's sympathy for nostalgia. He has retained the original '55–'57 front turn signals, as well as the horn grilles and wheels—although the rears are widened slightly. But how neat they look with a lick of paint, beauty rings, and early Porsche hub caps with Wolfsburg centre crests

Above For comparison and admiration, a fully-restored '54

23

Above There was a time when all Cal-look Bugs were painted in straight, primary or pastel colours, but nowadays almost any shade is acceptable—certainly with graphic stripes as nice as these. They're done in Pagan Gold, Tangerine and Brandywine Candy against metallic copper enamel, and represent the imagination of 25-year-old retail clerk Michael Feser. With its colour-matched eight-spoke Empi-style rims and other Cal touches, 'Feez's' '68 is a modern-day Looker through and through

Above 'Refined' is the only way to describe this very un-Volkswagen-like striped interior. Upholstered in camel-coloured leatherette with 'new wave' in-lays, it is a superb piece of work, both in design and execution. The seats were carefully selected from a junkyard Honda, while the padded dashboard surround and centre console are both custom-made. Wall-to-wall carpeting, a four-spoke leather-rimmed 'wheel and the mandatory megawatt sound system help to make this VW the neatest on the streets of Roseville, California

Overleaf 'Okay, Angie, hold it there.' Robert K. Smith, Features Editor of *Hot VWs* magazine, is one of the most popular characters within the SoCal VW scene. Here he's shooting a feature on Angie DiGiacomo's slick '66 *CAL DUB*, with Angie playing the model role. The beautiful black Bug was put together by Angie's husband, Jack, and in many ways it represents the archetypal Cal-look Bug; lowered, dechromed, with chromed nerf bars, Porsche alloys and superb detailing throughout. And that means it's not just a Looker, but a 'cooker' too. Under the 'lid sits a hot, dual-Webered 1835 cc engine, enveloped in chrome and polished aluminium and with enough 'go' to make this car a possible contender at the stop light grand prix. Not that Angie or Jack are into street racing though. They prefer cruising to the shows and 'meeting all the good people'

Above Check this for a slick rewiring job! It takes a lot of time, patience and know-how to rewire a car to a show-winning standard, and this meticulous piece of work has helped Rick Ohlandt pick up loads of trophies on the California circuit

Above When Greg Aronson lowered and dechromed his mag-rimmed street Bug in 1969, he
couldn't possibly have conceived that thousands of
VW enthusiasts would follow his example. But,
thanks to an official classification of 'The California
Look' by *Hot VWs* magazine in February 1975,
that's exactly what happened. One of those
thousands is Bob Jackson, a professional VW
mechanic whose 'Peaches 'n' Scream'-nicknamed
$20,000 Volkswagen illustrates just how far street
fashion can evolve. Bob built his car purely to win
trophies at shows; it is never ever driven on the
street. It's a '62 with all the usual Cal-look
modifications expertly done

Above Rust-coloured Cadillac velour material was used in the upholstery work to complement the specially-mixed peach paintjob. The dashboard has been panelled-over and filled with an impressive array of VDO jet cockpit-style gauges, a stereo and graphic equalizer, and various switches. Who could resist the opportunity to drive this little screamer?

Above This is what it takes to win trophies for 'Best Engine'. The owner spent in excess of $5000 on parts alone for his 2084 cc engine, incorporating the best of everything. It would probably put out around 220 hp with the pedal on the metal

Overleaf Rick Perman's smooth '65 typifies not so much the SoCal-look as the *SoEnd*-look. SoEnd? That's short for Southend-on-Sea, Essex, a relatively small town with a big reputation for turning out some of the nicest California-inspired VWs in the UK. Rick's right-hand drive features a long list of body tricks—moulded-in fenders and running boards, Oval deck lid and tail-lights, to name but a few—a fully-detailed 1776 cc motor, and a truly unique candy-striped paintjob. And, like most of the growing number of Cal-look enthusiasts in Great Britain, he built his car for low bucks—like less than £1000 all-in. Way to go, Rick!

Previous page VW enthusiasts the world over love talking about their cars, and I'm no exception. Mine's a '68 Cal-look Bug, built in England as a Project Car for *Street Machine* magazine. I bought the car in 1981 for £60, which included a seized engine, the usual dings and European body rot. It had been imported from Holland two years previously, and the former owner had abandoned it in the local pub car park. Fortunately, it left Wolfsburg with a steel sunroof and left-hand drive, which suited my plans for an authentic California-style Bug to a tee. Unfortunately, some four years passed by before those plans reached fruition and the car was back on the street in its new guise. It has a '66 hood and a '57 deck, '73 doors and '65 tail-lights (with US-spec lenses). Early-style front and rear aprons and bumpers have been fitted, along with new fenders, Super

Beetle-type running boards and small, round Lucas front indicators. Not forgetting one-piece tinted door glass, Cal-look window rubbers and Baby Tornado door mirrors. The paint is VW Mars Red. Sway-A-Way adjusters were used to lower the front end, which also features early Opel Kadett-size Koni adjustable shocks and ventilated (drilled) discs, while the rear was brought down one spline and fitted with Bilstein gas shocks. For wheels 'n' tyres, I chose the traditional Cal combo: 5½ in. Empi-style eight-spokes wrapped in 135/15 Michelins on the front and 165s rear. Does a Cal-Bug turn heads in England? You bet!

Above left The area that fellow road-users never see and a good many VW owners prefer not to, is where the real freaks invest most of their time and money. Underneath the paint and polish is a 'sensible' 1641 cc that puts out about 90 hp. It's fully balanced with an eight-dowelled stock crank, 87 mm Cima pistons, Engle 110 cam, worked-on dual-port heads, Gene Berg oil pump, full-flow filter system, 13-row external cooler, $12\frac{1}{2}$ lb lightened flywheel, dual 40DRLA Dellorto carbs, Fourtuned exhaust, and a few other go-faster goodies. Not a Porsche beater, but certainly a quick enough runner and economical to boot

Above Throughout the project, there was a conscious effort to mimic the styling of the Bug's richer brother, the Porsche, hence the overall red/black theme and patterned cloth interior. The seats are aftermarket Cobra recliners, with the original rear seat and door panels upholstered to match. Grey cloth was used for the headliner, and thin pile black carpet on the floor and in the front luggage compartment. Either side of a late-model speedo, where the speaker grilles used to be, are tach and oil pressure/temperature gauges, while between the seats is a genuine Empi shifter. A four-spoke 'wheel and a four-speaker sound system makes cruising to VW events in England an altogether enjoyable experience

Left Balboa Boulevard, Orange County

Below Wanna be a 'low Cal' hero? Dump your Bug down-in-the-weeds and join the 'Locals Only' V-dub club of California. There are hundreds of clubs catering for all types of VW enthusiasts in the Golden State

Bottom As seen on the engine lid of a '57

VW action

Gather together more than 300 of the world's most colourful Volkswagens between LA and Sacramento and what have you got? A *California Caravan*, that's what! A two-mile long, rolling car show making its way to the Memorial Day *Bug-O-Rama*, 420 miles north. Beautiful Bugs and Buses, terrific Types 3s and a bunch of great-looking Ghias, bumper-to-bumper at the double-nickel speed limit, paintjobs and chrome sparkling in the sunshine. To witness such a sight is to appreciate the phenomenal level of enthusiasm for air-cooled VWs in California.

This annual pilgrimage, organized by some of the numerous VW clubs and promoted by *Hot VWs*

Below The '84 California Caravan. It started with just a handful of cars in Buena Park, Orange County, at 6 am, but by the time it reached Sacramento the party was almost 200-strong. Here, after the third port of call, there were about 60 VWs waiting to rejoin Highway 99 North. The journey took 12 hours, and highlights were shown on Channel 26 TV's 'News at Ten'

Right *1L067VW* was one of the 300-odd Caravanners that rolled into Sacto in 1986, but the only one with turquoise paint, Baby Turbo door mirrors, louvres in the running boards, a protective bra *and* a custom-made Targa top. The two-fingered symbol means 'hang loose'

magazine (one of several specialist publications), represents just one of the many 'happenings' that make up the Pacific Coast scene. It began with the now-defunct *Bug-In* in 1968, and today includes such festivities as the *Bug-Out*, *Bug-Bash*, *Bug-Burn* and *Volkfest*. There are Transporter-only shows, Type 3 days, vintage events and VW swap meets, indoor and outdoor, whatever you prefer.

Apart from the extraordinary vehicles on display, most of these shows incorporate a variety of spectator attractions, such as the Club Car Push, Engine Pull and Beauty Queen contest. Then of course there are the traders and individuals offering a pot-pourri of parts, and, if you're lucky, the Drags. Wheel-standing ten-second quarter-mile Bugs—now that really is *unbelievable*. . .

Above and above right One wonders how the average Wolfsburg assembly-line worker of 30 years ago would react to seeing numerous pre-'58 Oval windows cruising with the Cal Caravan. He'd more than likely smile, like every other passing motorist on the road to Sacramento

Right How low can ya go? In the case of these three Lookers, to the max!

42

Left The Bug-O-Rama is a twice-yearly, one-day event held in Northern California, and since the demise of the world-famous Bug-In at Orange County Raceway in 1983, has grown to be one of the major happenings on the West Coast. It's a true showcase for some of the finest modified VWs, ultra-stock clean machines and fastest quarter-milers, attracting fans from all over the United States

Below Pacific Coast VW events include a variety of attractions and never least popular with the spectators is the Beauty Contest. At Bug-O-Rama XII, Sacramento Raceway, 18-year-old Tina Jeanette was the undisputed 'Queen Looker'

Above How about this for creative custom upholstery? As the Cal-look cult evolves, the competition at shows becomes greater, thus trophy seekers are forced to think up new ideas in order to score those all-important extra points. This neat piece of work was conceived and executed by top trimmer Howard Bennett from Orangeville, California

Above Cars like Frank Fabozzi's '56 Oval attract
all the spectators at every VW show. Literally
every part of this candy-coloured creation is either
chromed, polished or painted to perfection. The
early Sunroof body sits on a '67 chassis with disc
brakes and runs a full-on 2.2-litre motor, trick
custom interior and Porsche alloy rims. When
Frank acquired this VW, his sixth, he was
determined that it would be the best-looking Bug
around. It's a tough one to beat, for sure

Left and below The 'Engine Pull' is a contest in which several two-man teams must remove and reinstall a Beetle engine in the shortest possible time. They must drive the car into position beforehand, and drive it away after. This swift pair did it in just 3 min 6 sec and won a T-shirt each for their efforts! The world record stands at approximately $2\frac{1}{2}$ minutes

Dual Dellorto Blow Through
Sand Rail Turbocharged
$3195.- to 399/.-
ask for details
140 page Catalogue $3.-

Above Turbocharged engines of 200-plus hp are available off-the-shelf from several specialist companies, as are all manner of hop-up goodies from any one of the many air-cooled emporiums on the West Coast. Indeed, for a V-dub freak, any major VW meet in California is like 'shopper's paradise'

Right Heavy-duty wheelie bars and a 'stinger' exhaust are sure signs that this street-driven '67 Bug is true to its licence plate. Twelve-second quarter-mile times at close to 100 mph is nothing unusual for a hot street VW

Straight-line performance is an American institution. During World War 2, tales of racing hot rods on dry lakes and on the long, straight streets of an unpopulated Southern California spread throughout the infantry. Consequently, when young men returned home to various parts of the country, hyped-up on the idea of straight-line racing, pockets filled with severance pay, they built their own hot rods and made straight for the dozens of huge airfields or landing strips that lay dormant following the end of the war. Thus the sport of drag racing was born. For years, nobody even considered racing a VW; with its slow, horizontally-opposed four-cylinder engine and equally 'weird' appearance, it was the very antithesis of a hot rod. But then, as sales of the People's Car escalated in the US, the quarter-mile challenge became irresistible—at least to a few off-beat Californians. And so it was discovered that deep within every VW engine was the heart of a middle-weight contender, packing a knock-out punch that belied its overall displacement. . .

Left Bryee Jones actually sets his car up to wheelie and even goes to the trouble of removing the front shock absorbers. It does help the car to stand up, but you should hear the sound when it hits the ground! At Bug-In 31, the car came down so hard the battery came through the aluminium floorboard and both headlights popped out! Needless to say, Jones' VW is a real crowd-pleaser

Above Jim 'Granpaw' Upshaw never misses an opportunity to race his lime green Cal-Bug, and the fans love him for it. What's more, while the social-security-aged racer may only run in the 17-second bracket (always with his lady riding shotgun), he sure knows the meaning of 'cutting a good light'

Below Life in the pit lane

Above Most serious drag racing VWs are as impressive on top as they are underneath. This pearl and candy-striped quarter-miler proves the point

Above Steve Wade's fibreglass-bodied, tube-chassised 'Quarter Flash' is one of a growing new generation of VWs being used for a single purpose: to race the quarter-mile. Until recently, most VW hot rodders drove their cars to the dragstrip, raced them, and, if they were still in one piece, drove them home again. Steve's funny car-style sedan shows how far VW drag racing has developed. With this kind of weight, full-on turbo/fuel injection power, the right gearing and slicks, ten-second quarters are a dime a dozen. . .

Baja style

American off-road racing is a rough, tough and very exciting motor sport, and modified VWs are an integral part of it. The demands made on both the vehicles and the competitors is extreme, and events of up to 1000 miles over the worst possible terrain may take 20 or more hours of straight-through driving and severe physical punishment. Off-road racers must defy the hazards of boulders, sandtraps, gulleys and so on, and disaster can strike as quickly in the desert as on a smoothly-paved 200 mph circuit.

The sport was officially born in November 1967, with the inaugural running of the Baja 1000; a madcap dash down the rocky length of the Baja-California peninsula in northwest Mexico. Of the 68 vehicles of all types which had gathered in the bull-ring in Tijuana, a Meyers-Manx VW-based dune buggy was the first to slide to a halt in La Paz, 950 miles south. The Volkswagen's off-road capabilities were recognized and the words 'Baja Bug' soon became a household term—in California, at least.

Baja Bugs (pronounced bah-hah) are full-bodied VWs, modified for off-road purposes. They feature abbreviated fibreglass noses, tails and fenders,

Left Whereas the first-ever Baja race was staged to find out what type of vehicle would be the fastest over the harrowing trail, there are now more than 20 different classes of off-road vehicles, several of which are VW-based. Off-road racing has become big business and a finely-tuned science, and many of today's full-bodied racing Baja Bugs bear little more than a basic resemblance to the venerable Volkswagen, being stripped of all unnecessary weight and equipped with super-heavy-duty components. This shot shows such a vehicle careering through the silt at Johnson Valley near Barstow, California, on the first lap of the SCORE International 'Baja in Barstow 500 Km' in 1984

increased ground clearance and knobbly mud
tyres. All the bolt-on panels and parts necessary to
transform an ordinary People's Car are available
over-the-counter from countless specialists, thus
they represent one of the most popular alternative
forms of transport. Some more 'alternative' than
others. . .

Above While some take it to the limit for
potentially big rewards, others do it purely for
fun. Beefed-up stock suspension, big tyres and a
properly-built motor are the basic ingredients for
off-road action

Above Jim Cocores' Class 5 Baja Bug—seen here in action during the Baja 500—is a true state-of-the-art machine. Costing the best part of $25,000 to build, it features a sophisticated spaceframe chassis, a 2466 cc Porsche 914 (Type 4) motor, a beefed-up '78 Bus transaxle, rack 'n' pinion steering, and high-tech suspension at both ends. The front, with its extended trailing arms and massive shock towers, allows for 14 in. of wheel travel, while the rear provides approximately 18 in., thanks to ultra-trick CV joints and enormous air shocks. Jim has won numerous off-road events in this super-tough 'fiver', but on this occasion his was one of 87 vehicles which failed to complete the 321-mile race

Above Chip Lane drives this high-riding Baja, but rarely off the street. With its 33 in.-tall mud tyres, body lift kit, driving lights and other off-road accoutrements, most folk would assume that this clean machine was on its way to the Mojave Desert. But no. Chip's idea of fun is looking down on all-American muscle cars at the Saturday-night cruise. Different Volks for different folks, that's the name of the game in the USA

Above Just the thing for a backyard VW mechanic, the Mobilehoist runs on domestic electric or generator power and will lift a low-buck Baja racer in a matter of seconds

Above Yes, by it's very nature, the ubiquitous Bug
really is the perfect basis for a unique creation,
like this custom-built Baja-style truck

Left Full marks for attention to detail!

Above A lot of VW specialists in the US have their own specially-built VW for promotional purposes. Scotty's Foreign Parts put together this stubby little Baja

Right and overleaf This is what happens when you take 18 in. out of the centre of a Volkswagen—you end up with a *THINBUG*! After owning four relatively standard Beetles, mechanical engineering student Andrew Hancock figured it was time for something a little different. So, he took a $50 V W and spent approximately 1200 hours learning about the art of major body modification. Nine inches were taken out of each side of the floorpan before the ambitious sectioning operation took place. It involved all kinds of cutting, trimming, welding and metal shrinking, new glass, a new pedal assembly, gas tank relocation and much, much more. The good news is that Andrew's skinny sedan cost less than $1000 to complete, with the aid of many skilled and willing hands. From dead side-on at a distance, there's nothing especially different about this '69 V-dub. But, if you happen to glance up and see it in the rear-view mirror—as they say, it could only happen in California. . .

65

Above Adaptor plates are available to mate a wide variety of engines to the VW transaxle. The Mazda rotary, for example, will even fit under the standard Beetle engine cover. A V8, on the other hand, requires slight cosmetic surgery. . .

Right And now for something *completely* different. Young Mitch Walter must be the envy of every high school kid in Downey, California. At just 16 years of age and without a driver's licence, he owns what is undoubtedly the hottest rod in town; this unique V8 front-engined VW! Starting with a $300 'Dub minus motor, Mitch and his street rodder Dad spent the best part of 12 months constructing this ground-pounding creation. After stripping the car to pieces and selling the floorpan, trans and front end for $250, they began by designing and fabricating a new 2 x 4 in. tube chassis. It utilizes a narrowed '68

Chevy Corvair front suspension unit and steering, together with a super-strong Ford nine-inch rear end. The latter had to be narrowed a full 16 in. in order to accommodate a pair of ten-inch-wide Centerline racing wheels under the stock VW rear fenders, following contemporary street machine trends. Where once sat a fuel tank there's now a hopped-up 327-cubic inch Chevy V8 that will put out at least 300 hp should Mitch so desire. In relative terms, that's around six times the power of a standard 1600 Beetle! The engine is mated to an auto trans and cooled with the help of a GM radiator positioned where the spare wheel used to be. Much of the necessary cooling air enters the rad through the inverted louvres in the lower area of the squared-off hood and exits via several rows of conventional louvres higher up. The car has a full integral roll-cage for safety and strength, a Ford Mustang shifter, a race-style aluminium fuel tank under the deck lid—in fact the only thing 'sedate' about this '69 Sedan is its relatively stock sheetmetal. From the outside, with the hood down, it could pass for a regular Cal-Bug. But when the driver turns the ignition key, there's no mistaking that this is one red-hot VW with a difference!

Convertibles

Convertibles are cool! Leastways, that's what it says on the back of one of the best-selling VW T-shirts in Southern California. And there can be few Convertible owners in the world who would disagree—or 'plain Jane' Bug owners come to that. After all, when you take the virtues of a Volkswagen and add a convertible top, what else can it be other than a 'cool' mode of transport with tremendous pizazz?

The VW Convertible—Cabriolet, to be more precise—was built by Karmann in Osnabrück, West Germany, right up until January 1980, two years after the demise of the hardtop. Ever since the first one appeared just four years after the war, the Convert' was always considered superior to the standard Beetle on which it was based. Furthermore, this has always been reflected in its price. In 1949, when only the fortunate few were in a position to consider a People's Car, they actually cost 50 per cent more than a regular Bug, yet sold reasonably well. Such was the car's special appeal, which it retained for more than 30 years.

Interestingly, an international team selected by a French magazine once deemed the top-of-the-range Beetle as the vehicle with the biggest snob value. While *Road & Track* magazine described it as 'looking like an old English perambulator—you almost expect to see a nanny pushing it along'. That may be so, but one thing's for sure. In sunny California, Convertible Bugs are fun cars to drive.

Left *Let's go surfin' now, everybody's learnin' how. . .*

Right The VW top is vinyl on the outside. And leatherette on the inside (to prevent shiny metal bars from showing off). In between there's a one-inch-thick hand-padding that actually cushions sound. All in all, this top makes the Convertible as airtight and weatherproof as our regular sedan. And that's a nice thing to know. Unless of course, you live on the desert

Above This Cabriolet has been made to look earlier than it actually is with the addition of broad whitewall tyres and two-tone paint. Enchanting paint scheme was applied to many Cabrios in the late 1940s and early 1950s—though the colour combinations weren't usually as eye-catching as this

Above Thanks to the benevolent climate and the huge car-orientated population, automotive swap meets are as traditional on the Pacific Coast of America as the Saturday-night drive-in. Amongst the wide variety of cars and parts for sale, one usually stumbles upon a gem—in this case, a 1955 Volkswagen Convertible. To quote a well-known line from Jan & Dean's 'Surf City': *It's not very cherry it's an oldie but a goodie. . .*

Right Mid-1960s Converts, which colour would you like?

Previous page Following World War 2, the British military authorities took control of the bombed-out People's Car factory—the giant industrial showpiece built by Hitler to fulfil the dreams of a nation—and managed to get production of the Volkswagen going for the very first time. Anxious to capitalize on their efforts, the army offered the plant to a number of British car makers and the Ford Motor Company as a going concern, only to be met by an overwhelming negative reaction. So, in 1948 they handed it back to the Germans, and a new man took control. His name was Heinz Nordhoff, and under his leadership production and sales figures rose steadily until the Beetle eventually overtook the Model T Ford as the world's most-produced car. A lesser-known fact is that back in 1948 Nordhoff gave orders to two German coachbuilding companies; one to produce, in prototype form, a full four-seater convertible, the other a luxury two-seater version. The firm of Wilhelm Karmann handled the four-seater and went on to produce more than 330,000, while Joseph Hebmüller created the two-seater. This is one of the 696 Hebmüllers built before the Hebmüller Coachworks was tragically destroyed by a fire in 1950. Fully restored to as-new condition by Maurey Cole, it now rests in Huntington Beach, SoCal, valued at $25,000

Top row The Hebmüller is perhaps the most valuable of all coachbuilt VWs, since only 60 are still known to exist. This '49 Heb' was the 12th to leave the German *Karosserie*, as stated by the chassis number and the owner's personal licence plate. When Maurey acquired the car it was in a more-than-sorry state; almost every panel had to be remade and every single part required refurbishment. The convertible top had long since met its demise, but the bows remained, which enabled the owner to have a new, original-type top made incorporating the letter-box-sized rear window. All in all it was a painstaking exercise, but one which every VW enthusiast lovingly admires

Left Late-model Super Bug on the Pacific Coast Highway. During its 31 years of production, the Karmann Convertible, like the Wolsburg Sedan, went through countless changes and refinements yet always retained its natural charm. Moreover, with its unique mixture of quality, craftsmanship, sportiness and fun, there will only ever be *one* Beetle Convertible

Above What a showpiece! Cameron's flat-four is the ultimate *pièce de résistance*, a built-to-the-hilt 2110 cc which even the late great Dr Porsche would hardly recognize. The engine is based around a late-model crankcase with an 82 mm counter-weighted Berg crank and 90.5 mm pistons and cylinders. Internal goodies include Carrillo rods, a hot Engle V26 cam, and 11:1 compression big valve heads. Notable visible parts are the enormous 48 Webers, centre fan shroud, and a brass-plated alternator stand. No wonder this car is flamed!

Overleaf These off-road racing fans have the perfect mobile base—a Convertible Baja full of cold beers

Right While only the lucky few can achieve individuality on the street in a production car, most accomplish their desire through customizing. Cameron Atchison falls into the latter category. He picked up this '60 Convert' for $2000, then spent about six months and a further $14,000 turning it into a flamed showpiece. The owner has since won numerous trophies for Best of Show, Best Paint, Best Engine, and so on, although he only drives the car about once a month. The list of body tricks includes full-dechroming, recessed tail-lights and front indicators (in bumpers), painted running boards and one-piece door glass. Rather than swap the original link pin/swing axle chassis for a later model better suited to high performance, Cameron went for chrome, polish or paint on *everything* in order to score maximum points at shows. The car is lowered front and rear, and rolls on Pirelli P7-shod Porsche-style five-spokes

Type 2

It has often been said that the Beetle is a car which people either love or hate. If that's the case, then the same must surely apply to the equally-characteristic VW Bus. With its box-like shape, flat face and traditional Volkswagen peculiarities, it is anything but a regular means of transport—but then Bus enthusiasts aren't usually 'regular' sort of people.

The Type 2 Transporter was introduced to the world on 12 November 1949. It must have raised quite a few eyebrows. Though it featured the same wheelbase and 25 hp engine as the Beetle, the bodywork was welded to a sub-structure comprising two steel girders lengthwise with five cross-members between the axles. But thanks to its utilitarian nature it was an instant success,

acquiring the nickname *Bulli*, meaning 'general workhorse' in German. Just under 10,000 Transporters left the factory in the first year, though by 1964 annual production was no less than 20 times that figure.

'Bus freaks' in California generally focus their attention on the pre-1968 split screens, the *real* Type 2s. They were manufactured in many forms over the years—Kombi, Panel Van, Microbus, Deluxe Microbus, Single Cab and Crew Cab Pickups, as well as umpteen special conversions— and it's a case of the earlier the better for the true *aficionado*. By far the most sought-after Buses are the 'Barndoors', those with enormous engine lids built before March 1955. Certainly there are an increasing number of enthusiasts breathing new

life into old Transporters, but that's not to say they're all purists. . .

Above VW Station Wagons are as much a part of Pacific Coast imagery as the proverbial sun, sand and palm trees. The 'Wagon sold well back in the 1960s, partly because of its dual-purpose appeal. By simply undoing six wing nuts and pulling out the two rear bench seats, it turned from a nine-seater car into a 170-cubic-feet-capacity van—ideal for the small businessman with a large family. However, in spite of all its attributes, it was found that American wives particularly disliked the vehicle. Maybe the slightly unorthodox appearance had something to do with it?

Above Volkswagen of America first imported VW Buses into the US way back in 1952. Only ten were registered in that first year, and this two-tone Deluxe model is believed to be the one-and-only survivor. The 17,000-mile '23-window' belongs to vintage VW enthusiast Mike Hornbecker, and it's all original—even the tyres! The Bus spent its first 22 years in America at a VW dealership in Muskogee, Oklahoma, where it sat on display most of the time and was rarely driven. Then, as the story goes, the dealership changed hands in 1975 and the new owner took one look at the Bus and said something like, 'What's that old thing doing around here? Get rid of it!' Evidently he didn't care too much for

Wolfsburg's earlier products. Unlike Washington's Steve Wood, former President of the Split Window Club of America, who saw the subsequent ad ('1952 Deluxe Microbus, 11,000 miles, $2000') and promptly became the vehicle's new keeper. Three years later it was sold to another enthusiast who let it 'mature' under wraps for five years until avid collector Hornbecker eventually bid the right price. Now the present owner has this super-rare VW in rust-free California, he doesn't intend to part with it or drive it too regularly either. After all, with a 25-horse motor and a fully non-synchromesh transaxle, it wouldn't be too much fun anyway

Above What better for a grocery-getter than a topless Type 2? Built for low bucks (and a high-speed suntan), this cut-down cruiser makes for ideal transportation in the Golden State

Left It's hard to believe that Mike Hornbecker's 35-year-old Bus is in original condition, and not the result of a painstaking restoration. The only visible proof lies in the fact that the exterior paint is slightly faded, compared to the dash. All pre-'55 Deluxe Buses had three painted Bakolite dash pods; one housed the speedo and switches, another a clock, but the third was simply a frame for what later became a universally-familiar symbol

Above Plunkett Motor Company's 'Volks Toter'
takes the form of a shortened split-screen single-
cab pickup with a custom-built fifth-wheel trailer.
A truly unique little rig which proves that Type 2s
never die, they're just made to work harder!

Above The Volkswagen Transporter was manufactured in various forms, but none rolled off the assembly line looking quite like this! Orange Plaza Muffler obviously thought that a short commercial would be the most effective means of advertising. . .

Above and left Crew cab pickups are considered 'cool' in California, and Rob Anderson's lowered and louvred '60 must be the *koolest* around. The bright yellow truck features umpteen custom modifications and captures attention wherever it's driven—especially when the crew are on board! *KOOL CAB* was actually the handiwork of previous owner Dennis Thorp, an aircraft painter by trade, and his son, Danny. Obviously a family of louvre lovers, the Thorps had no less than 334 hot rod vents punched into this old Volks—even the lower dash panel received the treatment. Other body changes include a rubber front airdam, steel side skirts, aluminium nerf bars in place of the bumpers, and the removal of the characteristic VW emblem from the truck's face. And, of course, that Corvette Yellow paintjob with contrasting graphic stripes. Inside you'll find new brown vinyl and velour upholstery, a three-spoke wood-rimmed 'wheel, and the mandatory modern-day sound system within the painted steel dash. Rob's ride is powered by an ultra-reliable stock 1600, all polished and painted. As the saying goes, this one's for show, not go

Right English events attract all kinds of individuals too. Witness this much-adorned post-'68 Camper at 'VW Action'. The owner takes his European touring pretty seriously, judging by the badges

Bottom right Nicknamed the 'Samba', the Deluxe Microbus was VW's top-of-the-line Transporter prior to the up-date in 1968. With its huge canvas sunroof and eight 'sky windows', it gave passengers the feeling of being in a sort of mobile aquarium. This one looks stock, apart from the noticeable lowering job, but it's got a hot one out back. What a nice way to travel

Far right Less windows, more privacy

Right and below Jim Riddle's beaten-up, bullet-shot Bus is anything but 'Cal-look', but he always manages to take home a trophy from the shows. But then it always carries the same inscription: 'Worst of Show'!

Left The Society of Transporter Owners (SOTO) is a California club serving the interests of pre-'68 Type 2 enthusiasts. In June 1984 they held their first anniversary meet in Orange County, and this line-up represents just a small fraction of the flat-faced VWs that attended. It's a fast-growing club, with most of its members hell-bent on 100 per cent restoration

Above The song 'Six wheels on my wagon' holds a special significance for the owner of this stretched, six-wheeled Greyhound-style Bus. Some folks will go to extraordinary lengths in order to stand out from the crowd

Above Two-colour paintjobs separated by mid-tone graphics are very popular, and late-model Buses provide the perfect canvas for any would-be creative painter

Overleaf Late at night, Newport Beach, SoCal

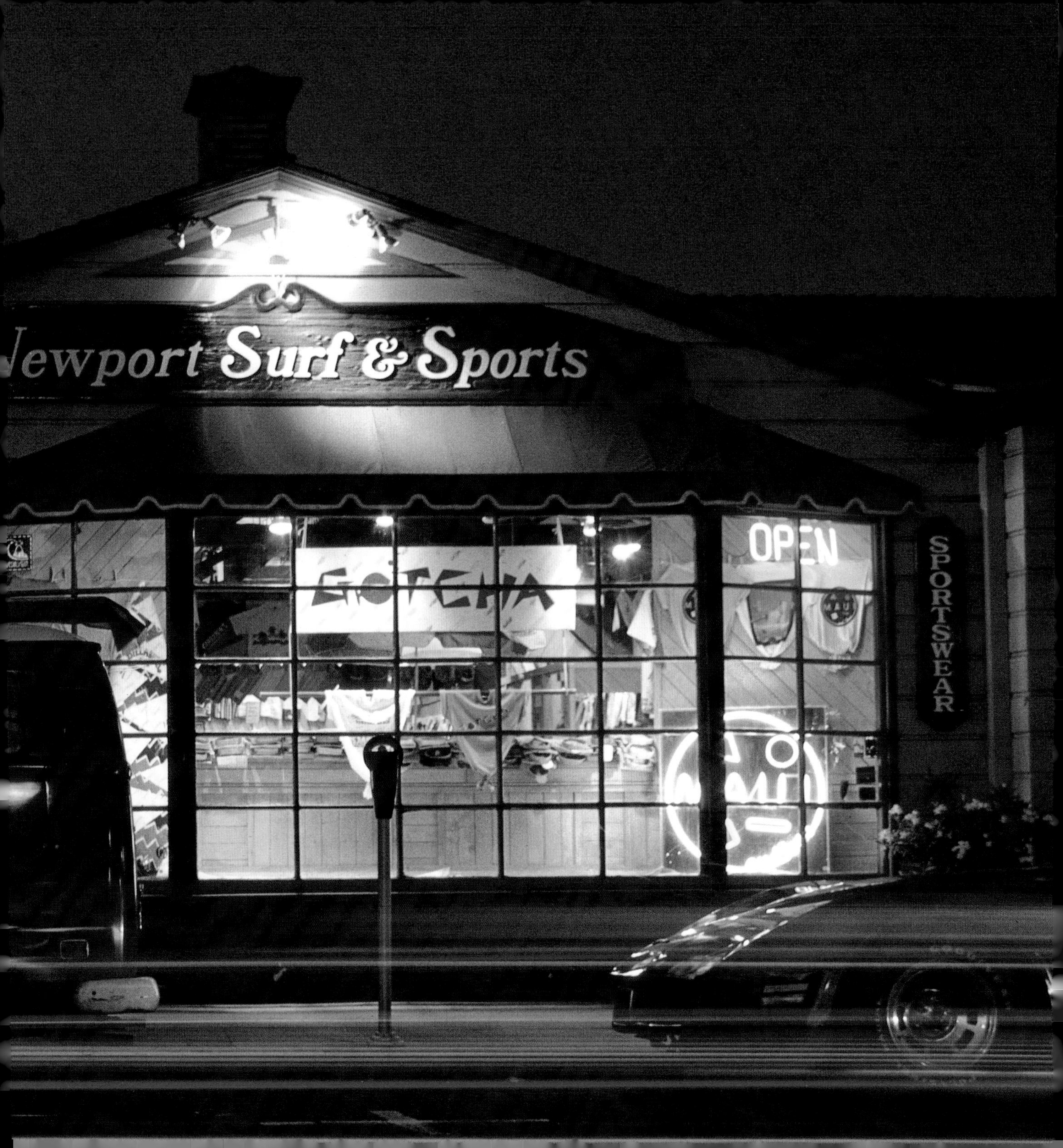
Newport Surf & Sports
GOTCHA
OPEN
SPORTSWEAR

Type 3

By the late 1950s, the Bug had well and truly established itself in the world's car markets, and Volkswagen were looking forward to an expanding future—and model range. The Type 1 series—Bugs and Karmann Ghias—were to be supplemented by a new line of passenger cars. Since designation 'Type 2' was already applied to the Transporter range, the new line, logically enough, was called the Type 3. It came in four forms, all incorporating the same floorpan.

The 1500 Notchback and its Type 3 Karmann Ghia derivative, the 'razor-edge', were launched at the 1961 Frankfurt Motor Show, though neither of these two cars was ever exported to the USA. Unlike the Type 3 Variant, or Squareback, which went into production four months later, followed by the 1600TL Fastback version in 1965. They all had basically the same engine as the Bug, but with a different fan/carb arrangement which meant that the motor was only 15 in. high. This facilitated a very unusual feature in a car—luggage compartments front and rear.

The Type 3 extended Dr Porsche's pre-war concept up-market, offering all of the Volkswagen's traditional advantages, along with more room, a more modern appearance and better performance. And it was well received by the American public, particularly the Squareback. However, the same cannot be said of the relatively short-lived Type 4 411/412 (basically over-glorified Variants), the last range of air-cooled cars VW built. Today, a lot of VW customizers are looking at the Type 3 as a 'different' basis for their individual style and taste.

Left In 1965, actor Dustin Hoffman introduced the new VW Fastback to the American public in a TV commercial. In his inimitable way, he used words like 'jazzy', 'powerful' and 'roomier' to describe the new-look Volkswagen, and went on to say, 'It's got a trunk up front where most cars have their motors and in the back, where most cars have their trunks, we have a . . . it's a trunk, large trunk!' As Hoffman stared into the trunk, scratching his head in bewilderment, the ad finished with a voice-over: 'Call in at your VW dealer. He'll show you where the motor is.' Today, if Hoffman saw the Fastback pictured here, he'd have good reason to wonder whether it had any suspension. That's *radical*!

Right The 1500 Sedan or 'Notchback' was never exported to the US, consequently they're much sought-after in California. Those relatively few examples that exist in America have all been imported by individuals. 'S' versions, like this superb '65, came with a 54-horse dual-carb motor and extra trim

Above Station wagons have always had a role to play in the American way of life, therefore it's not surprising that the Type 3 Squareback sold well in its day. What's more, they're now an increasingly-popular basis for the Cal-look treatment. R. K. Smith of *Hot VWs* magazine built this super '67 Square several years ago and, in so doing, did much to initiate the trend. Unlike lowering a Beetle front suspension, it only takes a few hours and basic mechanics to dump the front of a Type 3; it's simply a matter of rotating the lower trailing arms upwards by the required number of splines. R.K.'s is down two splines in front, and with its Riviera wheels and custom paintjob, it never ceases to attract admiring looks

Above Gary Dean's super-clean '69 Notchback is
different in more ways than one. Not only has it
been lowered drastically, repainted in Porsche Red
acrylic enamel and fitted with highly polished
Empi-styled eight-spokes, it's also right-hand drive!
The Notch was imported by a friend of Gary's
from Japan, but when Gary saw the car with its
unusual steering position he just had to have it,
knowing that it would be a guaranteed head-
turner on the street. Needless to say, the 21-year-
old owner spent hundreds of hours and several
thousand dollars bringing it to its present state of
perfection. What a stunner!

Left Top Notch is the most appropriate
description for Gary's 'weekend driver'. All of the
original exterior trim, with the exception of the
bumper over-riders, has been retained and
refurbished, and the paintjob is absolutely flawless.
The super-low stance was achieved by adjusting
the front end five notches, and the rear by two

Below Beneath the lid inside the fully-carpeted
rear luggage compartment sits a rebuilt 1600,
pirated from a junkyard Squareback. All of the
engine tin has been sprayed red, the crankcase
black, while most of the other visible parts are
either chromed or polished. The motor mates to
the original fully-automatic transmission

Previous page Keith 'Kid' Dean is the son of legendary West Coast customizer, Dick Dean ('Dean's the name, chopping's my game'), so it's hardly surprising he drives the most outstanding Squareback in California. In simple terms, this candy-red custom has been roof-chopped four inches, although chopping any automobile is anything but simple. The usual method involves sectioning all the pillars and quartering the roof so that the inclination of the pillars remains basically stock. However, on this altogether-special Squareback, the rear 'C' pillars have been re-angled further inwards, and the roof pushed forward and down to meet the four-inch-sectioned windshield posts. Thus producing a wicked-looking wedge-effect top chop, enhanced by forward-sloping 'B' pillars and one-piece tinted door and side windows. But that's just for starters. A pair of Type 3 bumpers were cut 'n' shut to make up an early Corvette-style 'split' front bumper, which is tied together with a grille guard from a '62 T-Bird—and there's even a custom-made grille, behind which lies a six-row oil cooler for the stock 1600 mill. The car's been lowered front and rear, relieved of its trim, and has limited-edition VW wheels with early Porsche-type hub caps and beauty rings. Not to mention cut-down Cal-look window rubbers, street rod-style door mirrors, and the ultimate custom touch, a genuine 1933 Maserati single-loop roll-bar!

Above The 'one-of-a-kind' theme was carried through to the interior, retrimmed all-red using a combination of vinyl, corduroy and carpeting. The original Type 3 dash has been cut out in favour of a 'floating dash'/centre console arrangement, hand-formed in aluminium. It houses the original gauges and a VDO tachometer, plus the mandatory sound system. A Ford Thunderbird donated the power seats, while a trick three-spoke 'wheel points this streamlined baby in the right direction

Top left In terms of pure paint beauty, nothing beats a deep, dazzling candy-apple paintjob. Candy is a translucent paint, normally applied over a gold or silver base, therefore its shade depends on its thickness, or the number of coats applied. Spraying an entire car evenly is a real art, and this super-slick '66 proves that it's one of many which Keith Dean has mastered

Bottom left In order to fit within the re-angled rear pillars, the upper half of the rear door was likewise inclined at a more acute angle. The stock licence plate recess in the lower section of the door has been skinned-over, and the 'plate relocated between a matching split rear bumper, beneath a Fastback light. European tail-light lenses are also fitted

Karmann Ghia

The Karmann Ghia: 'For people who can't stand the sight of a Volkswagen', wrote VW's ad copy writers in their typically witty style. The charismatic KG was designed by the Ghia design studio in Turin and coachbuilt by the craftsmen at Karmann, and looked every inch a racy Italian sportscar. Beneath its sleek lines, however, were the same basic chassis and mechanical components, and hence the same basic performance, of the Bug.

Even the most dedicated Bug lover of the mid-1950s would have been hard-pushed to find any sporting appeal in the fast-selling People's Car. Of course Porsche had been producing their 356 model for some time with VW-inspired mechanics, but that was an out-and-out sportscar for the well-heeled minority. So, in the summer of 1955, just before the millionth Beetle left Wolfsburg, Volkswagenwerk filled the gap between these automotive extremes by introducing the Type 1 Karmann Ghia. Roughly 443,000 were manufactured over the following 19 years, including 81,000 Convertible models.

The amount of labour involved in the creation of one 'Ghia body was incredible. Almost 20 different seams were welded, ground down, filed and sanded by hand. It took two skilled men no less than $4\frac{1}{2}$ hours to stitch up a convertible top. Each car was worked on and fussed over until numerous inspectors had passed judgement over it. There was no way the Karmann Ghia could have been produced in larger numbers—there just weren't enough hours in the working day.

Left With its sensual Italian-styled body and dependable Beetle mechanics, many enthusiasts see the Type 1 Ghia as having the best of both worlds. Volkswagen produced 44 Bugs, or thereabouts, for every KG coachbuilt by Karmann, and today's prices reflect that the VW-built-for-two is in short supply. This cherry-looking coupé is a used-car salesman's dream

Above Roughly 80,000 Type 1 Ghia Cabriolets were produced by Karmann between 1956 and 1974, and the majority were exported to the US. Indeed, style-conscious Americans found its good-looks and wind-in-the-hair freedom even more appealing than Mom's apple pie. The young lady behind the 'wheel of this pre-'67 Cab' (recognizable by its painted steel dash) was *lookin' good* at a stop light on the Pacific Coast Highway

Above The licence plate says *LIL2LO*, but any Cal-look *aficionado* would tell you this dark pink Ghia sits 'just right' on its Michelin-wrapped, polished Porsche alloys. Just perfect for puttin' around town

Below A colourful quartet of Cal-look KGs, captured beneath a rare English sunset. Andy Barry's pearl-painted coupé in the foreground took a mere two months to transform, and that included replacing the bottom four inches of the whole car and repainting it twice. The most enjoyable part of the build-up was 'finally getting it in primer', while his one-and-only complaint about driving the car is the lack of illumination from the six-volt headlights. He says 'they're worse than candles'

Below Richard King a.k.a. 'El Ritchie', is one of Britain's best-known car customizers as well as being *the* Karmann Ghia restoration specialist. Based in Westcliff-on-Sea, Essex, Ritchie says 'coupés are cool but Cabs are cooler'—what's more, his '65 Cal-Cab is the coolest in the UK. It features genuine Empi five-spoke rims, full colour coding, and lots of trick touches throughout. 'Silly Sid the BMX kid' is a pro racer who jumps Ghias as a hobby

Overleaf El Ritchie's previous creation was this mega-smooth '71 Type I coupé. It is now owned by Gary Clift but Ritchie performed all the mods including smoothing out the wing tops, rolling the sills, semi-shaving the gutters and adding Vauxhall PA Cresta tail-lights and Fast Lemon paint

Left Tri-coloured trunk upholstery matches the exterior stripes line-for-line on Bryan Houston's multi-prizewinning KG. That's show business

Above Happiness is . . . cruisin' Highway 99 in a fine lookin' Ghia

Below Dennis Hyde's sanitized '69 is nothing short of Cal-look perfection. The car was stripped down to every last nut and bolt and, over the course of two years, rebuilt to a standard that even show judges find hard to believe. Each and every part of this car, whether visible or not, has been treated to the same quality of finish. It's flawless—in fact it's *unbelievable*

Below The engine compartment is a work of art, reflecting Dennis' two-year addiction to detailing. The actual motor is a stock 1600 with dual Solex carbs. . .

Below Dutchman Rens Ruts owns one of the slickest-looking Cabriolets in Europe, with a drivetrain to match. It comprises a hot Porsche 914 motor mated to a 911 five-speed trans. Rens rebuilt the engine incorporating 100 mm Mahle pistons with the standard 71 mm crank (2.2 litres), a warm cam, ported and polished heads with bigger valves, dual Solex P11 carbs, and a custom-built fan/drive set-up. It fits so neatly many European show-goers believe it was some kind of factory option. Hardly!

Below Ten minutes later it ran a 14-second quarter-mile

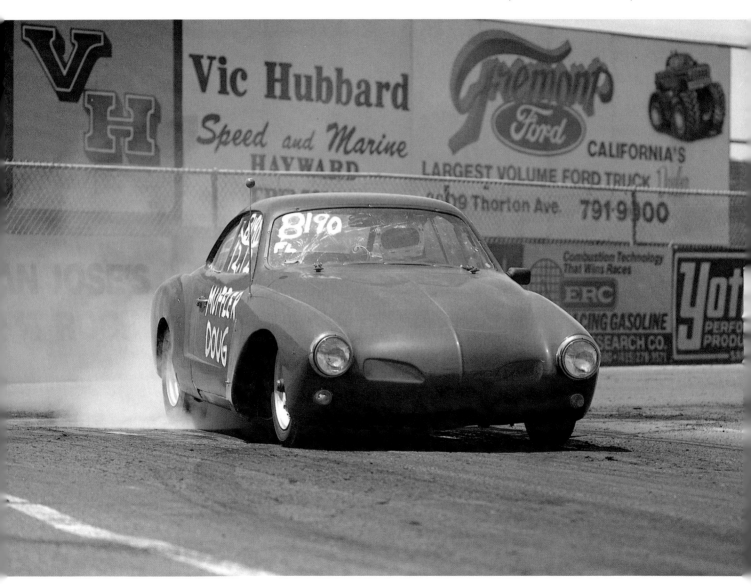

Below Jim Larsen's '68 Ghia launches off the line at Baylands Raceway thanks to a 'killer' 1800 with dual 48IDA Weber induction. Like most serious drag racers, Jim's ten-second machine features a fibreglass flip front end and lightweight Centerline wheels, and he has also moved the front axle forward by several inches. This both increases the car's high-speed stability and decreases its chances of wheelstanding

123

Below Hawaiian Mark Deacon races the fastest full-bodied VW in America; a highly sophisticated, alcohol fuel-injected, turbo'd Karmann Ghia known as 'Red Rider', which runs low-nines at 150 mph. It's a tough act to follow, but this is the car that he hopes will do it; a twin VW-engined 800 hp dragster complete with a stretched fibreglass Ghia body on top! Unveiled at the Baylands Nationals, it never ran but its awesome looks sent the fans wild with anticipation

Below What started out a thrashed $175 Karmann
Ghia coupé is now Bob Godfrey's topless,
turbocharged racer which frequently runs high
nine-second elapsed times at more than 140 mph.
Motivation takes the form of a Rajay EB-60 turbo'd
1941 cc (73 mm crank, 92 mm pistons) that is red-
lined at 8000 rpm. It's a hot one

Left Until fairly recently, nobody would have considered off-roading a Karmann Ghia. But nowadays those racers seeking real individuality are scouring the wrecking yards for front-ended Ghia bodies, adding new one-piece 'glass fronts, eliminating all excess weight, and bolting them to up-rated Type 1 chassis'. Is nothing sacred?

Below Dump it, dechrome it, prime it and drive it. There's no law against having fun in an unpainted Cal-coupé—especially one with hot rod-type hood louvres

127

Other interesting titles from Osprey

Porsche 356
The full developments of the Coupé, Cabriolet, Roadster, Speedster and Carrera
Denis Jenkinson
136 pages hardback, 80 b/w photographs, 8 pages of colour, 0 85045 363 1

Porsche 911 Turbo
The full development story of the road-going Porsche 911 Turbo—3 and 3.3 litre and Project no. 930
Michael Cotton
136 pages hardback, 90 b/w photographs, 8 pages of colour, 0 85045 400 X

Ghia—Ford's Carrozzeria
A sensational look at the work of Ford's Italian design studio
David Burgess-Wise
192 pages hardback, 220 b/w photographs, 0 85045 625 8

Tri-Chevy
A colour pictorial celebrating those classic Chevys of 1955—'56 and '57
Mike Key
120 pages, 123 colour photographs, 0 85045 615 0

Lead Sleds
A colourful look at chopped and lowered customs—1935 through 1954
Mike Key
128 pages, 124 colour photographs, 0 85045 547 2

Street Machines
A full colour review of post—'49 street machines and customs
Andrew Morland
128 pages, 122 colour photographs, 0 85045 546 4

Available from all good bookshops or write for a catalogue to:
Osprey Publishing, 27A Floral Street, London WC2E 9DP, England
Motorbooks International, PO Box 2, 729 Prospect Avenue, Osceola, Wisconsin 54020, USA